Green Isle in the Sea

Green Isle in the Sea

An Informal History of the Alternative Press, 1960–85

Diane Kruchkow & Curt Johnson
Editors

December Press
Highland Park, Illinois

A special issue of December Magazine,
comprising vol. 27, nos. 1-4, 1985

Green Isle in the Sea: An Informal History of the
Alternative Press, 1960-85

**Cover drawings, and occasional drawings in text,
by Montana Morrison**

ISBN: 0-913204-15-3
Library of Congress Catalog Card Number 85-72963

**Publication of this book was aided by a grant from
the National Endowment for the Arts.**

Distributed by Chicago Review Press
213 West Institute Place
Chicago, Illinois 60610

Published by December Press
3093 Dato, Highland Park, Illinois 60035

Contents

For Bob Wilson

&

All Those Who Helped

A Green Isle in the Sea

About half a dozen years ago, Curt Johnson and I were sitting around a wood stove, discussing the small press—past, present and future. We realized that the real energy of the grassroots movement that sprang up in the mid-'60s to early '70s had not yet been documented and we decided to set about doing that.

An old *Twilight Zone* serial showed a girl who fell through the wall next to her bed into the fourth dimension. As I remember it, her parents and others tried to pull her out, but she never fully returned.

The small press did something like that to me. Back in 1969, as a senior in college, I hit upon the world of the small press, and proceeded to fall into it like Alice falling down the rabbit hole. Only it wasn't a dream. I've lived more than 15 years of my life there, trying to understand what was going on around me and peering back up the hole from time to time trying to figure out that world, too.

The small press provided an environment, back in the late '60s, in which one could discover literature first-hand (not third-hand, as in academia), meet people with real commitments not only to literature but also to social and political movements, and generally establish an alternative way of life. I was looking for that "green isle in the sea," as one littlemag editor from the '20s put it—a spot of purity and flowering among all the protest and destruction.

It quickly changed my life: I became a born-again small press fanatic. Writers, to me, back then, were the people with the right stuff. They were steeped in the absurdities of life or overflowing with appreciation for the little details. Their eyes were sharp and their actions didactic. To be involved in the world of writers was tremendously exciting. I had mentally transported myself back to Paris in the '20s early on, and was sure I would now come in contact with some of the vital minds and talents of our time. Needless to say, editors of little magazines were merely writers who took the publication process just one step further and helped keep the whole scene jumping.

Surprisingly, I have not entirely abandoned this vision. Fifteen years of active involvement, of course, has knocked down a few idols here and there, but the ideals are still strong. The small press has changed, surely. Organizations have brought some editors together and separated others, while grants have become a prime topic of debate. Not all writers or editors are gods, I've discovered. There is jealousy, backscratching, competition and even conservatism. Many editors have gleefully followed in the footsteps of big business. Quite a few are not movers and shakers but just want to know how to get a book into people's hands. Small publishers compose a strong and quickly growing segment of the total publishing world today.

But it's been the energy and the ideals behind it all which initially caught me and kept me going and still keeps me on my toes. It's still there, albeit a bit hidden in the mass of publications and a bit disguised by fancy multicolored offset covers. It's matured a little, gotten more sophisticated. But it's still there in the heart of things. The small press has aged like a septuagenarian, surprised to find himself with white hair when he still feels 30.

During the period we've tried to cover in this book, that energy was much more raw. Poets on the streets gave out free broadsides in San Francisco. Editors lived on the sales of poetry magazines sold at Harvard Square. Most editors were writers and most writers knew at least one or two editors. Magazines ("littlemags") outnumbered presses. Poetry was an instrument of peace. Quite a few of us were active participants in Vietnam protests and student rebellions. Len Fulton, in fact, traces the '60s renaissance of small press publishing back to the free speech movement at Berkeley. But no matter whether we were in California, New York, New Hampshire, Chicago, or anywhere else, we were part of a simultaneous surge of independent publishing, little known to most people but passionately embraced by those involved—soon to be known as the small press movement. Whether or not this movement is over is not our concern here. It is the roots of this movement and some of its participants which we bring you in the following pages.

Diane Kruchkow

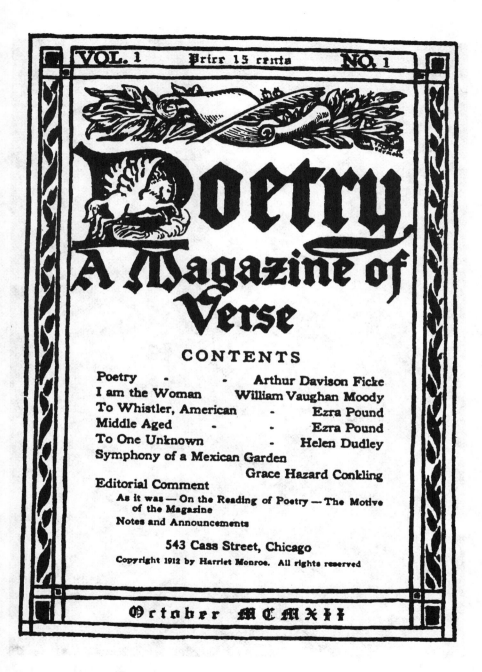

VOL. 1   Price 15 cents   NO. 1

Poetry

A Magazine of Verse

CONTENTS

543 Cass Street, Chicago

October MCMXII

Title page of first issue of *Poetry*, 1912

Richard Morris

Camels Coming

Richard Morris

Richard Morris was born June 16, 1939, in Milwaukee, Wisconsin. Studied physics at the Universities of Nevada and New Mexico, 1958-68. Ph.D. in theoretical physics, University of Nevada, 1968. "Live in San Francisco. Somewhat more than half my income is derived from writing, somewhat less than half from my salary as Coordinator of COSMEP (Committee of Small Magazine Editors and Publishers, founded 1968).

"I am not married, and have no children. Edited *Camels Coming* magazine, 1965-68; published poetry chapbooks and poetry broadsides under the Camels Coming Press imprint, 1968-71; published *Camels Coming Newsletter*, 1972-79."

Publications—Poetry: *He Dreamed; Prey; Don Giovanni Meets the Lone Ranger; Ginsberg Smoked Some Dope While Einstein Played His Violin; Reno, Nevada;* Plays: *Poetry Is a Kind of Writing; The Board of Directors* (aka *Grape-Nuts*); Nonfiction: *Light; The End of the World; The Fate of the Universe; Evolution and Human Nature.*

Attaining Respectability

The '60s and '70s were an exciting era for those involved in literary publishing, and I am tempted to take a nostalgic look at that era, and to recount some of my experiences as an editor. I won't, however, because there are some observations which I think may be more significant.

It seems to me that literary publishing today is quite a bit different from what it was 15 years ago. I am not exactly delighted with the changes that have taken place.

During the '50s and early '60s literary publishing in the United States was dominated by the university-affiliated quarterlies. The most prestigious ones functioned primarily as journals of criticism. They allotted the majority of their pages to the publication of critical articles, while publishing a short story here and there. Poems were used as fillers. Even those magazines which emphasized fiction and poetry tended to accept material which conformed to prevailing critical standards. It was, in the words of the poet Randall Jarrell, an "age of criticism."

One of the most obvious characteristics of the fiction and poetry that was published was its respectability. The academic magazines accepted little that was innovative, or outrageous, or revolutionary. On the contrary, they published material which seemed designed to please the academic practitioners of the then-dominant "new criticism." Works which did not conform to these standards were dismissed as "beat" writing, whether they had anything to do with the beat movement of the '50s or not.

During the early '60s, many of the younger writers began to become aware that certain kinds of writing—often the only kinds that interested them—were simply not getting published. They responded by doing the natural thing: they started magazines of their own. Suddenly, the few dissident publications which had been publishing the work of the beats, the Black Mountain poets, and other "underground" writers were joined by hundreds of new periodicals. It soon became obvious that a literary revolution was under way.

Many of these magazines tried to seem outrageous. But this was only natural. After all, the best American poetry has always had a certain outrageous quality. Perhaps it has something to do with the fact that we in the United States do not feel the weight of centuries of literary tradition. Or perhaps it has something to do with the need to be heard above the din of our all-pervasive pop culture. Nevertheless, I think it is clear that the best American poets, from Whitman to Pound to Bukowski, have tended to spurn the literary models that would be foisted upon us by the professors of literature, and by those who believe that "literature" is spelled with a capital "L."

Something of the same spirit can be found in American fiction. Such books as *Huckleberry Finn, Tropic of Cancer, Catch-22*, and certain novels by such authors as Vonnegut could never have been produced within the context of European culture. Sometimes this quality is even captured in critical writing. Leslie Fiedler, for example, bears little resemblance to the typical European literary intellectual.

And yet when I look at the literary magazines that are being published nowadays, the uniquely American quality of outrageousness seems to be absent. Instead, we are inundated by a flood of bad writing that fills hundreds of well-produced but unexciting periodicals. One must have a masochistic streak if one wants to plow through the work that fills literary magazines today.

It has been said that there are too many writers being published, and that the best fail to gain reputations because their work is buried in an avalanche of mediocrity. I am really not sure whether this is the case or not. The magazines, at any rate, are the focus here, not the writers.

The most obvious characteristic of the magazines of the '60s was that they injected a little fresh air—and often a few well-placed farts as well—into what was then a suffocating literary atmosphere. Some of them were mimeographed and quite sloppily produced; others showed evidence of care in production and design. They all, however, lacked respectability. The material that they printed would not have found a welcome in university English departments.

To be sure, there were conservatively edited journals which aped the quarterlies. There were "sewing circle" magazines which printed work that was quite amateurish, and there were publications which were simply inept. However, there were quite a few which seemed wholly disreputable, and constantly exciting. If they were sometimes cheaply printed, if they contained misspellings and typographical errors, it didn't seem to make any difference. If anything, such faults only added to their outrageousness, and became assets.

Even their names were outrageous: *Entrails, Marrahwannah* (pronounced "marijuana") *Quarterly, Atom Mind, Open Skull, The Willie* (so called because it was edited by a poet known as Willie Gobblecunt), *The Buddhist Third Class Junkmail Oracle, Fuck You, Meatball*. Those are a few which come to mind; there were many others. Some magazines, of course, were rather demurely named. It is not necessary to have a magazine with an outlandish title to participate in a literary revolution.

But of course the revolution has been over for some time now. Like the political revolutions of the '60s, it was co-opted by the larger culture. As a result, literary publishing, much to its detriment, has gained respectability. More and more writers are being cranked out of creative writing courses and the MFA factories. As their work finds its way into the burgeoning numbers of magazines, we find ourselves being fed an increasingly bland literary diet. Meanwhile, editors clamor for grant support, and forget about literature in the process.

At the risk of seeming to digress, I would like to ask why it is that so few people listen to serious contemporary music. Could the fact that most of our composers are now people who have Ph.D.s in composition have something to do with it? Could literature be falling victim to a similar fate?

I have no desire to go on an anti-academic tirade. I have a Ph.D. myself, and if I did not make my living in the literary world, I think that university teaching would be my occupation of choice. However, I cannot make myself believe that universities provide a healthful environment for the arts. As institutions which are dedicated to the upholding of cultural tradition, they can only have a conservative influence. Paradoxically, it is only in the sciences that universities encourage the exercise of creative imagination. I have heard many poets say that they feel that creative writing courses and formal literary study have had a harmful influence on them as writers. I do not believe that this is an accident.

The various grant programs, too, have had a baneful effect. I don't mean to imply that grants programs are set up with anything but the best of intentions. On the contrary, they are set up by well-meaning people who understand that the arts need patronage, and who are concerned about the need to find some kind of support for contemporary literature. Unfortunately, they do not stop to consider the effects of the fact that grants are awarded by committees.

It has been said that a camel is a horse that was designed by a committee. This is grossly unfair to the camel, a creature which is marvelously adapted to

3

life in the desert, and it is probably unfair to committees too. Committees, after all, are generally made up of dedicated, intelligent people who work very hard to make equitable decisions.

The only problem is that committees almost always favor work that is mediocre. Perhaps this can best be illustrated by the following example:

Suppose that a committee is awarding grants to literary magazines. Magazine *A* is the first to be considered. The work that it publishes is amateurish, and the editors appear to be rather dumb. So far, there is no problem. The grant application is turned down.

But now suppose that the committee comes to magazine *B*. One or two members find this publication to be very exciting. The others—who constitute the majority—see no value in it at all. There may be a variety of different reasons for this lack of interest. Perhaps the magazine does not appeal to their literary tastes. Or perhaps the fact that the committee members have had to read something like a hundred magazines in a two-week period has caused the majority to give the publication less attention than it deserved. In any case, their inclination is to put it in the same category with *A*. As a result, the committee either denies *B* a grant, or gives it a small sum to placate its supporters.

Magazine *C* is considered next. This time one or two members speak in support of the publication. They are not the one or two that favored *B*, but they are again a minority, and so they are voted down. *C*'s application suffers a similar fate.

Finally, magazine *D* comes up for consideration. No one gets very excited about this publication at all. On the other hand, no one hates it either. At last, the committee is in agreement. *D* has some modest literary value; no one disputes that. Since the editors of *D* have obviously put a lot of effort into the production of their magazine, it is quickly agreed that they deserve a substantial grant.

The mediocrity of magazine *D* is rewarded. Is this really so terrible? It is true that some government money has been wasted. But does this really do so much harm? After all, no one is going to want to read magazine *D*, whether it gets a grant or not, right?

If this was all there was to it, I would be perfectly willing to see grants committee members go on playing at being government bureaucrats. But unfortunately, this is not all there is to it. The chances are that *D* will go on getting grants. Because it is "successful," it will become a model for the new magazines that are started. These will, in turn, get grants themselves. The granting process, in other words, establishes the legitimacy of *D* in the eyes of the literary community. Not only does blandness triumph, the process becomes self-perpetuating.

I realize that the argument sounds a little contrived. It must be remembered, however, that it is intended to be an example of the ways in which mediocrity is fostered by grant-giving programs. A committee may not behave in precisely the way that I have described. Nevertheless, I think that it is clear that it will tend to favor that which is acceptable to all to what is exciting to only a few. The publication which is inoffensive will be favored over the one which is controversial. The more often grants are given, the more frequently this will happen.

I'm not sure what can be done to eliminate the literary mediocrity that has been fostered by the universities and by the grants committees. Even if we went so far as to assassinate the professors of creative writing and to blow up the building in which the National Endowment for the Arts is housed, they (the professors and the building) would only be replaced. Very little would have been accomplished.

Perhaps the solution lies in recognizing that small literary publishing has come to serve the purposes of the Establishment. Perhaps what we need to do is to become disreputable again, and start a new revolution. After all, we have nothing to lose but the NEA.

Robert Fox

Carpenter Press

Robert Fox

Bob Fox's stories and poems began appearing in 1964 in such little magazines as *Trace, Prism International, The North American Review, Salmagundi, The Remington Review*, and *Mundus Artium*. Originally from Brooklyn, New York, he is a blues guitar and piano player. He lives with his wife, Susan, and their two children, Joshua and Jessica, on a 73-acre farm in southeastern Ohio and—farming being what it is—makes his living as Writer in Residence for the Ohio Arts Council in Columbus. A collection of his short stories, *Destiny News*, was published in 1976.

A Brief History, and Some Observations

I. *History*

My own fiction and poetry began appearing in little magazines for 10 years before Carpenter Press was established. A brief chronology will help put the history of the press in order.

1970—My wife Susan and I, Brooklyn transplants, moved from Athens, Ohio, to suburban Carpenter (known locally as "Hippie Holler") in Meigs County where Ambrose Bierce was born and supposedly acquired his contempt for man. I taught English part-time at Ohio University and had a student who wrote moving dreamy mythological poems about cowboys and horses. Two of my neighbors were artists/illustrators who did striking line portraits of cowboys and horses. A fine edition of Ron Davis's poems, illustrated by Baker and Lynas, would make a lovely book I thought (*see* 1980, below).

1971—During summer session when Susan was finishing her BA and I was teaching a survey course in American Lit, Curt Johnson sent me the manuscript

7

of *Nobody's Perfect*. I stayed up past midnight turning the canary pages, and Susan complained my laughter kept her from studying. I wrote Curt that if he could not find a publisher elsewhere I'd find a way to get the ms. into print. But I was sure that one of the commercial publishers would recognize Curt's vast talent and make a bestseller of the book.

At the end of the summer we moved to Levittown, PA—the only housing we could find near Rider College that accepted couples with dogs or children. I mentioned the idea of starting a press to several of my Rider colleagues whose general response was "Why bother?" and "There are too many small presses already."

1972—We moved back to southeast Ohio where I was more comfortable as a writer. We planned to buy a farm, raise sheep and start the press. No one at Rider thought we were serious since we were both from Brooklyn. What was I going to write about? Cows? Pigs? Didn't we know from experience that the U.S. did not exist beyond the Delaware? No. We were pretty dumb. We rented a farm north of Athens and I incorporated Carpenter Press and applied for tax-exempt status. The application was turned down for the same reasons publishers of Bibles are rejected.

1973—I decided that Carpenter Press should not be tax-exempt. I was not about to become engaged in all sorts of other activities so that my press, or charitable foundation could obtain tax write-offs or grants.

Curt asked me if I was serious about offering to publish *NP* two years before. Yes, I replied.

We found our dream farm in Snowville, back in Meigs County. Our savings were gone. I lost my part-time teaching job. Susan did not have a job. We were dead broke through the summer, except for a settlement with Science Research Associates, which had reprinted a story of mine in a textbook without permission. We had a big garden, with large Irish cobbler potatoes, and tomatoes into November. In the fall I found a job as a part-time editor and got back to *Nobody's Perfect*. The money became available privately and after going through revisions with Curt I put the book into production.

I designed a flyer composed of blurbs from big press editors who panned the book. Why, people asked me, was I publishing the worst book in the world? I used the flyer for an advance order sale and it was enormously successful. Other writers clamored to buy the book.

1974—*Nobody's Perfect* was published in January. It was a special day, a clear cold one, meeting the semi in Middleport, loading the cartons into the back of my old International pickup, then unloading them into an unfinished end-room in the house. I shipped out cartons of orders that first week.

Then the reviews began to come in, from the *Chicago Daily News, Fiction International, Small Press Review* and numerous other mags. And the reviews were all good! I had overprinted the original flyer and returned it to the printer to have the good reviews printed on the back.

With the initial sales I began to repay part of the borrowed money.

1975—Along with full-length fiction, I wanted to do poetry chapbooks and Carpenter published Alfonso Tafoya's *Confrontation at Calvary*, a small but

8

strong first collection by a young poet.

With two titles I applied for an NEA small press assistance grant and was turned down because the Endowment's grants office lost the copies of *Confrontation*: Insufficient support materials.

1976—Chapbook publication vigorously supported by the NEA across the country. Some East and West coast publishers doing fiction chapbooks with NEA support. Still, little or no full-length fiction from small presses.

1977—Joshua Fox born. I risked some personal money and some borrowed money and Carpenter published two more full-length novels: James Norman's *The Obsidian Mirror*, a well-crafted mystery rich with a knowledge of Mexican folklore and Aztec mythology and Curt Johnson's *The Morning Light.* Quite an experience doing both books. Norman's ms. was virtually flawless. Johnson's had been meddled with by numerous editors since 1960. But it was another wonderful experience working as an editor with Johnson. We spent a long evening over a fifth of bourbon in the summer of 1976 arguing over the ms. My suggestions were followed by long silence, then the rewrite, and good justifications for not going along with some of my ideas. I was amazed at his strength, doing the rewrite while his life was in personal crisis. Both novels got excellent reviews.

I became Poet in Residence for the Ohio Arts Council to rejuvenate and reorganize the Poets in Schools Program. The job came at a fortunate time, for our savings were gone once again and Susan had left her job when Josh was born. No matter that I have to commute 100 miles each way to work—I have experience as a long-distance driver. We had to sell the cows though. (We never did get sheep.)

1978—(Here I shift into the present tense—does this mean the modern era?) Carpenter Press gets a $5,000 grant from the NEA and puts three new full-length fiction titles into production.

1979—The three new fiction titles are published: Daniel Lusk's novel *O Rosie*, Matthew Paris's novel *The Holy City*, and Brian Swann's short prose collection *The Runner* is substituted for Hugh Fox's "Leviathan" whose rewrite was never returned. The author had disappeared in Brazil. Swann's book receives brilliant reviews. Otherwise, reviewers are impatient with Lusk's daring shift of point of view in an otherwise realistic and lyrical novel, and with Paris's orchidaceous style which parodies the dross in contemporary S-F. Both writers should be winning prizes for their work.

1980—Carpenter receives an $8,000 grant from the NEA and puts four books into production: two beautifully illustrated poetry chapbooks, Jane Teller's *Love Poem for a Bank Robber* and Ron Davis's *Women & Horses* (illustrated by Baker and Lynas—at last!) and two full-length fiction works: Jerry Bumpus's second story collection *Special Offer*, and Hugh Fox's *Leviathan* (finally glad he tracked down the ms. before returning from Brazil). His novel is a mammoth copyediting job at this end, and typesetter Kathryn King in DC (who also set the three 1979 titles) comes through with wonderful proofreading, and David Lynas spends months studying photos of whales and aquatic life for the cover art and

9

interior illustrations. (Lynas is responsible for the Carpenter logo and the cover drawings for *Nobody's Perfect* and *Special Offer*.)

1981—All four titles are published. Jessica Fox is born. The fiction receives superlative reviews from *Library Journal, Booklist,* and National Public Radio's Morning Edition calls Carpenter "a king of the underground fiction publishers."

Numerous phone calls and letters arrive from writers, reviewers and potential mass-market reprint publishers wanting to know if Hugh Fox is really dead. Ask Connie.

1982—Stories from the Swann and Bumpus collections are nominated for the Pushcart Prize but aren't selected. NEA grant denied.

1983—Carpenter publishes Steve Kowit's first full-length collection of poetry—selected poems—*Lurid Confessions*, 96 pages. Good reviews so far from the *L.A. Times Book Review, Poetry Flash*, etc.

Small press assistance again turned down by NEA. According to 1984 Guidelines, Carpenter now ineligible for further NEA support. Has not published at least six 48-page books in the last three years. Carpenter has published five titles totaling 480 pages. Six times 48 = 288. Guidelines seem odd . . . oh well. Carpenter plans 10th anniversary celebration without NEA support which scratches the catalogue and puts proposed new novels on hold for the time being.

Now for a few words about the chronology. As my own work appeared in the little mags, it began to dawn on me that some mighty fine writers were also editors. Maybe I too had a responsibility to fulfill. I was also reading full-length fiction manuscripts from writers like Johnson and Matthew Paris. Paris's first novel *Mystery* was done as an Avon original paperback in 1973 because the editors thought it was a parody of *The Godfather*. I read the ms. of *The Rabbit Club Mystery* in 1967 or '68, a year or two before *The Godfather* was published. After getting numerous runarounds in New York, Paris sent me the manuscript of his *Holy City*. Like *The Morning Light*, it was a mess, having been meddled with by numerous editors at trade houses.

So, after 10 years, I find myself still in business, though ineligible for public support. No matter. As NPR said, Carpenter is a major fiction publisher. It is the only independent fiction publisher in Ohio and in any of the neighboring states except Pennsylvania and Kentucky, and it is the major independent fiction publisher in the Midwest. Very few small presses across the country publish full-length fiction. Despite the increase in fiction publishing by university presses, very little new fiction is being published that shows a unique and individual taste. Even a number of small presses who began to publish fiction show the mark of consensus, the stamp of mediocrity that marks so many university press fiction titles.

So, I can be proud of what Carpenter has achieved to date, for even with 12 titles in 10 years, 8 of them are full-length fiction—each a mammoth undertaking. My taste (mine only) is justified in the reviews the fiction has received, reviews which were not solicited, begged, or bought with advertising bucks.

While I am proud of Carpenter and its reputation, there are a number of things which make me sad about being a publisher. I'm troubled most because many of the books I've published should have gotten into print years before. *The Morning Light* was a novel of the early '60s. *The Holy City* and *Leviathan* were each written a decade or more before they were published. These books are good enough to stand above immediacy, yet in ways we may never know they have not spoken to their time.

Second, it is odd that I have had to turn down manuscripts by fairly well-known authors. I am amazed at the number of fiction writers of national repute who have queried Carpenter in the last three years. I have had to say no, for neither the money (nor my time) is there. Well, you might reply, couldn't I borrow it? Wouldn't revenue from their books provide income for books by lesser known writers? No. It would not be enough. I'll explain.

Carpenter books have not been getting out to their full audience. While not mass market items, Carpenter fiction titles have an audience of from anywhere between 5,000-25,000 readers. Yet, I have been able to reach only 1,200 or fewer readers with each title. (In contrast, Paris's mass-market *Mystery* sold about 80,000 copies off drugstore racks with less advertising than what I put behind his *Holy City*. And James Norman's reputation in the trade was no guarantee that *The Obsidian Mirror* would sell, despite superlative reviews. Comments his agent received from editors on the ms. were similar to what *NP* received. Yet the books continue to receive good to superb reviews in *LJ, Booklist,* the *L.A. Times....*) The problem of sales deals with public awareness, long the plague of independent publishers.

II. *Observations*

Part of the problem lies in the paradoxical unwitting censorship that dominates our culture. A renaissance has been occurring in all the arts, particularly literature, for more than the past two decades. Federal and state funds have helped bring the renaissance to small towns, rural areas and inner cities all across the country. Yet the mass media continues to portray art as the plaything of the rich.

Not long ago Dick Cavett hosted several well-known writers and critics who bemoaned the merger of commercial publishing with the entertainment business. Though they called for an alternative (reform from within?), not one of them mentioned the small press. A sympathetic professor I know recently told me he wished the small press was a viable alternative to commercial publishing. I replied that according to *Publishers' Weekly*, small presses collectively make up several million dollars of the book trade annually. He was astonished.

In the Soviet Union, manuscripts are exchanged underground, hand to hand, and reach large audiences. In this country, the underground manuscripts are published with the help of tax dollars, yet rarely reach a large audience. You can't find the books in the stores or read about them in the major newspapers or magazines.

In October 1981 I was invited to the annual convention of the Ohio Library Association to talk about "The Plight of the Small Press" (an unfortunate title of their choosing). A dozen or so librarians out of the thousands at the conven-

11

tion attended my talk; none of whom (except the editor of the OLA *Bulletin*) had read my well-publicized article "The Survival of Contemporary Literature"—though it had appeared in their own organization's publication (and was quoted in *The Christian Science Monitor*'s first small press book review feature, August 1981). At such a convention one might expect the keynote speaker to be someone whose main concern would be literature and publishing. However, the keynote speaker at this meeting was Bettina Gregory of NBC who prattled Washington gossip.

During the late '60s and early '70s when the entertainment conglomerates bought heavily into the book business and found it not very profitable, they tried to convince the reading public that the novel and the short story were dead. Today the conglomerates are doing even greater harm to their own book businesses by blockbuster deals for books which don't bring returns. Eventually it will be to their financial advantage to do away with books altogether and mass market us into robot-like consumers of electronic games. My own brother-in-law, a well-educated lawyer, will spend hours playing video games and then tell me he'd like to read new fiction but there just hasn't been any since Cheever and Updike.

The written and spoken word has managed to survive various onslaughts and will survive the present censorship. Literature is too vital an expression of the human psyche to be easily suppressed. The cultural renaissance I alluded to earlier is not over. Rather, it is part of a great social upheaval occurring internationally. The revolution in the arts is part of a new assertion of the individual, a spiritual revolution concerned with self-worth. It started sometime after World War I and accelerated greatly since World War II. It has expressed itself in numerous forms such as interest in Eastern religions, individual psychology, organically grown food, rock and roll music, etc.

The opinion-molders in this country would like us to believe that the '60s are dead, and that the '70s were the "me" decade, a period of irrelevant selfishness. I lived through it all and don't see it that way, for there has been a continuous evolution, taking various forms through the last three decades. During this period of great spiritual change, there has begun a deep-seated social and economic change as well. As conglomerate mergers continue to increase there is also a shakeup in corporate management.

The hierarchy as the management structure that effected the industrial revolution is no longer viable, yet it remains in wide use. In visual terms, the model for the hierarchy is the pyramid, with power concentrated at the apex and filtering down to the broader, lower levels. It is a closed system based on power, secrecy, and manipulation. The hierarchy is slowly giving way to the open system represented by the sphere as model, a system based on mutual trust and respect, appreciation for every participant's role, function, and worth to the system. Many corporations unable to alter their hierarchies are going under. In the automobile industry, for example, General Motors is frantically trying its Quality Work Life program, where the assembly line is replaced by teams, each responsible for assembling their own automobile. Each team forms a "quality circle," where each of the members is responsible to another for their time and the quality of their work. Two of GM's biggest obstacles are old-time managers who won't yield "power," and the unions, who don't know how to deal with the change.

The pyramid and sphere as hypothetical models can also be applied to the current literary world, as poet Jim Bertolino has pointed out in several articles. The independent press movement, today's literature, can be represented by the sphere which encompasses a wide range of literary activity including readings, book fairs, poets and writers in schools programs . . . . Bertolino uses the term "literary biosphere" to describe the wide-ranging activity. The old model, the pyramid, is no longer applicable. Many writing styles currently coexist, as if the history of literature were being recapitulated before a new birth. Bertolino borrows a metaphor from Dr. Lewis Thomas's *Lives of a Cell* to compare today's literary folk to termites erecting their astonishing cathedrals. As writers, editors and publishers, we are all involved in shaping an edifice much greater than our individual selves; it is time that the reading public become aware of an emerging new literature.

Elsewhere in *Lives of a Cell* Thomas writes, "Language is *the* biologically specific activity of human beings—holding us together at the core of our existence." Contemporary writing, exemplified by the collective activity of small presses, is witnessing a recreation of the English language comparable to what occurred in the Elizabethan age; it is a quantum leap of the human spirit.

Today's literary establishment, centered around academic writing programs based on the Iowa model and commercial and university publishing, views contemporary writing in terms of the pyramid or hierarchy. Certain literary styles are fashionable as are certain literary superstars. A handful of academic writing programs spawn large numbers of neophyte writers who write like their mentors (or the current superstars whose pictures appear in the literary tabloids) and embark on professional careers in a manner reminiscent of 19th-century capitalists on their way to the top. Financial success (or a good teaching job) has come to be regarded as an indication of a writer's true worth, and the apex of publishing is represented by a few big fiction writers and poets tied to commercial houses.

The literary establishment in this country is becoming increasingly conservative, with universities, which were once hospitable to diversity and new ideas, playing a key role. In the early 1970s, university presses recognized the need to publish new poetry and fiction as the conglomerates withdrew from the market. And indeed, some university presses have been able to survive the consensus mediocrity of the reader system, and introduce dynamic new writers and new works by neglected older writers. But there is an increasing appearance of supposed "new" novels imitating the fiction of the '50s. Critics have come up with appropriate jargon to deal with this—a return to pre-postmodern humanism! Novels about adolescents coming of age and bourgeois sterility abound. And poems in university quarterlies dazzle technically; they are personal yet disengaged.

13

The climate at universities cannot be very positive in a time of massive financial cutbacks. But according to management specialists, universities are responsible for much of their own ills. They are administered by awkward and unresponsive bureaucratic hierarchies. In this context it's easy to see why many editors are afraid of intimidating boards of trustees and other funding sources. But it also appears that many editors themselves are not widely read and simply cannot recognize a good piece of writing that does not resemble an already familiar author or style. It is regrettable that the least responsive, most chauvinistic segment of the literary community is the best funded.

Many funding sources adhere to the old view and want to know who or what is best. Such absolutes tend to rely upon the known and familiar and don't respond to what is new. Absolute criteria of quality are as inappropriate to the literary renaissance as classical mechanics is to quantum physics; Newton's Laws cannot be used to explain the behavior of subatomic particles. The new view of literature recognizes subjective judgment, accounts for a multiplicity of tastes. It is pluralistic and truly democratic. Rather than abdicating responsibility, the new view opens up an exciting, virtually limitless road of discovery.

The spirit of individualism that librarian Felix Pollack wrote about so eloquently in his introduction to the 1969 COSMEP Catalog still remains as the publishers' reason for being. While some of the memorable magazines of the '60s have bitten the dust, there are a number of good new ones, independents such as *Black Messiah, Affinities, Pig Iron, Live Writers!, Gargoyle, Sing Heavenly Muse!* and academically affiliated magazines like *Cutbank* and *The Colorado State Review*, which is articulating a new vision of latter 20th-century fiction.

Writers, like artists in all disciplines, have had to become administrators and fundraisers in order to survive. The new "professionalism" one sees in the independent press in no way lessens a commitment to serious writing nor does it impair an editor's ability to stand on taste and judgment. Publishers need either an outside source of income or must publish cookbooks. (Bill Truesdale of New Rivers Press writes eloquently about this problem in this volume.)

There is no financial reward or personal glory involved in literary book publishing. Books, not their publishers, get the reviews. Grants and sales don't reimburse a publisher for the amount of time spent in putting a book together, regardless of printing method. Publishers become publishers because they must.

Part of the excitement of publishing for me involves the vast amount of discovery and sharing that occurs with other publishers through the mails and at bookfairs. Behind it all is a continuing sense that each of us makes a contribution to a much greater whole. We may each be small, but we are part of the energy of an evolutionary leap forward.

III. *The Triumph of Contemporary Writing*

(What follows is a re-titled and very slightly revised version of my OLA *Bulletin* October 1980 article referred to above.)

14

Contemporary writing in this country is in a time of exciting renewal which the general reading public does not share. An inadvertent censorship exists, which is slowly breaking down. But two persistent myths about writing and publishing must dissolve if the present rebirth is to pervade society, enabling our literature to survive and grow. The first myth maintains that commercial publishing houses exercise superior taste and judgment, making available to the public the best of what is written; the second implies that the small, independent press (the site of our literary renaissance) is either a vanity network, subversive conspiracy, or a minor league farm system for the big leagues of commercial publishing.

I once believed that commercial publishing was the apex of a hierarchy, and also, while in graduate school, believed that little magazines and small presses were the minor leagues. I started out as a writer in the early 1960s believing that commercial publishers would love nothing better than to discover new literary talent. They were printing most of the big names of the period—Salinger, Malamud, Bellow, etc., and so the myth seemed to have a firm basis in reality. I did not know at the time that a careful examination of the history of modern publishing indicates that the majority of classic writers have been either self-published or published by friends. A partial list of writers who published their own major work includes Pope, Blake, Burns, Irving, Whitman, Twain, and Upton Sinclair. Self or small press publication tends to be the rule and not the exception; and numerous writers like myself who came of age in the '50s and '60s were and still continue to be deluded into believing they must be commercially published to be truly successful. Many young writers still do not realize that it remains virtually impossible for the unknown writer to get published commercially.

An examination of the history of publishing in England and America helps put the present situation into perspective. Publishers as such did not exist before the 18th century. Until the publication of *Johnson's Dictionary*, bookstores published books. Samuel Johnson's project was so costly, it required a consortium of bookstores to foot the bill. Within ten years, publishers as such emerged in England. It was not until the mid-19th century that publishers recognizable by name emerged in the United States. When the book publisher did emerge, he was not always a scrupulous businessman with the interests of the author at heart. Mark Twain describes in his *Autobiography* how his relationship with the publisher of *The Adventures of Tom Sawyer* led to his self-publication of *The Adventures of Huckleberry Finn.*

Len Fulton, publisher of Dustbooks, has estimated that since 1912, commercial publishers have discovered and sponsored only about 20 percent of the writers in this country—small presses and magazines have sponsored the rest. Schools such as dada, surrealism, beat poetry, and concrete poetry, were all first published in the small presses (1).

However, the general reader might argue that John Updike, E.L. Doctorow, and John Gardner, among others, have all been discovered by large presses, fueling the first myth that commercial publishers exercise superior taste and judgment. The partial truth behind this myth is that in the late 19th and early 20th centuries, publishing had become a gentlemen's profession. The kind of man who became a publisher was a man of good family with a literary inclination, who regarded his work as a profession first and a business second, an attitude that led to a privileged relationship between authors and publishers. Only a handful of commercial publishers remain who have lasting commitments to their authors.

The great change began to occur in the late 1950s and early '60s. According to the Authors Guild, over 300 mergers have taken place in the past 20 years (2). The mergers have been motivated by the American obsession with growth and expansion which has dominated industry since the end of the Second World War. According to *Publishers' Weekly* statistics, the number of books published in the U.S. has grown from 13,000 in 1950 to over 40,000 in 1974 (3)—a figure that remains constant today. Government tax policies have contributed to this expansion by encouraging owners of small companies to convert their holdings into shares of stock in large ones. It is interesting to note that the number of small presses has grown as the number of mergers and takeovers has increased. Just in the recent past, the number of small presses listed with the *International Directory of Little Magazines and Small Presses* has grown from 997 in 1974 to 1,950 in 1978 (4).

In response to the increasing difficulty writers had in getting published, many writers decided, "To hell with Godot, we'll do it ourselves." (5) The rise of independent publishing in the '60s corresponds with the return to traditional crafts, such as leather, ceramics, and furniture making, just as the increased interest in natural foods is related to the mergers and takeovers occurring in the food industry.

A thorough listing of who owns what in the book industry can be found in the *PW* article on "concentration." Many of the parent companies, such as MCA and Gulf-Western, are Hollywood studios, or corporations that own vast timberlands from which pulp for book paper is produced. The influence of conglomerate corporations on their subsidiaries cannot be understated. CBS and *The New York Times* are two parent companies that have been sued over anti-trust law violations. While the legal aspects of conglomerate control of the book industry is an interesting and revealing area for study, my concern here is to describe some of the most important changes conglomerate ownership has brought to the book industry. These changes can be itemized as follows: the lost identity of book publishers, mass marketing techniques, demoralizing effects on editorial staffs, the peculiar economics of book publishing, and the devastating effects upon writers.

Several years ago, Robert Giroux of Farrar, Straus & Giroux summarized the commercial book world as follows, "Book publishing is hardly related to literature." (6) Indeed, Doubleday now calls itself a communications company on its letterhead, as if to disassociate itself from books, and many other parent companies are multinational corporations which can no longer be thought of as making an identifiable product.

The corporate takeover of book publishing has had its most visible effect in the vast changes in marketing techniques. The typical trade book will not remain on the shelf for longer than the original order, which is usually two weeks for ten books. In the words of one editor, "Books are produced like steers to be slaughtered monthly." (7)

The practice of producing and marketing books like beef cattle or soap has changed the personnel who staff the editorial offices. The editor with a sympathy for new currents in writing or with an eye toward innovation, has fled the industry. Literary people have been replaced by management personnel, and the mediocrity in editing that has resulted is laughable. A successful book brings numerous imitations. Many agents, as well as authors, specialize in producing books that are copies of genre bestsellers.

A late '70s experiment conducted by Chuck Ross raises questions that resonate far beyond the issue of mediocrity. Ross submitted, in typewritten manuscript, copies of Jerzy Kosinski's prize winning novel *Steps* to numerous conglomerate publishers, including the publisher of *Steps* and the publisher of Kosinski's earlier books. Ross used the pseudonym Demos. An editor at Houghton Mifflin, publisher of the earlier novels said, "Jerzy Kosinski comes to mind as a point of comparison, but the manuscript as it stands doesn't add up to a satisfactory whole." (8) How could two publishers not recognize their own author, a National Book Award winner? Even if they couldn't recognize the work, why couldn't they recognize its quality? Yet the myth persists that big publishing houses exercise superior taste and literary judgment.

Those few remaining editors who have tried to retain the trust of their authors have been finding their confidence undermined by the huge, unwieldy bureaucracies that have consumed their companies. Impending mergers also demoralize editorial staffs, who are the last to learn about such takeovers.

From the point of view of the businessman, publishing is not very profitable. It is so unprofitable that one wonders why conglomerates have been so eager to enter the field. Publishers have generally acknowledged that it takes the sale of 10,000 copies of a trade book to break even. Seven out of every ten trade books lose money. The loss of federal Title II funds from the Library Services and Construction Act, in the early 1970s, coming at a time of economic recession, made the economic pinch apparent. Publishers agreed to eliminate "marginal" books, those that sell less than 5,000 copies. Many university presses also proceeded to abandon their poetry series. Many commercial publishers declared they could handle no new authors, and have hardly affirmed their commitments to their established ones. Poetry was the first but not the only genre to suffer. First fiction and "serious" fiction (9), the publication of short novels and books of short stories was virtually eliminated from publishers' lists. After 140 years of publishing, Bobbs-Merrill scratched fiction from its list after being purchased by ITT. A survey conducted by the literature program of the National Endowment for the Arts (reported in and available from *CODA*) covering the period 1952-77 found that the number of titles of new fiction did not rise, while the number of trade books published in this country more than tripled (10).

In 1976, profit margins on trade books fell below 2 percent, reaffirming publishers' dependence upon the sales of subsidiary rights—primarily paperback

17

and film. The effects of the search for higher profits has been disastrous for writers, and for all literature. Publishers used to take pride in keeping a title in print. Some books sold well, but slowly over a long period of time, and some found their readership years after being introduced. These books were called "sleepers," a bygone phenomenon in the world of commercial publishing. When books are removed from their shelves after the original order has not sold out, they are remaindered—sold at a fraction of list price to dealers, or pulped. Some books are pulped before being bound, when not enough advance orders are received. Pulping an unbound book provides a convenient tax write-off for a publisher.

Low profit margins encourage publishers to seek the big book, the potential multi-million dollar movie. Editors are under tremendous pressure to focus on such properties. The Big Book gets showered with attention—many other manuscripts don't get published. To a large extent, the success of a book is determined by the sale of film rights. There have been complaints, denied by the industry, of the parent company keeping the title "inhouse." The parent may be a film company, outbidding others for its hard-cover subsidiary's film rights, and also seeing that its paperback subsidiary also outbids its competitors. Such wheelings and dealings can be disastrous for authors. One writer complained that he could not reach his editor by phone once the parent film company lost interest in his book.

Books not targeted for films don't receive prime exposure in the review media. Books supported by major advertising *are* the ones reviewed. In a sense, the big companies buy the reviews.

Writers are under pressure to do what the publishing establishment feels it needs if they are to be commercially published. Upton Sinclair tried that over sixty years ago and it didn't work then. And more recently James Norman, a well-established author, was not able to sell his experimental novel, *The Obsidian Mirror*, despite his reputation. It was eventually published by my press, Carpenter.

Among some of the recent practices of publishers to increase profits are choosing subjects first and finding suitable authors afterward. John Jakes was selected by Fawcett to be author of the Bicentennial Series; and it's no secret that the subject of *Jaws* was chosen by computer, the author selected later. Another recent phenomenon is the novelization of movies and television shows. *Mork and Mindy* is the latest addition to the paperback racks.

In addition to novelizations, the newest paperback phenomena in this country is the photonovel, copies from Latin-American countries with low literacy levels. Photonovels are collections of stills from popular movies like *Grease*, with a line or two of dialogue superimposed. The decline of literacy in this country is, at least in this respect, directly encouraged by the practices of big publishing.

I had spoken earlier of an inadvertent censorship that has been keeping news of our literary revival from the general reader. Small press books are rarely reviewed in the major media because small presses cannot afford advertising space, and because well-crafted, literary books are not media events. Novels that are most frequently reviewed are those targeted for television or Hollywood. The advertising dollars for these books dictate the reviews. The *New York Times* (which was sued for providing free ad space to its own subsidiaries) is as much a tool for industry profits as *Publishers' Weekly*. *PW* has never carried small press reviews because it is solely a marketing tool and has nothing to do with literature. So, although we are in an era of excitement about language, a veritable rebirth of the written and spoken word, we are in a literary "dark ages," where the general reading public does not share the excitement.

Despite publication and distribution assistance to small presses from the literature program of the National Endowment for the Arts in Washington and state arts agencies, and despite the recent efforts of several university presses in publishing serious fiction, the financial resources available to independent presses cannot keep up with writers' backlogs. It takes up to ten years for a writer to get a book into print. A classic case is Jerry Bumpus's *Anaconda* (11), definitely the sort of first novel that would have been published commercially in the early 1950s, unfortunately written after the big mergers began to make themselves felt in the early '60s—the novel, finally published in 1967, is now out of print.

When a writer does not get a book out to its audience within a reasonable amount of time after it is written, he is often hurt and changed as a writer. But in the context of all of literature, and of the spiritual and intellectual life of the nation, the effects are potentially disastrous. To paraphrase author Jonathan Baumbach, it is a real problem for the life of the country when the imagination, the inner life, is suppressed (12). The question of the survival of our literature is ultimately tied to our spiritual survival.

Notes

(1) Len Fulton, *Tribal Energy*, a flyer advertising the *Whole Cosmep Catalog*, Dustbooks, Paradise, Calif., 1973.

(2) *CODA*, Poets & Writers Newsletter, Vol. 6, No. 3, Feb./March 1979, 201 W. 54th St., NYC 10019, p. 23.

(3) Remarks by Peter Davison, *The Publication of Poetry and Fiction, A Conference*, Library of Congress, Washington, D.C., 1977, p. 6.

(4) "The Question of Size in the Book Industry Today," a special report reprinted from *Publishers' Weekly*, July 31, 1978.

(5) Len Fulton, *op. cit.*

(6) Harry Smith, "Publishing and the Destruction of Values," *The Smith*, 5 Beekman St., NYC 10038, No. 22-23, New York, 1973, p. 5.

(7) *Ibid.*, p. 19.

(8) Chuck Ross, "Rejected," *New West*, February 12, 1979, Beverly Hills, Calif., p. 40.

(9) Clarence Major, "The Crunch on Serious Fiction, Part I, Commercial Publishing," *The American Book Review*, Vol. 2, No. 1, Summer, 1979, P.O. Box 188, New York, NY 10003, pp. 14-15. Major provides some long-needed definitions.

(10) *CODA*, *op. cit.*

(11) Jerry Bumpus, *Anaconda*, December Press, Chicago, 1967.

(12) Jonathan Baumbach, *The Publication of Fiction and Poetry, op. cit.*, p. 12.

Selected Bibliography

1. *International Directory of Literary Magazines and Small Presses,* Dustbooks, P.O. Box 100, Paradise, CA, 95969. The most comprehensive reference book of its kind. Timid librarians have not stocked this unique reference tool because some of the presses listed are politically radical.

2. *The Small Press Review*, edited by Ellen Ferber, Dustbooks. Short reviews, articles of interest, Small Press Book Club a regular feature. Source of many of the leads for this article.

3. *The Publish It Yourself Handbook*, edited by Bill Henderson, The Pushcart Press, P.O. Box 3801, Wainscott, NY 11975, 1973. Source of historical background in this article. A history rather than a manual. Pushcart is also the publisher of the annual *Best From the Small Presses*, an excellent introduction to the breadth and scope of the contemporary scene.

4. *Literary Politics in America,* Richard Kostelanetz, Sheed, Andrews, & McMeel, New York, 1978. Paperback reprint of the famed *The End of Intelligent Writing,* a careful study of the incestuous New York publishing and reviewing scene.

5. *The Passionate Perils of Publishing*, Celeste West and Valerie Wheat, a special issue of *Booklegger* magazine, San Francisco, 1979. Special articles on the literary-industrial complex, guides for publishers and authors, the feminist press, etc.

6. *The Blockbuster Complex*, Thomas Whiteside, Wesleyan University Press, 1981. Fascinating study of how private publishers became corporate, leading up to the mergers with entertainment conglomerates. Also contains a detailed study of how the B. Dalton Co. has revolutionized the book-selling industry. Makes no mention at all of the small press. Originally published as a series of articles in *The New Yorker.*

7. *Publishers' Weekly*, September 10, 1982, a small press feature issue with a lengthy study by Judith Appelbaum. The import of the article is that collectively, small presses do a multimillion dollar business, a small but significant portion of the trade. The issue also contains a number of blurbs by editors of small presses about their operations. Many literary presses are included. My initial skepticism about this issue has given way to a new sense of its importance, for the fact of small presses *as a collective* is going to be of great significance in future studies. In that sense, this article is an unwitting breakthrough.

PW's parent, R.R. Bowker, has since (fall '83) launched *Small Press*, a how-to mag for publishers!

8. Review media:
   (a) *The American Book Review* (cited in the article), interested in the best books being published. Covers small press, university press, commercial press. Intelligent, well-written.
   (b) *The New Boston Review,* 77 Sacramento St., Somerville, Mass., 02143. Excellent national review.
   (c) *Stony Hills*, Weeks Mills, New Sharon, ME 04955. Good coverage of national small press scene, with New England focus.

Carpenter Press's first office

Carol Berge

Center

Carol Berge

Carol Berge was born on Manhattan Island in 1928. "Grew up in New York. Studied with Louise Bogan, Kimon Friar, M.L. Rosenthal, Warren Bower, Ralph Bates, Margaret Mead, and others. Attended college(s) for eight years; no degrees. Sociology, Psych. and Geology, mostly. Current absorption with history and economics and physics plus the physical sciences in general. Twenty books —one son, Peter (born 1956). I earn part of my living by teaching at university level—very challenging and ultimately worth it; though it doesn't pay well, one meets some very fine people. I've taught all over the country. I had a NY State Council CAPS Grant in Fiction in 1974 (just after the publication of the three Bobbs-Merrill books—a collection of poetry, a collection of stories and novellas, and the novel *Acts of Love*)—this was also the year that *Acts* came out in paper from Pocket Books, and the year that both Peter and I 'left home' and sold the farmhouse in Woodstock. Since then, I've bought, remodelled and sold three more houses and enjoyed it immensely—this is one way I earn a living. I received an NEA in fiction in 1979."

Literary Magazines and *CENTER*

By the time I finished college (1954), I'd read into *The Dial, The Sun, The Little Magazine* and others. By 1959, I had read or was reading *Chelsea, Poetry Chicago, Partisan, Paris Review*. In San Francisco, I read (and was later published in) *Genesis/West* and *Beatitude*—I suppose they were my introduction to the contemporary excitement of the ecstatic little literary mag, and Barney Childs and Chester Anderson were my earliest inspirations of what could be done. Then came Ed Sanders, who's still a giant and an example; I was published in (actually, one has to say, I participated in) several issues of *Fuck You*, and Ed published my "Vancouver Report" on his back-room mimeo press. *FY* was the apex: fresh, audacious, defiant and utterly *au courant,* the core of the mimeo revolution. I read and liked *Yugen, Floating Bear, Noose, Kulchur* and *Big Table* and thought them exciting. I met, heard and was energized by Burroughs, Gysin, Ginsberg, Ferlinghetti, Kerouac, Kesey, Roi Jones.

In 1970 I began gathering material for *Center* as a forum for innovative and experimental new prose and fiction; it seemed to me there were too few places for new writing to be seen. I never considered editing a magazine as a way to make any money. The first issue was run off on a Gestetner by friend Susan Sherman in NY (I was living in Woodstock) and I had the cover done in Kingston and mailed it out (200 copies) myself. #s 2 through 13 were published from anywhere I happened to be—Ohio, Mississippi (concurrent with my work as Editor-in-Chief of *Mississippi Review*, a lit mag of a whole other color, as they say, and that was the first time I rode straddling two horses), New Mexico, Calif., N.Y., anywhere.

People have received *Center* well: I have a copious folder of comments—it had good reviews in *Margins, SPR*, and *TriQuarterly* and was chosen as one of the litmags in NY State's pilot project for State Libraries. It's in various university libraries in USA and Canada. I stopped publishing in 1981, feeling I'd done what I set out to do and would like to take a break. I'm currently Contributing Editor to *Woodstock Review* and to *Shearsman*, two good litmags. And that's enough for now. If it changes, I can always begin doing *Center* again.

From issue #2, *Center* was partly funded by CCLM/NEA Grants. I got as little as $300 and as much as $4,800 in grants and stretched them as far as they'd go. I had an almost religious precept of paying my authors and got grants to do so—even if it was as little as $3 a page and copies. I'd say that each copy of *Center* was read by at least two writers, and with an average print run of 400-500 copies, that meant *Center* was seen by over 1,000 writers and students of writing, which I considered successful. And the feedback was energizing and exciting for all.

Certainly I was writing my own prose and poetry while editing and publishing *Center*. It's always been my theory that energy breeds energy; I like being involved in two or more projects at the same time. I don't believe in "writer's block," I've never experienced it. I suppose the most significant aspect or accomplishment of my having published *Center* is the room it gave to really exciting writers—the encouragement it afforded to writers of experimental prose—to know that there was a place where they could see it in print, fast, and get feedback from other intelligent writers, pronto. People who published in *Center* networked, exchanged good words, came to know each other. Sure, I'd do it again —if there's a need and if I get the urge. As far as its being "worth it," editing and publishing *Center* took a lot of time and a good deal of money and a tremendous amount of energy, often cooperative (parties to put it together, sometimes, and always mailing-parties)—these were good events for all concerned, a fine *communitas*.

As far as regrets, very few: one writer hassled me endlessly, making changes and corrections ad nauseam in his ms., diddling, fiddling and rewriting till I was out of patience, and then, when the issue was printed, complaining that his final version was different from the one printed, and giving me an Errata sheet to insert in each and every copy. I removed them almost at once. There was no noticeable difference, believe it; the piece was a series of non sequiturs, deserving house-room because I had imagined some integrity it turned out not to have. Another regret would be having to receive guff from those whose works I had to reject; I'm sure I sympathize with writers but I'd imagine the last thing a writer can afford to be is thin-skinned. But at any rate, I can count these nerds, these incidents, on one hand, so they are proportionally few: I printed some 250 writers in the 11 years that *Center* existed.

Center was *all* psychic energy. I thought of it that way and I still do. A lot of love, a few serious mistakes, a few minor ones, but the majority were a success: the appearance in print of new writing from fine writers who deserved to become better-known. Some 40 books have appeared which contain material first printed in *Center*, by such writers as Toby Olson, Carol Sturm Smith, Al Drake, James Mechem, it's a great list, and anyone can have the list who wishes it: write to me.

Part of the reason for stopping publication of *Center* was the shift in the economy. James Mechem and I sat down in some pizza joint in Wichita two years ago and talked about little mags when I was on my way across country with my son Peter; James told me his *Out of Sight* was selling for $300 the complete set, to libraries, and a few months later, that figure seemed suddenly rational and attractive: I would get that last issue out, and would charge that or more for full sets of *Center*. That's what I did: the last issue, #13, is priced on the cover at $15: it's a signed, limited edition of just 200 copies, really beautiful and chock-full of the kind of fine writing I've always tried for in *Center*. I am also selling sets of the first-three-issues, as a collector's item, for $150 the set. Back copies are limitedly available, again for $15 each. *Full* sets—#1 through #13, with a facsimile #4, are $350. Send checks to me at 222 W. 23rd St., NY, NY 10011. If any writer and/or contributor wishes to complete her or his set, a different price applies; write to me and query.

As to my concept of the background of any editor/publisher of a literary magazine: she or he should be literary. I mean that in the same sense that I think creative writing should be taught by creative writers, not theoreticians or pedants. The prime requisites for editing are intelligence, sentience, literacy and just plain pure drive/energy. I think there are too many little mags, and I'm thinking now of *Antaeus* on the one extreme and *Bitterroot* on the other. I don't want to be bored when I pick up a lit mag; I don't want to go on some guy's ego-trip, or on some other guy's pedantry-trip. I think the mags who publish Alfred Dorn should be outlawed.

Some of the lit-mag editors and magazines I have really enjoyed and respected: James Mecham and his *Out of Sight*; Ray Federman and *Mica*; Ed Hogan's *Aspect*; Jeanne Lance and Peter Holland with *Gallery Works*; Stella and *Back Roads*; George Bowering's *Imago*; Cid Corman's *Origin* series; *The Ant's Forefoot* (I don't know who did that); Anna Banana's *File* (together, I suppose, with the Canadada people), Jane Creighton's *Sail the Road Clear,* and (enormously), Donald Phelps' *For Now*. I confess that I don't read literary magazines

25

much any more. What I do read: *The Harvard Medical Newsletter. TIME. Financial World. Barron's. MONEY. Bestletter. Antique Trader News. The Wall Street Journal. New York Magazine. IWS Newsletter.* And whatever books my friends have written and send me or I buy from them. And books I review.

I like oriental cooking best of any and seafood next. I've gained 25 lbs. in the past six years. I feel fat and fiftyish. My hair is pewter-color now. I smoke too much and would like to quit but I may not. At present I am conducting two workshops at home (at the Chelsea Hotel, in New York)—one in Poetry Writing, one in Fiction Writing; they are *great.* I love them, I love the people and the energy and doing them, I look forward always.

I have, I think, a realistic perspective about the kind of writing, and the kind of editing and publishing, I do. I don't create a mass product—I don't, as my advertising executive brother recently pointed out, deal in "multiplicity"—that is, I don't make a product that caters to the multitudes. I'm an elitist. I write for the 1/10 of 1 percent and I edit for that narrow group as well. That's why I'm not rich. I wish I were rich. But when I went through the Est training some five years ago, I understood that if I really wanted to be rich, I would be. So the point is moot. Anyway, I do like challenges. I suppose that's apparent. Why else would anyone start up a literary magazine and continue it for 11 years? Why else would one write avant-garde prose? I tried twice to write a commercial novel and failed utterly. What a cliché—I mean, simply, I failed. Period. What I succeed at is writing non-commercial stories and novels and non-commercial magazine editing.

What I despair of most, probably, is academic little-mags which specialize in the tried-and-proven, the pat and dead and boring, things with plot and narrative and dialogue all in their proper proportions according to Hoyle. What I despair of next, surely, is the clutter, self-pity and trash of the two Owski's among us: Di and Chas, the Prince and Princess of Overproduction. What I delight in and treasure is those of us who keep the line clean and fresh, deal straight on with the reality—I mean, don't come from an old script, don't come out of reaction but out of action.

The poets I never tire of are those who write from historical perspective: always, Olson; Rexroth sometimes, Pound, Bishop, Snyder. The cold shiver down the spine, the in-touchness, the lack of trivia, the absorption into history/ physics/earthscience. A grandeur, a grace. As for prose writers, William Eastlake, Amiri Baraka, Dave (D.E.) Steward, Dennis Williams, Ed Sanders are writing today's excellence—more, of course; but not too many more. See list of those published in *Center*; they've had my vote. George Hitchcock is always good. I like those writers whose style is unmistakeable without seeing the signature—or, let's say, I respect that. Jackson Mac Low, in a class by himself, or in with the other composers. What John Cage writes is there: with Soleri and Lilly and Fuller; you can't separate it into history or philosophy, poetry or prose, it's all of them. Certainly the voco-verbal work of Meredith Monk is purest poetry, as is the dance of Phoebe Neville and Yvonne Rainer. But then we'd have to get over into film, as Yvonne has, as Carolee Schneemann has, and into video, as Nam June Paik has—aren't his video works poetry, isn't Harry Smith's Heaven

26

and Earth film pure poetry? I don't want to see a separation that calls what I do poetry and what these people do something else; it's all the same stuff. It connects into, defines and shapes how we live, how the life will be lived next.

TERRY STOKES
GAYL JONES
DON CUSHMAN
DAVID KELLY
ALEX GILDZEN
CAROL NAST
ROBERT BRADY
NINA KHINOY
LYN HEJINIAN
TOM WHALEN
JOHN BENNETT
TOM OLSON
TOBY OLSON
JORY SHERMAN
JULIA VOSE
TOM CUSON
BRIAN SWANN
BINNIE KLEIN
LAURA CHESTER
ROGER ANGLE
MARVIN COHEN
RON SUKENICK
ED SANDERS
TOM AHERN
CAROL BERGE
STANLEY BERNE
TED ENSLIN
PHILIP CORNER
TERENCE WINCH
DONALD PHELPS
NANCY SCOTT

BRUCE McALLISTER
ANTHONY EDKINS
GEORGE HITCHCOCK
MELVYN FREILICHER
JACK MARSHALL
LINDA STEPULEVAGE
GEORGE CHAMBERS
ROBERT BONAZZI
KATHLEEN FRASER
STEPHEN E. SAMUELS
SAM EISENSTEIN
HENRY H. ROTH
DAVI DET HOMPSON
GEORGE MONTGOMERY
STEPHEN DIXON
LUCY R. LIPPARD
R. KOSTELANETZ
WILLIAM V. DAVIS
WILLIAM PLAYER
MARJORIE SIMON
ARLENE ZEKOWSKI
LAURA BEAUSOLEIL
ROBERT PETERS
HOWARD McCORD
NORMAN SOLOMON
LINNE GRAVESTOCK
SUSAN HOLAHAN
CHARLES PLYMELL
MICHAEL GORMAN
JONATHAN LONDON
BARBARA SZERLIP

Robert Wilson

December Magazine / December Press

Robert Wilson

Robert Wilson (1928-83) graduated from Lincoln College, Lincoln, Illinois, and from Roosevelt University in Chicago. He was the recipient of a 1974-75 National Endowment for the Arts writing fellowship. He edited *The Film Criticism of Otis Ferguson* (Temple University Press, 1971) and co-edited with Dorothy Chamberlain *The Otis Ferguson Reader* (December Press, 1982). His book of stories and essays, *Young in Illinois*, was published by December Press in 1975. He was Movies Editor of *December* from 1965 to his death.

"The Movies"
From May to December

In the spring of 1963, the new Publisher of *December*, Curt Johnson, dispatched a weary talent scout named Frank Nipp to the University of Chicago neighborhood of Hyde Park in quest of manuscripts for his fledgling issue (Vol. 5). Frank returned with a story about the grim aftermath of a game of mumble-peg lifted from the 1950s hope chest of one of his former students at Roosevelt College, along with an option to publish a second story by the same writer about the same type of kid playing basketball.

Since my literary vein had been tapped by the spring of 1965—the roundball epic appeared in *December* Vol. 6, 1964, a printing fiasco of such proportions that it would have stopped any publisher who was not a hardened lemming dead in his tracks—I needed a transfusion if I was not to be left behind at the very start of what has turned out to be a long, long march.

As it happened, Hyde Park in those days was a hotbed of youthful Sarrisites rabid to spread the Gospel according to St. Andrew. I asked Frank to file a report with the Publisher stating that I was prepared to edit a complete section of *December* devoted to the lively art of film criticism. The Publisher agreed.

Volume No. 7 contained most of the ingredients that were to characterize "The Movies" section through nearly a decade of ongoing vitality. (Although the section survives as a sentimental addition to the by now increasingly rare "regular" numbers, a note of heavy breathing and agitated age could already be detected in the last continuous appearance in 1973, when the Academy overtook us all.) Andrew Sarris himself blessed that first section with one of his most graceful essays, "The Movieness of Movies"; youth and the University of Chicago Doc Films Group were represented by William Routt and 19-year-old Richard Thompson, who settled in to become an old pro (Thompson is now Chairman of the film department at Latrobe University, Rundoora-Victoria, Australia, where Routt also teaches); Professor T.J. Ross of Fairleigh Dickinson University arrived over the transom with "*The Servant* as Sex Thriller," his first of what was to become a record number of published manuscripts in *December*; and, not least, Frank Nipp carried forward a kinky *December* tradition by signing his wife's maiden name, "Rita Ann Mayfield," to a book review (on sex and sadism). Ever onward.

And so, as the Benny Goodman-Ziggy Elman-Martha Tilton version of "Thanks for the Memory" echoes softly in the background, we shadows on the landscape of his mind lift our glasses in a toast of all good health and cheer to the Publisher on this the 20th Encampment of his journey to the restful waters and the peaceful night.

december

$2.50

a magazine of the
arts and opinion

PRATT & LAMBERT PAINT

a Mag for
ALL YEAR!
Fiery Polemics
Movies!
Pictures!!
Poetry!
STORIES
plus: the REAL
LOWDOWN on
THE LIT ES-
TABLISHMENT

Drawing of Lee Wallek by Marty Pahls

Explication du Preceding Texte

Lee Wallek

Lee Wallek was born in Lachine, Quebec, Canada, in 1919. He has worked as a freelance text and reference editor in the Chicago area since before World War II (editing, among other projects, two chapters of the 12th ed. of the University of Chicago *Manual of Style*). He has been literary editor of *December* magazine since 1962, and is the author of *The Forbidden Writings of Lee Wallek* (1977), a collection of essays.

. . . I am a farmer's son and a farmer myself. I have also published some short stories. Three altogether. They were included in *The Yen River Magazine*. This is a literary periodical . . . published by the Sian branch of the Writer's Association.—Tsao Chan-Kuei, "The Little Author," in Jan Myrdal's *Report from a Chinese Village* (1963)

It falls to me, as *December* magazine's literary editor, to elucidate Robert Wilson's rather recondite prose—and certainly arcane essay—for those of you who weren't there.

Wilson, of course, was the movies editor of *December*, but he was always much more than that to the magazine. Personally, in spite of his predilection for the slivered screen, I always liked him. All he was asked to do in the present instance, however, was to write a simple response to the same 21 questions all the other contributors to this volume were asked to write a response to. But like almost all the other contributors, he chose to go his own merry way . . . . Well enough and good, I suppose, but murky to the uninitiated.

So, then, there are five paragraphs to Wilson's response; in expanding and explaining I will refer to these paragraphs by number.

Paragraph 1:   Self-effacing as always, Wilson does not elaborate about his two short stories. Both were *almost* published by large-circulation magazines in the mid-'50s, including *New World Writing*, which kept the manuscripts 2½ years before finally rejecting them. (Thirty years ago quite a number of large-circulation U.S. magazines still published quality fiction. Had Wilson been published

33

by them back then—who knows?) And in 1966, another of his stories, "The World Outside Illinois," was cited by Martha Foley as a "notable" story of its year. Moreover, only three years ago (1982) his roundball epic was translated into German as "Betonbasketball" and anthologized in *American Freeway* by MaroVerlag (8900 Augsburg 1, Bismarckstr. 7½, West Germany), the same year that a 7-foot West German transfer student played center for Wilson's hometown high school team in Lincoln, Illinois. Noblesse exchange.

The "weary talent scout named Frank Nipp" referred to in Paragraph 1 is a veteran Chicago reference and textbook editor—ofttimes researcher for, advisor to, and editor of the celebrated journalist, freelance writer, and diplomat John Bartlow Martin. Nipp was confidant and mentor to both Wilson and Johnson early in their working-for-a-living lives and is still, more than a good friend to them both and to *December* through the years.

Finally, with respect to Paragraph 1, and not to belabor the obvious but rather in hopes of clarifying the almost hopelessly obscure, the former Roosevelt College student/writer referred to near the end of the paragraph is Wilson himself. It's passing strange: the two mid-'50s Wilson stories are exceedingly detailed and clear; it is only over the years that Wilson's style has become as elliptical as I find it—and as it must surely be, for I am, after all, the world's foremost litcrit.

Paragraph 2: The printing fiasco happened this way. By 1964 *December* was being typeset in Korea by Samhwa (today a huge Asian conglomerate). Wilson had steered Johnson to that far country, where for a decade skilled Oriental fingers hand-set each issue (many interesting typos as a result) letter by letter for wages approximating ten dollars a month (even so, above average wages for the country). In a misguided effort to save even more money, Johnson had a close friend from high school, who by then was a partner in a job shop in Rapid City, South Dakota (that's right), print Vol. 6. Halfway through the Rapid City print-run the sheriff padlocked the job shop (bankruptcy) and only 300 copies were delivered to Chicago. Another 300 copies were printed at Speed-O-Lith here from the Rapid City plates, but—yes—it was a fiasco. But not of lemming-like proportions. Gracious! And besides, Johnson printed the roundball story again, in a later issue (Vol. 13, nos. 1/2) to make amends. Authors are, in the main, petty ingrates, aren't they?

Paragraph 3: The Publisher agreed to include a section on the movies, yes, but little did he realize what he was letting himself in for. He was forced to feign an interest in an art form to which he had been theretofore marvelously indifferent. And he was dragged kicking and screaming by Wilson to screenings of such turgid silent classics as *Greed* and *The Battleship Potemkin* and, worse, to Norman Mailer's *Maidstone*, a disaster from which most of the rest of the audience—the U of C Doc Films membership, deep-dyed cinema aesthetes all—walked out, leaving Wilson and Johnson (non-members) sitting nearly solitary to view the final torn images of a prose genius gone bonkers behind the boom.

Paragraph 4: Thanks to Wilson, *December* was the first little ("literary") magazine to have a regular section devoted to the movies. Its regular (non-book) issues still feature such a section—most recently Vol. 23, Nos. 3 and 4 (1981), which in addition to its "regular" fiction, articles, and graphics, and 90 pages devoted to feminism (a special), had 45 pages on the silents (Part I), including a 20-page biog/critique of the director Rex Ingram. What Wilson fails to mention is that one of the contributors he names in Paragraph 4 could have (still can) write an exposé based on personal experience of being blacklisted that would skewer the Eastern Literary Establishment. The Publisher and I *begged* Robert Wilson to ask that contributor for that (non-movies) article but he refused . . . . So (must) be it.

Paragraph 5: This is the 23rd Encampment (1963-85) for the Publisher on the long, long march, not the 20th. (Though when Bob wrote his piece it was only the 21st.) The hallmark of little magazines and small presses is the condition of being late. Which is only fair, given their financial constraints, but which calls for some history and statistics.

The founders of *December* were a disaffected quartet from the University of Iowa's Writers Workshop: Richard Schechner, Deborah and James Trissel, and Louis Vaczek. Jeff Marks took over from them when they left the Workshop and in 1962 gave the magazine to Johnson because he (Marks) could no longer afford it.

December is not a quarterly, though many U.S. libraries think it is, and subscribe to it as if it were, and thus some have as many as 16 numbers coming to them. *December* is published irregularly—as often as cash can be got together to pay for an issue—and only four volumes thus far have had four numbers.

The publishing record of *December* (high notes appended) is:

Vol. 1, No. 1—1958—published in Iowa City; Maxwell Geismar, Vance Bourjaily
Vol. 1, No. 2—1958—published in Iowa City
Vol. 2, No. 1—1959—published in Iowa City; Jeff Marks on staff
Vol. 3, No. 1—1960—Marks moves magazine to Chicago
Vol. 3, No. 2—1961—Richard Stern interviews Ralph Ellison
Vol. 3, No. 3—1961—Leslie Singer interviews Tristan Tzara
—No issue in 1962
Vol. 4, No. 1—1963—Jerry Bumpus—third time; Marge Piercy
Vol. 5, No. 1—1963—Raymond Carver—first time; new publisher, Curt Johnson
Vol. 6, No. 1—1964—Henry H. Roth—first time
Vol. 7, No. 1—1965—first Movies section
Vol. 8, No. 1—1966—Carver's "Will You Please Be Quiet, Please?"
Vol. 9, No. 1—1967—the Jerry Bumpus novel *Anaconda* (1st special issue)
Vol. 9, Nos. 2 and 3—1967—first double issue; first John Bennett
Vol. 10, No. 1—1968—Joyce Carol Oates' "By the River"
Vol. 11, Nos. 1 and 2—1969—Richard Hugo interview; Maxwell Geismar; Gershon Legman's "The Fake Revolt"
Vol. 12, Nos. 1 and 2—1970—"Living the Logic of Lunacy in Vietman," Chandler Thompson, and James Drought novella
Vol. 13, Nos. 1 and 2—1971—Richard Kostelanetz, an excerpt from *The End of Intelligent Writing* (then unpublished)
Vol. 14, No. 1—1972—George Chambers' novel *The Bonnyclabber* (co-published

with *Panache* magazine)

Vol. 15, Nos. 1 and 2—1973—Kostelanetz with another *End of . . .* excerpt (still then unpublished)

Vol. 15, Nos. 3 and 4—1973—Curt Johnson's novel *Nobody's Perfect* (published by Carpenter Press)

Vol. 16, Nos. 1 and 2—1974—Jay Robert Nash's war stories, *On All Fronts*

Vol. 17, No. 1—1975—Matthew Hochberg's novel, *Sweet Gogarty*

Vol. 17, No. 2—1975—Robert Wilson's stories, *Young in Illinois*

Vol. 18, No. 1—John Bennett's stories, *The Night of the Great Butcher*

Vol. 18, Nos. 2 and 3—1976—a further excerpt from Jack Conroy's autobiography

Vol. 18, No. 4—1976—Robert Fox's stories, *Destiny News*

Vol. 19, Nos. 1 and 2—1977—Johnson's novel *The Morning Light* (published by Carpenter Press)

Vol. 19, Nos. 3 and 4—1977—*The Forbidden Writings of Lee Wallek*

Vol. 20, Nos. 1 and 2—1978—Norbert Blei's *The Second Novel*

Vol. 20, Nos. 3 and 4—1978—Hugh Fox's novellas, *Honeymoon/Mom*

Vol. 21, Nos. 1 and 2—1979—Henry H. Roth's stories, *In Empty Rooms: Tales of Love*

Vol. 21, Nos. 3 and 4—1979—Dennis Lynds' stories, *Why Girls Ride Sidesaddle*

Vol. 22, No. 1—1980—Thomas E. Connors' stories, *Abstract Relations*

Vol. 23, Nos. 1 and 2—*R.V. Cassill*, a festschrift

Vol. 23, Nos. 3 and 4—*December*'s feminist issue

Vol. 24, Nos. 1 and 2—1982—*The Otis Ferguson Reader*

Vol. 25, Nos. 1-4—*The Dillinger Dossier* by Jay Robert Nash

Vol. 26, Nos. 1-4—Curt Johnson's novel *Song for Three Voices* (published by Carpenter Press)

Back issues are available from Kraus Reprint Corp. and on microfilm from University Microfilms International.

Up to this issue, since 1958, *December* and December Press have published:

1) Seven novels
2) Six collections of short stories
3) Three novellas
4) Three books of essays
5) One non-fiction book
6) One chapbook
7) 162 short stories (exclusive of collections)
8) 61 articles on the movies
9) 895 poems
10) 96 book reviews
11) 77 general articles (essays, editorials, etc., exclusive of book-length collections)
12) 3 plays

13) 7 interviews
14) 429 pages of photos
15) 310 pages of graphic arts
16) 6,674 total pages

I totaled all of the above with a pencil—look, Ma, no pocket calculator! A sum total in 26 years of 38 separate publications. Whew!

Lastly, to give an insight (oh, misbegotten, much-abused word) into the editorial policy of *December*, I reprint below a take-out from an essay by Johnson published in the library and subscriber editions of Vol. 14, No. 1:

"I publish exactly what I like" is probably not specific enough to serve as an editorial policy pronouncement—even though it is completely descriptive—so let me try to embroider it, using as a hoop some questions sent me in 1966 by a young man who said he was "a prospective magazine major in Syracuse University's School of Journalism." He said he was "especially intrigued by the question—what do editors do and why?" and was "consequently conducting a survey of fifty magazines of various types with the hope of . . ." etc. His *Q* and my *A* follow:

Q. How did you get where you are today, what is your background? What is the best preparation for a magazine editor and where can one get this preparation?

A. As close as I can figure it, I'm nowhere today. My preparation for editing a little magazine is 15 years as an editor/writer for how-to-do-it magazines, encyclopedias, and textbook firms. The best preparation for an editor (in my opinion—and that will be understood hereafter) is to edit and produce magazines (even if it's *Rock Products* or *Modern Laundry*) or books (even if it's the commercial idiocy of *The Adventurers* or the mindless idiocy of *Trout Fishing in America*). Experience is not the best teacher only; it's the only best teacher.

Q. What skills are necessary to become a competent editor? How great a role does instinct, curiosity, enthusiasm play in your profession?

A. The skills necessary to an editor are, first, mechanical: how to cut to fit, how to mark and correct type, how to crop pictures, like that; second, enthusiasm. Make that first, instinct and curiosity being handmaidens to enthusiasm. And always, per that great Hoosier philosopher Abe Martin, *L'audace*.

Q. What kind of character does your magazine have and how close is the magazine's character to your own personality, ideas, interests?

A. *December*'s character is the short story. And as close as I can make it.

Q. Norman Podhoretz, editor of *Commentary*, has written that the editorial process boils down to four major phases—doubt, deliberation, labor and negotiation. Does your view differ much from this?

A. Yes.

Q. Are most of your articles commissioned by the magazine or submitted independently? How do you go about getting your articles and persuading the "good" writers to write for you? Is there much cajoling on your part?

A. Most are submitted independently. No cajoling, or very little, on my part, because of function of little mags: to print unknowns—most of whom the editor hopes are "good" or will become so.

Q. How do you negotiate with an outraged writer? Do you find that most writers are grateful or indignant when they see their articles edited?

A. Don't negotiate with them. Have had only one outraged (see vol. 7, no. 1 of *Dec*, pp. 192-93) and simply let him rage. Since we print mostly belles-lettres, we don't (I don't) edit much. Bob Wilson does and the writers are grateful, as they have reason to be.

Q. Do you personally examine each manuscript you get? Do you find it hard to reject most pieces? What fault do you find most common in rejected manuscripts?

A. Yes. No. Amateurity.

Q. How do you encourage your writers? How important are relationships with writers and their agents to the editor? How can the writer and the editor benefit each other?

A. By printing them. Not at all. Don't know.

Q. What factors restrain a magazine's creative energy? How much influence does the publisher have on the creative spirit of a magazine?

A. Time and money. On independent little mags the publisher is usually also the editor. Therefore . . .

Q. How does an editor encourage his staff to produce beyond its capacity?

A. He can't because they can't.

Q. How do you begin a publication—to write for a specific audience or to fulfill a need, or both?

A. Both.

Q. How do you know who your audience is and what they like? Do you feel your magazine is benefiting its readers? The community? How?

A. Don't know. Yes, I feel mag benefits its readers—but, as important, it benefits its writers by giving them an audience, however small, and also some distance from what they are doing. Could benefit the community—by shaking them up a mite, maybe—if community read it. Which it doesn't, en masse.

Q. Do you ever ask yourself if being an editor is all worth it? Do you ever have any regrets?

A. No. Yes, but not about being an editor.

Q. As an editor, what do you care most about, professionally? Do you believe magazine editing can contribute to the betterment of the English language?

A. *December*. Magazine editing contributes daily to the standards of usage of English, not necessarily the betterment, not necessarily the worsening. What are your absolutes?

Those were the questions and those were the answers six years ago. They'd be the same today. I never heard from the young man again, however, so quite possibly my answers were unsatisfactory—and may still be. Therefore I have constructed a set of searching, rigorously logical questions especially to clarify, once and for all, the editorial policy of *December*, and will now ask, then answer them.

38

Q. What is the world of the little magazine editor like?

A. Like most every other world in the world: Unlimited authority with no power at all.

Q. What is the world of the little magazine *writer* like?

A. Read Gilbert Sorrentino's *Imaginative Qualities of Actual Things* (Pantheon, 1971).

Q. What are your prejudices in fiction?

A. I'm against stories with teachers or writers in them . . . .

Q. Do you have any strong opinions or prejudices?

A. Not me. But, of course, being a WASP Midwest male raised in lower middleclass circumstances, I "instinctively" fear and distrust people with money, brains, or power. Also poolsharks and women. After that, I suppose everything follows. These slightly skewed inclinations I am aware of, however, and thus lean over backwards to compensate for them, so that finally—

Q. Yes. And as your friend, Abe Martin, the Hoosier whizbang, also said, "Give me six words from the pen of the most honest man alive and I'll hang the sunuvabitch." Now then, what about fiction in *December*? How would you categorize it?

A. I wouldn't. But in *submissions* of fiction to *December*, 40 percent of all the stories submitted are *apparently all* meaning—but since, if this *is* so, almost invariably the meaning is *not* enunciated in either plot or character, and the intended meaning (theme) remains obscure; 30 percent are all character, 20 percent are all plot, and 10 percent are all character and setting. Or, put another way, 45 percent are plot and character, 54 percent are setting and plot, and 1 percent are a workable combination of all the elements necessary to a story. That 1 percent is what is published in *December*—together with some few stories not quite finished but published simply because the author is a hard worker, has talent, and should be encouraged, or he may quit writing. This is known as the "A-for-effort" editorial approach and is very much frowned upon by all other editors—and writers.

Q. On the subject of prejudices—which probably define an editorial policy as well as anything, what are some more of your own?

A. I am prejudiced in favor of the individual, decentralization, and freedom, as long as I define all terms . . . . You nod . . . . The background that qualifies me to hold this prejudice is that I pay taxes and can read. I also edit this "little" magazine. This last qualification has never gotten me any place in the worlds of power, wealth, and celebrity, or in the worlds of culture, knowledge, and sensibility, either, and that it hasn't has pissed me off considerably over the years. It *has* helped me get my own stories published, though—you look shocked?—and it *has* got me a number of good evenings of fellowship while smoking mary jane and/or drinking whiskey. Also a split lip. Also some good friends. (Though I was happier putting out *December* when I didn't know any writers or editors personally, truth be told. Life was less complicated.) At any rate—are you listening still?

Q. You were saying?

A. I was saying I'd never gotten anyplace editing *December*, never "made it" like Normie P., editor of *Commentary*, did, for example, and that this has pissed me off. Some years back, though, I decided to live with it. (As far as I could see, there was only one alternative.) Just now, though, mentioning mary jane and whiskey and using the term "pissed me off," I was wondering, is that the sort of language a father's teenage son and daughter should hear? And I—ho-there! Are you listening?

Q. Whu—? Oh, yes. Next, I wanted to ask you why it is in the cinema that the good guys hardly ever say anything? Is it—?

A. On account of Abe Martin's six words and hanging bit. But I was asking about the kind of language proper to use in front of one's teenage son and daughter. In the ten years I've been putting out *December*, not only did I outgrow Norman Mailer (or *he* did), but also my son grew from six to 16 and my daughter from three to 13. (I was 34 and too old to trust when I started.) That does raise the question, doesn't it, whether (or not) it's proper to use certain kinds of language? Or worse, to tell them that their father makes most of his living today by writing pornography? (Which must also say something about our country and its values, huh? Or their father?)

Q. Not really, do you?

A. Yes or no, depending on what's proper.

Q. Well, let's leave your family out of this, can we?

A. They're very important to me. Would I be working as a garbageman if it weren't for them? And both of my children are very sensible people—a lot more than you or me, or little mag editors or writers. Most kids are, you know. But all right. I just want to say that through working on a little magazine I've met a goodly number of people with paper assholes, but never so many—not nearly such a high percentage—as when I was working for textbook firms and encyclopedias (and I include Britannica most emphatically) and (1984 addition) the American Bar Association (I speak of the lawyers who belong). The higher echelons there are staffed almost exclusively with such. In fact, the higher you go—say on up to the Presidency of the United States—I mean, for crissake, money-grubbing liars, cheats, frauds, and killers. Wot the hell, the corporations and their stockholders made *record* profits last year, and the rest of us—the *most* of us—were told we had to cinch in our belts and fight inflation and the recession, and have our wages frozen (*if* we could find a job), because—I mean, Jesus H. Kee-*rist*, man! . . .

Q. Is there anything final you'd like to say about the editorial policy of *December*?

A. Only that I wish we could get more—and more readable—articles on politics in it. For as Edward Abbey once said, "If the heavy-assed oligarchy which now owns and operates America does not get off our necks and begin to respond to human needs, we are going to have a revolution—maybe a civil war." That is totally true, and—

Q. I see. Do you have any other plans?

A. Only to lose eight pounds. I was hoping you'd ask me if I'd ever been tempted to sell out during the past ten years. That's usually a big question where litmags are concerned. They're very proud of their editorial integrity, un-

40

fettered by commercial considerations, so to say. The answer is that no, I haven't ever been tempted to sell out, but I wish I had been. If somebody came to me this instant with a bundle of money and wanted *December*, I'd sell out on the spot . . . . And then maybe I'd start another little magazine—another independent. I think I'd call the next one *The Yen River Magazine* . . . . It's as my daughter explained to me last Sunday when we were having this Italian food at Gennaro's in Little Italy, and I was trying to persuade her to become *December*'s business manager. I have no head for figures, anyway, or skill at wrapping packages (which is a lot of work), and I was telling her how this was her big chance . . . . But she refused . . . . Anyway, she said to me, "You get a lot of fun out of it, don't you."

There it is. Those curious as to a fuller history of *December* are referred to the Afterword of this volume. They may find it there. Incidentally, the name of the magazine comes from the month in which the first issue was *supposed* to have been published. (It arrived about three months later.)

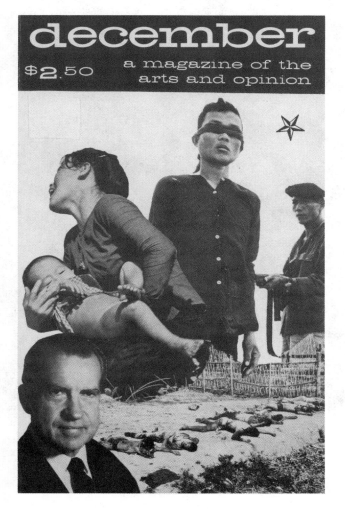

Len Fulton

Dust and Dustbooks

Len Fulton

Len Fulton was born in Lowell, Massachusetts, in 1934. He has been editor/publisher at Dustbooks since 1963, was chairman of COSMEP, 1968-71 (that is, at the *beginning*), and also in 1973, is the author of the novels *The Grassman* (1974) and *Dark Other Adam Dreaming* (1975) and co-author of *American Odyssey* (1975). Among many other services he—and Dustbooks—render to the alternative press, he is consultant on small presses to the American Library Association.

An Odyssey

Somewhere in the shadow of a north New England hill there are two sticks. They are smooth at one end from my hands, and they are chopped and battered at the other from the miles of ground they covered in running out my dreams. They were my front legs. Their heft in my hand had been the heft of my imagination, and those sticks gave me my first real measure of it. When, later, real horses and words came to replace them I planted them in that shadow, and they grew in my memory like seeds. Now it is later by 35 winters, by a dozen horses, 2 novels, a publishing company, and 25,000 books within the reach of my hands. What I learned from those marvelous old sticks (hewn from pine slabs they were) was something about will and idea, how the reach must be always for the grasp to be ever—and how the frozen mud of one dream thaws and becomes the germinal soil of yet another. All that from sticks.

And it is the smell of fields I remember as we cut them down in the northern Vermont summer. She was a hard land and the late '40s were hard times. The winter was white—I remember that too. We broke through adamantine snow and the ice to get the animals to water. In the morning the only warmth came from the cows we were milking, and the manure had to be pickaxed out of the gutters. The nights were long and tuneless and marked the days with ghosts. One winter as we huddled in that farmhouse under the northern shadow of Mount Mansfield, my father took to writing. I think he had always coveted the enterprise—or at least possessed some prideful hint of a secret talent. A Canadian Scot he was, whose people were northern lumberjacks with a literacy hard won and carried high. In those few bleak months as the temperature edged to 30 and 35 below, he bent seriously to it, wrote poems, stories about region, and an allegorical novella called *Our Town*. I think what touched me most and first was his privacy of self, the luxurious loneliness of his own world of mind. I sensed what he was up to those hours and nights and weeks behind the keys— just as I had come to sense him as a man of the soil and as a hunter. He was making a hard world over according to his own passions; he was putting his private mind (and his loneliness) into a *form*. I had an almost immediate and organic faith in the effort, as I had in the beauty of those deep Vermont woods— which could be any place you wanted to make them.

Writing, then, for me grows out of the private self and gives form. Publishing is (or *should* be) a further natural step in that formation—which is why I feel the small magazine, for example, is itself an art form. It presents a life-style, a personal bout with some devil or dolphin. The form of the work determines its published shape as it slips from its private to its public world. The form must be true to its private origins and the shape to its formal ones, so you then have the craft of publishing keeping faith with the art. I can't imagine publishing a magazine, book or newspaper that lacked a continuity, or in whose continuity I took no part. Well, yes, I can *imagine* it, but it jars.

I started *Dust* magazine in 1963 because I had the urge to do it—and because I had lain fallow long enough thank you under the largely self-inflicted notions that there were higher arbiters of taste. The "quiet world" of the '50s (actually more comatose than quiet) was falling in, and in Berkeley, California, where I lived and worked, the collapse was as big as they get. Mario Savio was making speeches about "putting your bodies on the wheels and on the gears to stop the odious machine"—and the machine to which he referred, the University of California in Berkeley, was one with which I possessed intimate familiarity.

I had learned publishing early, and had learned it under the hard, bedeviled fist of Maine's icebound Yankee soul. A friend, Bob Fay, and I, new idylled from the University at Portland, started with no more than some innocence and charm a weekly newspaper at Kennebunkport in 1957. From that we embedded ourselves deeper yet into the Yankee soul upcountry at Freeport where we purchased a letterpress print shop and two more local weekly papers. If it had worked (I was 21), I might still be there, but as it happens the winter of '57-'58, riding in on seawinds that only a Melville could love, slapped us breathless. I strung south, working for a weekly in Massachusetts, and spent my last year east of the Mississippi (1958-59) on a daily just outside New York City. From there I returned to college at the University of Wyoming at Laramie, and moved to Berkeley in '61 to work on a doctorate in psychology. Well before Savio and the Free Speech Movement (FSM) I had come to know and feel the insular and indurate heart of academe. Psychology was on the make everywhere for grants, crying out for a scientific name—and pulverizing those who resisted.

I resisted. I resisted because I had paid my price in austerity before the north New England snows, and "experimental rigor" in the study of the human mind often reduced to absurdity the merest creative impulse. (We used to say of this experimental rigor, that it had *rigormortis*.) I had studied literature, and done some writing, so resisted because I sensed a more than chance connection between human behavior, language, and mind. Those Berkeley psychologists skirted that issue by using rats, monkeys, frogs and other animals who did not confuse the issue with words. I proposed to study the literary roots of Freud for my dissertation; they handed me to a faculty advisor named French, from Maine, with no "r's" in the soul of his language, and a herd of laboratory monkeys with their brains ablated. I proposed novels and poetry as the matter of my study; they proposed the English Department—though my talent for statistics frustrated the clarity of this advice. "Symbols," I muttered to French one day. "It's all symbols." He looked up from my paper, written in the first person, active voice—a criminal thing in the academy. "You write that Freud *felt* a certain way about language. I doubt that many of us care how Freud *felt*," he said, leaning forward on that word as though he'd trapped the fingers of a heretic defiling a sacred fount. "Stated, postulated, yes—felt, no!"

Five years of academic psych plus a dime got you a cup of coffee in those days, and very little more. However, as an undergraduate at Wyoming I had been forced through a course in research statistics, something used to terrorize students in the social sciences. I found it in fact a quite sensible pursuit, took further studies in it, and when I went looking for work again in Berkeley I discovered I'd unknowingly gotten myself an ace in the hole. No one needed a psychologist, but every project in even the borderline sciences screamed out for a statistician, a person who could arrange raw and often carelessly acquired data into sophisticated tabular form, charts, graphs; who understood "confidence" and "testing" and the use of computers. I was not long in landing good and steady employment with the California State Department of Public Health, a position I held until retiring in 1968, and without which there would've been no *Dust* and certainly no Dustbooks.

Dust magazine was founded in a breech. It was personal for me, and also spiritual, ideological in the social sense, a response to a new *Zeitgeist*. I found a number of others too, with modest writing or publishing experience: Andrew Curry, black, brilliant, a product of Cleveland's Hough District, a psychiatric social worker, painter, poet, musician, dancer; George Kauffman, a staffer for the *Berkeley Barb*—a man from the '30s who'd never lost his angst or his consciousness for the world's dismal; Emil Strom, a composer, witty, good with language in a piecemeal fashion, an unruly conservative, like Kauffman a product of the '30s, who would argue that he'd "seen it all before"; Frank Lapo, a geneticist who couldn't find work precisely in his line and so took blue-collar jobs in defiance, a complex and unpredictable person whom I understood least of all, given to an absolute distaste for conventional expression (Lapo was our

45

"Treasurer" and showed a transcending compulsion for the job); and Bob Fay, my old friend and partner from Maine newspapers, at that point an ad man for a paper in Richmond, California.

Just before starting *Dust*, in 1962, Kauffman and I had both been directors of a newspaper in Berkeley, a co-op weekly modeled on the food co-ops and titled *The Citizen*. By early '63, with nothing published, the paper was already foundering in the wash of Berkeley's upper-middle class liberality, reminding me more than anything else of academic rigormortis. What wiped out *The Citizen*, however, was not the unending harassment by its reader-owners, or by the California Corporations Commissioner, or even the hostility of Berkeley's merchant class. What wiped out *The Citizen* was *The Berkeley Barb*, a hip, flip and grainy harbinger of the underground press movement. *The Barb, The Los Angeles Free Press*, and New York's *East Village Other* all started circa 1963, and by the time they had organized the Underground Press Syndicate in '65 there were some 100 such papers in the country. It was a primal year for change.

Dust faced two struggles, fiscal and editorial, both hitting crisis proportions by the third issue (Fall '64). At that time the "editorial board" had shrunk to four: Curry, Fay, Strom, and me. By the fourth issue Strom had quit, and by the eighth, Fay. Curry, bless his soul, stuck with it through the 13th issue (Summer '69), mainly as poetry editor, having given up all financial involvement in the magazine with Fay's departure in 1966. To this day I don't know whether to blame the fiscal or the aesthetic/editorial problems more. Anyone who's tried it will probably know that a publishing operation with six editor-partners is a unique form of madness, and it *is* in retrospect marvelous that anything got out at all. Yet those first seven issues were regular, 64 to 88 pages, costing $600 apiece. This prorated at $100 per partner, minus subscription receipts which were boosted by having six people with private circles as disparate as their artistic biases. By Number 4 there were 518 paid subscribers, virtually all individuals, no institutions. Subscription money covered roughly two of the first four issues, with the other two costing those of us left about $250 each—considerable when the final product was destined never to satisfy all investors. At first renewal (#5) the real thunder of periodical publishing clapped me awake. Subscriptions plunged to 300. And with each succeeding issue more atrophy occurred, with huge gouges at #8 and #12 when new volumes began. When *Dust* suspended publication in 1972 it had 290 paid subscribers.

The personal and editorial conflicts were simply inevitable, numerous and rending. Lapo, always unpredictable, dropped the records and bank book on my doorstep one day and drove off forever into the sunrise. Kauffman, who thought we should publish only ourselves and refused even to read unsolicited manuscripts (which by #2 were pouring in), quit when we voted not to print one of his short stories. Strom objected to a lesbian poem titled "A Pretty Story" by someone named Lake Purnell from Kansas. We voted to print it anyway—and Strom withdrew the day #3 was published. By #7 Fay had amassed personal problems—and an obvious weariness for the repetitive process of periodical publishing—struggling through one issue only to get to the next. We agonized on this for a day, for neither of us took the other's plight lightly. It was clear he must leave.

46

And it was clear by then to me that though the founding deal had been a six-way split, the operant deal was me, and five others who had tentatively agreed to the thing as long as it pleased them. Everyone but me thought always of the magazine as ultimately mine, and as a result felt a certain freedom to walk away from it. At Fay's departure Curry said he would edit the magazine—as long as I would publish it. Faith, I must say, drove me after that. It was a faith in literature as an enduring human pursuit, a faith in the times—the '60s—as a sort of renaissance which neither I nor anyone then could precisely name, but being *in* them was proof enough. It was a faith which measured the medicinal power of independence by the natterings of its many detractors, and a sense somehow of the intrinsic value and dominion of the freedom of print. It was a faith in the essentially tribal spirit under which the small press functions, a spirit dwelling on the one hand outside the corporate octopus, but on the other inside the cultural stream of real possibilities. And it was a faith, more than the rest, in myself—as my father had known it in himself to survive the cold blowing blizzards of the eastern northcountry.

I decided to be a publisher again.

Throughout the summer and fall of 1963 we had held many meetings, towards the first issue, planned for Spring '64. We spent one of those meetings finding a title, which we came to after casting out the "journal of" stigma (stronger then than now, believe me), "quarterly of" which was too entrapping in the periodical sense (and also possessed of some stigma), and Thales' four elements. I suggested *Dust* as something that existed in literature and life without regard to style, age or place; and as a title under which we could maintain an editorial posture sufficiently open (read "loose") to accommodate all of our aesthetic proclivities. We quickly began to use its literary references in ad copy, from "dust into dust" to "fear in a handful" of it. Issue #1 carried a 17th-century subscription pitch:

> Golden lads and girls all must
> As chimney-sweepers, come to dust.

We defined a "shovelful" ($3.50) as "four handfuls" ($1 each), and when the mag died in 1972 one long-time subscriber wrote: "It is hard to believe that never again will another dust bite the day." Several scientific organizations subscribed, clearly planning to advance their laboratory knowledge of dust as a ubiquitous substance—but no one ever wrote back admitting an error, hanging on instead through four issues. We received, starting early, many poems and stories either titled "Dust" or about dust (I don't recall ever publishing one of these), and one day I found a copy of Yael Dayan's novel *Dust* lying on my desk with never an explanation as to how it got there. I became known in the post office as "Dusty," and had a printer once who would address my mail:

> Dirt Books
> Len Fulton, Chief Pornographer

47

In the early '60s poetry was still struggling to escape the aesthetic regulations of the "formalists" (Eliot, Ransom, etc.). Language in general was still struggling for the full measure of its freedom against suppressive social forces as well as academic ones. The Beats had made gains in both these matters in the '50s, but it truly remained for the little magazines and underground newspapers of the '60s to take up the cause with their sheer number and diversity. While they had been limited in number and located in either New York or San Francisco, these early efforts were easily isolated and harassed, as with, for example, "Howl" or Lenore Kandel's *Love Book*—or Miller's *Tropic of Cancer* which was prosecuted in Marin County, California, in 1962. Once magazines, presses and newspapers began to appear everywhere in the country it became a futile business to track them down—to say nothing of a demand for literacy that outran most county prosecutors. Furthermore, the Free Speech Movement at Berkeley in '63, which drew masses of street-bodies to its cause, and the burnings of Watts and Detroit, soon created a perspective against which a free and open press looked least mean of all.

The small magazines, which began to proliferate in 1963-64, took up such causes as "concrete" poetry, a mix of visual and grammatical material in experimental form imported from Brazil, Switzerland, England, and Canada. This led to the whole testing of "intermedium art," wherein old structural genres were reworked in new, fluid and functional ways. The "Meat" poets, who began as followers of Charles Bukowski, stretched the subject matter of poetry via their mimeo mags: "Every inch of the planet earth, every curse word, every thimble, every spot of dirt, every slam, bang, jing, every chug in the harbor is poetry" (Douglas Blazek in *Ole* #1). And dope, war, prison, race, ecology, and sexism all eventually worked their way into poetry, as content which affected form, mostly by loosening it. Rhyme and meter in the old sense fell into final disuse as the "projective line" (that of the natural breath) became dominant, through oral presentation. When we started *Dust* there were two readings per week in the San Francisco Bay Area. Now there are literally dozens.

In a way *Dust* was a minicosm of the small magazine of its day. We published a little of everything and remained true to our founding sense of openness. We published Bukowski and Blazek, prison and dope poetry by William Wantling, socially satirical poems by L.C. Phillips, the street poems of Doug Palmer, translations from the Italian by Dora Pettinella, from the Japanese by Curry, and from the German by Gene Fowler. We published several hundred poets in the course of 17 issues. For reasons unknown in my memory now we did not publish much in the way of concrete poetry until Wally Depew took over as editor with #14 in 1970.

We set out early to publish interviews and they, with some of the fiction, may be the most historically important features of the magazine. They covered modern poetry, black organizing, peace Berkeley style, street poetry, small presses, Zen philosophy, and novel writing. Here are the people interviewed and the issues in which those interviews appeared: Alan Watts, Zen philosopher (#2, #3; later published as a separate chapbook titled (*The Deep In View*); Louis Simpson, Pulitzer poet (#3, #4); Booker T. Anderson, black organizer (#2);

48

Doug Palmer, street poet (#5); Gene Fowler, poet (#6); Stephen Smale, anti-war activist (#7); John Williams, novelist (#7); d.a. levy, Cleveland editorpoet (#12). We published 35 pieces of fiction in the first 12 issues, most of it experimental, including work by Ed Bullins, Gary Elder, Ed Franklin, Sinzer James, and Nigerian Babatunde Lawal. I worked with a writer named Gene Gracer (whom I have not heard from since) through five rewrites of his grimly colorful story, "Shadows of Dawn" before publishing it in #7.

Some years ago I met James D. Houston (*Native Son of the Golden West*) and as we shook hands I said, "I remember reading manuscripts of yours for a mag I once edited." I wondered how good his memory was.

"*Dust*," he said quickly with a smile. "You even published me!"

"No shit?" The trick was on me.

"Yeh, a play I think."

"No shit! Really?"

Later he remembered the title: "Time to Kill."

We published work by two dozen artists, 50 letters from hate to love, and several dozen reviews. We published an article on atonalism in music by Strom, and Shakespeare's "Sonnet 50" which he'd set to piano music. This latter brought in a light-hearted complaint from a trumpet player who didn't "appreciate having to transpose his music from base to treble clef." Bob Fay wrote an article on Congressman Wright Patman's attack on the U.S. banking system, and Curry wrote several brilliant essays on Wallace Stevens, Issa, Hopkins, and James Baldwin. It was Fay who interviewed Booker T. Anderson one afternoon in Richmond, California, and Anderson had some unfavorable opinions about Richmond's black mayor. When the issue came out the Richmond city manager called me and asked if he could photocopy the interview and reproduce it with the mayor's comments attached. I checked with Anderson, who was incensed. I offered the City of Richmond as many copies as they wanted at a buck each, but informed them that to copy the interview would violate copyright laws. They checked with counsel, then bought whole copies of *Dust*.

With the fifth issue (1965), we picked up a British editor named Cavan McCarthy who published a little magazine out of Leeds titled *Tlaloc*. McCarthy contributed only one essay to *Dust*, a report on the obscenity bust of British poet Dave Cunliffe over publication of a book called *The Golden Convolvulus*, but he figured critically in other Dustbooks publications later. In fact, McCarthy mined the entire European continent and Russia for listings for the second annual *Directory of Little Magazines* (1966) and set up a momentum for collecting European information for us that is still going, though McCarthy quit in 1968 to disappear into Brazil and Nigeria. He was one of the best and brightest people I have ever worked with. In March, 1976, I was at the Gotham Book Mart in New York promoting my new novel, *Dark Other Adam Dreaming*. As the afternoon faded toward evening a young man materialized in the gallery, grinning because we were about to meet and he didn't want the moment lost too quickly. It was McCarthy, and it was 11 years later.

I would venture to guess that most small press editors active today have scarcely heard of *Dust*, and certainly have never seen a copy. Yet they know of Dustbooks, and contribute monthly and annual data, advertising, good will, and ideas to its several information titles, most specifically the *International Directory of Little Magazines and Small Presses*, and the monthly *Small Press Review*. It is the case of the tree bearing no seeming resemblance to its original seed.

Early in the course of publishing *Dust*—perhaps before its second issue was out—we began getting exchange copies of other mags from everywhere in the country. As early as #2 we printed reviews of Duane Locke's *Poetry Review* (Tampa) and Harry Smith's *The Smith* (NYC). In #3 (1964) we listed 36 mags as having been received, and 8 books, and devoted 5 pages to reviewing them. In #4 this list of magazines received had grown to 67, and I began to be fascinated by the fact that with each one also came a story, a human drama not unlike the one that had founded and was publishing *Dust* itself. The more I knew about it the more taken I became with what was obviously a larger movement somehow related by its literacy and publishing spirit. It was the first time in all my days that I'd found myself quite naturally and organically a part of something beyond the reach of my own hand, something that had not preceded me so much as it had simultaneously awakened with me, or I with it. I was drawn to it. At that point *Dust* receded in my interest and in the energy I would willingly give it. I devised the first of a multitude of forms for collecting information in 1965, and soon produced the first edition of the *International Directory of Little Magazines and Small Presses*—40 pages, 250 listings, 500 copies, a buck each. A year later, in an effort to track the movement's accelerating action in a more dynamic and immediate way, I started the *Small Press Review* as a quarterly. (It is now a monthly with 3,000 paid subscribers and earns $12,000 a year in advertising. The *Directory* now lists over 3,500 small presses and mags, is 650 pages, prints 10,000 copies and sells for $19.95.)

In 1967 an editor named Jerry Burns (*Goliards*) came to my home, and after we had talked and drank and talked some more he said:
"Let's join forces, man, a partnership!"
"I've done that one," I said—but he was wired.
"Then how about a meeting of little mag editors?"
A year later almost to the day we brought it off, Burns and I, in Berkeley on the U.C. campus, which five years before had prodded its last rat through the maze of my academic life. We held the meeting, titled the "Conference of Small Magazine Editors and Publishers" (COSMEP), and attracted 80 editors like ourselves from everywhere in the country. I chaired a panel on distribution which included Harry Smith (*The Smith*), Douglas Blazek (*Olé*), D.R. Wagner (*Runcible Spoon*), and Hugh Fox (*Ghost Dance*). It was out of that panel, the first of a thousand like it, in an effort to get funds for a catalog of small press publications, that the Committee of Small Magazine Editors and Publishers was born. By November of 1968 it had 110 paying members and a self-appointed Board of Directors. (Burns and I fought furiously over whether those Directors should be elected. By 1970 I had worn him down, and the first election was held at the

50

Buffalo conference that year.) It was Burns who, after the conference in Ann Arbor in 1969, concocted the COSMEP Newsletter. We "hired" Richard Morris in late 1968 to help get out that first *Catalogue of Small Press Publications*, typeset by Burns and printed by Ben Hiatt (*Grande Ronde Review*).

In mid-1968 I retired from my work in Public Health as a biostatistician under pressure from a nerve disease of still unknown origin or destiny. I broke with the urban madness and moved back to the mountains to spend time in the sun and the mud, and give the publishing and writing a chance to work its medicine. *Dust* had begun to be sporadic anyway in the flow of my other interests, and the move gave it a new setback. Number 11, published from the Bay Area, was dated Fall, 1967; #12, published from Paradise, was dated Spring, 1969; #13, all fiction, was dated Summer, 1969. At that point Andrew Curry, who'd been nothing if not a stolid co-editor and fast friend, quit—and I didn't blame him a whisker.

Finally I was, having quit gainful employment, running out of money, and out of energy for a magazine which had cost me $7,000 in seven years, and some editor-friends. It couldn't hold its subscribers (at #4 there were 518; after #8 there were 129), and it worked in some devilish way against the rest of my operation because it was forever unable to be as open spiritually as it needed to be to coexist with the *Directory* and the *Small Press Review*.

In late 1970, with subscriptions at 190, I hired Wally Depew to see what he could make of it. Depew was, along with Richard Kostelanetz and some others, one of the earliest and brightest experimenters in the U.S. in concrete art, games, probabilities and chance, series equations, permutations and the like. He had started a magazine called *Poetry Newsletter* in New York in 1964, and I had published his chapbook *Once*, as the fourth in a series of longpoems. Depew described his chapbook as "a contrapuntal, serially developed New Poetry long-poem using repetitive/progressive wood block series set against an expanding letter design." Depew edited four issues of *Dust* in 1970-71, one of which carried work by Folsom Prison poets and Canadians, and one, the 17th, having four contributors, all experimental, including Kostelanetz, Alastair MacLennan, and Depew himself. I liked the "new look" of the magazine, the fresh and intricate designs by Linda Bandt, and the tight no-nonsense editing by Wally Depew. I liked not having to decide on manuscripts and layout and rassling with complaints from contributors and subscribers. Though Depew would confer with me on the general size and shape of each issue, those issues were always an enjoyable surprise. For the first time ever I was able to concentrate on what had become my first interest: small press information. I applied for a $1,500 grant for *Dust* from the Coordinating Council of Literary Magazines in New York, which had turned me down several times before.

But a magazine like *Dust*, as any editor can tell you, becomes the child of a lifestyle, and you can partition it off no more easily than you can your personality or your face. I began to feel a vague, nagging sense that the all-fiction issue (#13), Curry's last, had been somehow an organic end, that I had started a whole

51

new contraption with Depew, and it was a contraption which was not a part of me. I had become a financier, and was otherwise excluded from the continuity.

On New Year's Eve, 1971, I walked with Depew, Gary Elder and others along a pathway through the brush, watching the stars and hearing the wind across the live oak. Depew talked about the next issue, a baseball issue (a non-literary interest we shared), and I knew in my heart it would never be. When, a few days later, the notice came from New York that *Dust* had gotten its first grant, enough money to see it through four more issues, enough perhaps under Depew's editorship to re-establish the magazine as an important vehicle of experiment in the country, I replied to CCLM:

> $1,500 is too little, and it is
> too late. I must turn it down.

But CCLM, unable to stop its wheels in time, sent the money anyway, and I put it in the bank. They stopped payment.

Dust had bitten its last day.

VOL. ONE   NO. ONE $1

small press review

A QUARTERLY REVIEW OF SMALL—PRESS PUBLICATIONS

In Memoriam: Alan Swallow 1915-1966

■ *A Quarterly Record*

■ *Mag News*

■ *Reviews*

■ *Bookstore News*

* * *and Features*

•SCENES:
NYC
Northwest
San Francisco
Arkansas

•Mags of South America

•The Making of an Anthology

Published by dustbooks in conjunction with
the annual Little Magazine Directory.
Printed in U S A

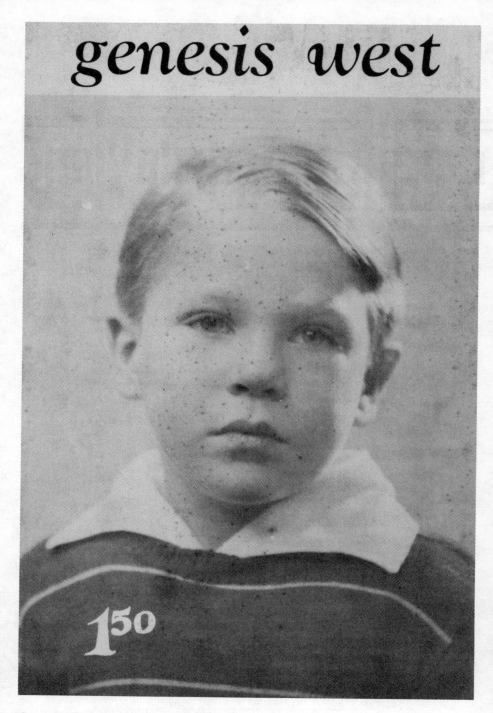

genesis west

Genesis West's **final cover (G. Lish, cover boy)**

Genesis West

Gordon Lish

Gordon Lish was born in Hewlett, N.Y., in 1934. He is a graduate of Phillips Academy and received a BA *cum laude* from the University of Arizona in 1959. From 1961 through 1965 he was editorial director of *Genesis West* ("a garden to grow the world again"); from 1969 through 1977, fiction editor of *Esquire* magazine. Since 1977 he has been an editor at Alfred A. Knopf, Inc. His books include *Dear Mr. Capote*, a novel, and *What I Know So Far*, a collection of short stories.

Gordon Lish Interviews Gordon Lish

Q. Why are you consenting to this interview?

A. I have a true thing to say.

Q. You could write an essay?

A. Too fussy, too formal, too effortful. Besides which, I'm a dynamic conversationalist.

Q. You prefer this farce to an essay?

A. I have a true thing to say.

Q. Okay. What qualifies you to edit *Genesis West*?

A. If I may speak dynamically, the answer is money. I had the money to print the first issue, so I appointed myself editor-in-chief.

Q. Is the magazine still operated on your funds?

A. Listen, I never had any funds. What I had was money, enough for one issue. After that, a corporation was formed, a non-profit corporation. It's a thing literary magazines devise in order to receive funds.

Q. Is there nothing else that qualifies you to edit such a magazine?

A. Well, I've always liked to read. So long as there's a box of Uneeda Biscuits handy, I could read for hours.

Q. You figure that's enough?

A. One box? Sure, it gets me started.

Q. I mean qualification.

A. I don't know. I suppose so. I did teach fiction writing for a time, but the college fired me.

Q. They fired you?

A. I think it was because my class enrollment grew from 12 to 73. It was an unhealthy environment for the students—legal occupancy, fire regulations, and so on.

Q. You were such a compelling instructor?

A. No, I *cried* easily. I would get so worked up over something I was reading as a model of good prose that I'd have to turn to the blackboard. But they could tell, anyway. I think a lot of those people came to watch me weep. Most of them were older women, you see. The ventilation in there was pretty risky for them.

Q. I take it you're quickly moved to passion.

A. That's right. I am.

Q. You are not guarded in your public statements, then?

A. No, I am not, therefore, guarded in my public statements.

Q. Suppose we test your candor.

56

A. I am prepared to have my candor tested.

Q. Why did you start *Genesis West*?

A. Well, I had to start something, you see. My friends were generally undistinguished. It seemed to Franny and me that if I were editing a little magazine we would meet all sorts of celebrated people.

Q. And did you?

A. Oh, yes. We met a great number of them.

Q. And was the experience satisfying?

A. Well, not exactly. Mostly, I think it depressed me.

Q. Why so?

A. I found out, you see, that the people I was meeting were also interested in making more distinguished friendships. Some of them even asked me if I were distinguished. They'd pull that on the telephone or in a letter—never to your face.

Q. You were disenchanted?

A. Profoundly. With poets particularly.

Q. Why poets?

A. They are forever on the make, intensely so. And they can be very nasty people when you don't cooperate.

Q. In what way must you cooperate?

A. First, you must publish their poems and then you must introduce them to distinguished people. Apparently poets thrive on distinguished relationships. I think it has something to do with acquiring funds or medals. It's all very complex, really.

Q. I take it you have had some personal head-knocking with a poet.

A. Yes, I have had some personal head-knocking with a poet. If I may speak dynamically, I knocked heads with a little lady poet in New York.

Q. She was nasty?

A. Unspeakably. I failed to cooperate and she became unspeakably nasty. This little lady will threaten to ruin your sales in the East. She will call you a fascist. She will write you letters, send you telegrams, poison your water supply.

Q. Her name, the name of this poet?

A. I never knew her real name. She worked an alias. New York editors tell me she's the war counselor for a bopping gang on 7th Avenue. I have saved all her letters. They are miracles of abbreviated lower case and not infrequently contain the word "zonk."

Q. Did you print her poems?

A. Of course. She's a good poet. After a while you get used to all the other crap.

Q. There were many such people?

A. Poets like that? Dynamically-speaking, yes. There's two guys who ship you fifty poems at a crack, each of them labeled with a long numeral. I think it's some kind of code.

Q. I gather your encounters with poets have not been altogether inspiring.

A. That's right. My encounters with poets have not been altogether inspiring. I am, in fact, learning to hate poets as a group.

Q. You are, perhaps, beginning to speak a shade too dynamically?

A. Look, let me tell you about poets who teach. They submit their stuff with a list attached showing all their publishing credits. Magazines like *Armpit 5* and *The Burning Crotch*. You *know* they teach because they always include this little note on university stationery. You don't dare reject them.

Q. But poets are simply people—subject to the same human failings that diminish us all.

A. You'll never get them to agree to it.

Q. Such a harsh judgement from such a young man!

A. Well, I told you I speak dynamically. Besides, I suffer from psoriasis and am consequently prone to irritability during the winter months. No more poets, not in *Genesis West*. Besides, there are thousands of places for poets to get their stuff in print, and damn few for prose writers.

Q. Did you say no more poets in *Genesis West*?

A. Yes, I did say no more poets in *Genesis West*. With the exception of Jack Gilbert.

Q. Is he not arrogant, too?

A. Jack? Jack is the most arrogant son-of-a-bitch who ever hoisted a pencil, but in his case the arrogance is earned. So far as I'm concerned, anyway.

Q. But you hassled with Jack Gilbert—publicly.

A. Well, you figured me for passionate and I already told you that I'm dynamic.

Q. I remember your complaining about Gilbert's arrogance when he attempted to edit poetry for *Genesis West*. You suggested he was cruel in his wholesale rejections.

A. That's right. Jack did reject them wholesale, and I did complain to him because the poets started complaining to me. I called Jack gratuitously cruel when he was simply being honest. You know what it is to deal with a man whose standards are impeccably high? Not easy, let me tell you. Very tricky stuff. I know. When I was teaching school, I made plenty of people miserable with my impeccably high standards. I was right, unimpeachably right, but they finally had to put me out on the street. That's what I did to Jack. Bounced him out of editing our poetry because he wanted to run blank pages where mediocre poems might have occupied space. Listen, I could turn toward a blackboard when I talk about this. The man's poems are the only ones that have altered my opinion of myself. That must count for something. That must mean he's a great poet. But the man is very demanding. Like his poetry, a heavy demand, a thunderous burden. To swing with it, you must match it with your own energy, an equally heroic courage. So there's Gilbert peppering the mails with his thoughtful, painful honesty on behalf of *Genesis West* and all I wanted to accomplish were a few distinguished friendships. Too risky. We were destined to clash.

Q. And now? All is forgotten?

A. Nothing is ever forgotten, I failed him badly. We forgive but we don't forget, and the thing is irremediably changed. The best that could come of *Genesis West* would be for Gilbert to take it over, make it strictly a vehicle for poetry, and edit the hell out of it. Nothing but blank pages! Such excellence the mind could not contain it! Listen, find me somebody with money enough—funds enough—and I swear to you I'll persuade Jack to do it.

Q. A moment ago you said that there were too many showcases for poetry and not enough for prose.

59

A. So? I contradict myself? In addition to speaking dynamically, I also contradict. It's a matter of editorial policy with me. You want contradictions? I'll give you contradictions! Be a thorough friend to Jack Gilbert and Ken Kesey in the same life! Try loving them both! For one night listen to them both talk and agree, agree! Three weeks ago my living room was the scene of a massive contradiction! Gilbert squatting here, Kesey squatting there, me in the middle— a regular nodding machine. Jack summons up pinnacles, I stand on them! Ken shapes a wilderness, let me be the first to grab a knapsack! Gilbert calls on restraint, I grin wildly and wink my eye! Kesey apostrophizes freedom, I chortle frantically and punch his arm! Both men are geniuses. Should I deny myself the rare company of a genius? I know so many I could afford to be spendthrift? Listen, what's an editor if he can't cough up a little contradiction for friends. For genius I'd lie myself straight to the grave!

Q. But I see where this issue presents work by another poet, James Spencer. James Spencer is not, I take it, Jack Gilbert.

A. No. James Spencer is not Jack Gilbert. I won't hesitate to concur with you on that.

Q. Why are you printing his poem, then?

A. Well, James Spencer started out being a distinguished friendship. It later turned out that he wasn't exactly distinguished, but he remained a friend. A fellow can do worse than a favor for a friend now and then. Excuse me, but what else is a literary magazine for?

Q. You can say that after praising Jack Gilbert's point of view?

A. I can say anything. It's my gift. As an editor, I'm entitled.

Q. You regard yourself with some importance?

A. I am all the time trying, yes. I also encourage my wife to make the same effort.

Q. Your wife has been a help to you with the magazine?

A. Actually, she has. She taught me to speak dynamically. Franny also packed me a nice lunch when I drove to New York for the ALMA meeting last year.

Q. That's the Association of Literary Magazines of America?

A. ALMA, that's right. A phenomenon called collapse; that's how you get the word, by collapsing down to the initial letters.

Q. What ever happened to ALMA?

A. I don't know. I tried to find out, but nobody was home. My guess is the thing flopped—collapsed, if I may express myself more dynamically—and nobody wants the responsibility of saying so.

Q. You did attend one of their meetings, then?

A. Yes, I did, in fact, attend one of their meetings. I was telling you about this nice lunch Franny made up and driving . . .

Q. What was it like?

A. The bread was kind of dry, but when you've been out on that road for a couple of days . . .

Q. What was the ALMA meeting like?

A. A polite streetfight. Aside from Reed Whittemore, every editor there seemed delighted with the opportunity to take a public shit on the editor he despised most. Editors, I have discovered, are even nastier than poets.

Q. Whittemore edits *The Carleton Miscellany*?

A. Correct. The only litmag I read from cover to cover.

Q. You like others, though?

A. Not so much that I would miss them, no. But I do like *Hudson*, their fiction, mostly out of loyalty for their having printed so much Ben Maddow.

Q. You have favorite writers?

A. I have favorite everything.

Q. Name some favorite writers.

A. I'll name one because it can do me some good.

Q. Go ahead.

A. Anatole Broyard!

Q. There's no one by that name.

A. I suppose not. I've got this embarrassing imagination, you know what I mean?

61

Q. Then I suppose you write.

A. I quit.

Q. Why so?

A. *Partisan Review* never answered my letters.

Q. I don't understand.

A. Neither did I. I had sent them this story, you see? My *best* story. So, I naturally tore up all the others because they weren't as good as my best. You want to hear a title? "Gasserpod, Gasserpod!" I confess to regarding that repetition as very dynamic, title-wise. Well, after six months I wrote those people and asked them where my story was. Every six months thereafter, I'd write another letter—a degree stronger, nastier, more ominous. I hinted at lawyers, great wealth, a litigious personality. Finally, I threatened to ruin their sales in the West, called them fascists, plotted their water supply. Three years later now and still no answer. So I quit writing.

Q. Letters or stories?

A. Both. Now I write textbooks.

Q. I gather you are content in doing this?

A. You are right to gather that I am content in doing this.

Q. Have you already published such a book?

A. Yes, my first is called *English Grammar*.

Q. The book is selling well?

A. Precisely, but that is not the best of it.

Q. What is, as you say, the best of it?

A. I am being sought out by people eager for a distinguished friendship.

Q. Will you disappoint them?

A. They aren't entitled?

62

The title page of the issue of *Genesis West* (vol. 3, nos. 1 & 2, 1965), in which the preceding self-interview appeared carried the following notice over Lish's signature:

It was decided at presstime. *Genesis West* dies. And there is this to say. Mostly it was an effort of love and pretense. And increasingly pretense. With less energy, always less energy, to sustain the pretense. What would you like to know? Gifts were variously insane and inspired. Thank Lou Swift and Bob Spaan for that, and B. DeBoer because he paid attention .... And Grace Paley because I love that person. Apologize to a few members of ALMA for flippant remarks printed herein. Some tried. Particularly Andrew Lytle, editor of *Sewanee Review*. He was ever the gentleman, an old soul, and therefore an expert on Hemingway's conceit. Say that this last issue is dedicated to Neal Cassady because I could produce no more compelling evidence of God's presence in man. Say that Opal Belknap was my only discovery. That she will one day write a great novel. That Ken Kesey has already written such a novel in *Sometimes a Great Notion*. That there is Jack Gilbert, and the fact of greatness. That there is excellence. That the world is happening and I am trying to watch. Say that I am tired, and that *Genesis West* dies. That as it dies it leaves a silence I would rather not hear.

Gordon Lish

Hugh Fox

Ghost Dance

Hugh Fox

Hugh Fox has been described as "the Paul Bunyan of American Letters, part myth, part monster, and, myself-as-subject, a magnificent non-stop storyteller." He is the author of literally dozens of books—including the non-fiction *Gods of the Cataclysm*, required reading for cultural historians in all disciplines—and the publisher of *Ghost Dance: The International Quarterly of Experimental Poetry*. The product of a Jesuit education, he teaches in the Department of American Thought and Letters at Michigan State University. His publications include the double novella *Honeymoon/Mom*, an Indian Ocean whale herd journal, *Leviathan*, and *The Dream of the Black Topaze Chamber* and *Blood Cocoon*.

Ghost Dance and Other Numbers

Caracas, 1965, there was this "Leftist" bookstore I was browsing in one day when I came across a copy of *El Corno Emplumado* out of Mexico, and at the back I found tons of ads about U.S. mags I'd not only never heard of but never guessed *existed*, like *Burning Water, Wild Dog, The University of Tampa Poetry Review* . . . . I wrote and got samples of them all, did a bilingual anthology that never got published. One copy was "lost" by *Orfeo* in Chile; I'm not sure whether it was a victim of changing politics or not. But the other copy I had was never returned by the editor of *El Cormorant y Delfin* in Buenos Aires who was SHOCKED by the de-pra-ved nature of the contents. What? Drugs and sex?

Actually I'd gotten my Ph.D. in American literature from the University of Illinois (Urbana-Champaign) in 1958 and I'd been living in Los Angeles from '58-'64, but LITTLE MAGS? THE ALTERNATIVE MAGAZINE WORLD? THE LIVING UNDERGROUND? THE INVISIBLES? Later I found out that *Dust* and *Olé* and everything else was starting out in the early '60s, but I had no hint that there was anything but *The Atlantic, Harper's, The New Yorker, Partisan Review* and the big New York book publishers. In fact there's a whole Limbo Zone in my life between 1958 and 1965 when I didn't get anything published but a story ("The Death of a Chinese Philosopher") in *Catholic World*, but when I had an agent (Howard Liebling of the William Morris Agency in NYC) and was furiously writing and submitting novels to Putnam's (Targ), Farrar, Strauss and Giroux, Doubleday, you name it. Some close calls like one time Farrar voted, YES, to publish one of the novels, but by that time it was already committee-run and he was outvoted. In fact the novels of those years, *Chicago Mau Mau, The Taffy Hills, The Fell of Dark*, etc., never have been published . . . .

Then in 1965 my first peek at the other ("real") world . . . .although I didn't really meet it face to face until 1968, April, Berkeley, when Len Fulton and Gerry Burns got together the Great Little Mag Jamboree that was to flower into COSMEP FOREVER! And it was there in Berkeley in '68 that I met Flying Dutchman Captain Harry Smith, Gypsy Satin Bluesleeves John Oliver Simon and his then in the background wife, Alta, static, morphine-white cadaverous Captain Zero (RJS), John Mind-Karate Banzai Samurai John Bennett, Doctor/Mr. Spock Outer Space Madcap Dada Morris, Sharon Asselin, long, lanky, langorous, Morris' Juliet, Wild One Motorcycle-Jacketed Doug Blazek, the Original Poet-Stripper Andy Clausen, Charles Potts then Trailblazer-Leatherstocking's LAFFING WATER, Curt He's-Walking-To-The-Mound-He's -Winding-Up Johnson, and of course Grassman Fulton, Machiavellian Gamester Ben Hiatt, Clamped-Up Brooder D.R. Wagner, Joel Deutsch looking like you always thought Jack the Ripper must have looked, Gerry the Pirate Burns, Alexandra The Good One (I named my youngest daughter after her) Garrett . . . who wasn't there? The era was just ending as I walked into it. (In the ending of *The Vanilla Gorilla* I tried to capture just that.)

Of course I'd already come to Berkeley with my first issue of *Ghost Dance* in hand thanks to Chilean David Valjalo and Columbian Dukardo Hinestrosa whom I'd known in L.A., part of the Latino Community. After all I was married to a Peruvian, I didn't hang with the Anglos. Dukardo, a very visually and verbally (a Nadaista) original artist, had ideated *El Cuervo International* (*Crow International*), had it printed, which triggered Valjalo to finally launch his *Ediciones de la Frontera*; and once I saw how easily the fucking offset worked, *Ghost Dance* emerged, the first copy printed in the printshop at Loyola University in Los Angeles. I wrote to Neruda for some poetry, he sent it, I put in a lot of other Hispanoamericanos, after all I'd met Borges and Sabato (Argentina) Icaza and Astudillo (Ecuador), Ciro Alegria and Vargas Llosa (Peru), Juan Liscano and Ramon Diaz Sanchez (Venezuela) before I'd met anyone at all in the U.S. My real "baptism" as a functioning writer had been in Caracas between 1964-66 . . . but that's another story. Certainly, though, the U. of Illinois Ph.D. in American Lit program had no visible practical function for the beginning writer—and ironically that's what I'd gone there for in the first place . . . to learn the trade.

What I wanted to do with *Ghost Dance* was . . . well, let's go to the title. Essentially the Ghost Dance Religion was the last (albeit unsuccessful) rebellion of the American Indians against Whitey. As a hispanized Irish-Czech Catholic from Chicago I automatically identified myself with outsider GROUPS and I wanted to make *Ghost Dance* a word-rebellion equivalent of the socio-economic rebellion of the original Ghost Dancer, in spite of the fact I knew that losing was built right into the effort. After all I'd seen the invulnerable-against-the-White-Man's-bullets Ghost Dance shirts at the University of Kansas museum—full of holes.

I never accepted anything I could understand (easily); I wanted to keep the mag on the extreme edge of the avant-garde. I felt that that's where reality was developing, that Art was involved with an evolutionary corkscrew like Science (I'd just come from pre-Med and Med school with a Darwinistic bias as DNA-molecule wide hadn't I?), and that TRUTH WAS TO BE FOUND ON THE LIQUID EDGE OF THE ALWAYS-NEW WAVE.

And that's the way I'm still functioning (on half a—$$$—cylinder), Millie Mae Wicklund's Marisol poems left out of the New Rivers Press edition, a new volume by Guy Beining, bilingual volumes by Cid Seixas and Ildasio Tavares, two new Brazilian poets. Of course *Ghost Dance* is in a (permanent?) holding pattern right now. I got back from Brazil in 1980 after two years in Florianópo-lis, disbelieving the rumors about how bad things were getting in the U.S., my wife immediately lost her job, I was forced into bankruptcy, CCLM moved and my grant-receipts were lost because they didn't forward the mail, it costs $200 just to have the Portuguese accent-marks put on my typewriter, the university where I work has been slashing tenured faculty, I'm lucky to have food and shelter, after all the poorer the tribe the more meager the art, there's no possibility of pyramids in Tierra del Fuego.

The year 1968 was a turning point for me. It was the year of the Big Jamboree in Berkeley, I left Loyola (Los Angeles), out of the Irish Catholic ghetto to what I hoped would be greener pastures in Michigan, got a summer fellowship at the John Carter Brown Library at Brown, met my second wife . . . what else? During the summer of '68 I made stops at Yale, Harvard, Hunter, the New York Public Library. Right to the Periodical Acquisitions Librarians (wasn't I a library-insect myself, after all?): "Hiya, my name is Hugh Fox, I've just started a new magazine called *Ghost Dance: The International Quarterly of Experimental Poetry*, might you be interested in subscribing . . . ?" Everyone subscribed, everyone I talked to. And I suppose that if I'd talked to a thousand people I would have gotten a thousand subscriptions. I wrote to Oxford, told them Harvard and Yale had subscribed, Oxford subscribed, and almost automatically I started getting subscriptions from Australia.

I was all enthusiasm. I got my own A.B. Dick offset press (Hitchcock—*Kayak*—had introduced me to the Mysteries of Offset on his old magic basement Multilith one time when I was in San Francisco). Number 2 I had printed at MSU, but 3 I had Valerie Jayne (Boston) draw pictures on offset paperplates and then I did the printing myself. I fled from white paper and any empty space on the page, did editorials every issue:

MINDMIND TRAPPED IN GRANDMOTHER-TIME and
gottamake it, MANSENSES UN-NONSENSING

67

the REALITY PUZZLE FLESHPERCEPTORS (IN LIQUID) PER-CEIVING ACCORDING TO THE LIMITATIONS OF THE PERCEPTIONS . . . .
(Number 3)

I used to take Eskimo drawings, get negatives, make aluminum plates, run through some thousands of sheets of paper, then print the issue on top of THAT. Or Zorita, my favorite stripper, negative and positive images of her, whole or dismembered and recombined into new surreal images. Every Saturday I devoted the whole day to *Ghost Dance*, got paper through the university at a super-low price, usually got a CCLM grant now and then, over the years printed lots of (mainly "new") wild-frontier poets. The "spirit" of those early years was very much related to my summer at Brown too. I'd had a chance (Hay Collection) to go through all the original files on Surrealism and Dada, Futurism, in fact all the original experimentalisms of the early 20th century, had written a critical book called *An Aesthetics for the Year 10,000*, the book of mediapieces called *The Vanilla Gorilla*, an essay on Harry Crosby based on his notebooks (pencil), edited the first as-complete-as-I-could-make-it *Works of A.I. Gillespie* (a never-printed victim of Something Else Press' bankruptcy) . . . my spirit was the Spirit of the '20s and I believed that there was something almost religious/kabbalistic/magic in experimental art, that somehow we most of the time saw things through a glass darkly and the purpose of the avant-garde was to take away that glass and let DIVINE REALITY shine in on us. I wasn't really *in* in '60s and '70s at all, I was in Paris, it was 1925 and the Cantos and the Prufrocks and the Portraits of Artists as Young Dogs were still to be barked out in holy defiance of the world that walked out numbed and wearing blinders.

I mean who haven't I published over the years? Books by Duane Locke, Bill Costley, Douglas Crow, Diane Kruchkow, Thomas Michael Fisher, Millie Mae Wicklund, Maria Land Patterson, Ascher-Straus, Richard Morris, Helen Duberstein, L. Cridisque, Harry Smith, Bruce Andrews, volumes with E.A. Vigo (Argentinian), and his Chilean counterpart G. Deisler (now exiled in Paris), and in regular issues you'd find everyone from Karl Kempton to Gene Fowler to Carl D. Clark, Gottfried Schlemmer, Sam Cornish, Ottone Riccio . . . Heinrich Böll . . . .

Of course there was NEVER any real sense of excitement when a new issue came out, mainly because in the U.S. there is next to no sense of literary "community"/"forum." I mean, say in Caracas, a new issue of *Zona Franca* would come out and it'd be an *event*—there was always a sense of "coterie"/"group"/ "movement." And when I'm in New York or San Francisco, OK, it still "happens," I even try to make literary-personal *pilgrimages* via Greyhound to create my own sense of literary community that encompasses the whole U.S., but,

1. There isn't any one cultural capital in the U.S. the way there is in, say, Venezuela, France, Argentina, Austria,

2. The widening splits between Mass Culture and Elite Culture, Media Culture and Print Culture, block any sense of large receptivity for a given book or magazine. Communication is super-developed viz a viz "The News" (say a hotel falls down in Kansas City), but the literary community is forever banned from

68

any sense of "newsiness," we're not News but Old Hat,

3. Whatever "outreach" programs that may have been starting via book buses or media-infiltration, given the overall Depression Climate of the U.S., are gonna be chopped to the ground. I mean Austria spends 25 times more money on funding CULTURE than the U.S. does, and in the mixed culture-bag of 1,800 symphony orchestras, etc., etc., etc., where does an experimental poetry mag fit in? In Detroit the PBS station has gone 24 hours a day and is doing Jack Benny Program reruns!

I mean the U.S. as literary encouragement climate is the wrong place, the wrong face, the wrong time, the wrong clime . . . so I've *always* felt that *Ghost Dance* was dancing in the dark, just the same way I've *always* felt that as writer I might just as well leave the ribbon out of the typewriter. CCLM was *some* help, and now . . . ?

I mean if it hadn't been for what happened to me in Caracas I don't think I EVER would have even "survived" in the U.S. non- (anti-) literary marketplace.

I wasn't in Caracas a day before Jim Smith (U.S. Information Service) took me around to all the newspapers and mags in town. I started writing for *Politica*, the big democratic ruling-power mag, for Juan Liscano's avant-garde *Zona Franca*, for Rafael Pineda's *Revista Nacional de Cultura*. Everyone paid, and when *Politica* had its big, what was it, 5th anniversary party, of course I was invited, the ambassador saw me (I was the only other American except him), "What are *you* doing here?" me triumphantly answering "I'm a contributor."

Every time I gave a lecture, the newspapers appeared; I'd get a photo plus a little write-up. And my lectures on race problems, economic problems, contemporary literature and music, you name it, I gathered together in a little book, *America Hoy* (*America Today*), translated into Spanish with the help of the Embassy secretaries, I wrote around to USIS headquarters in Chile, Ecuador, Bolivia, etc., sold copies and then arranged a lecture-tour based on the book. Which is how I got to go everywhere in Bolivia and Ecuador by jeep—I was EXPLAINING THE U.S.

So . . . that's how come my first books were published in Caracas. ENCOURAGEMENT. I mean confronted with submitting exclusively to *The Atlantic, Harper's, The New Yorker, Partisan Review, Kenyon Review*, etc., *I'd even stopped writing poetry*. In Caracas I revived, self-published my first volume of poetry: *40 Poems*. Then another volume of essays (*Problemas de Nuestro Tiempo—Problems of Our Times* . . . first delivered as a series of lectures at the U. of Carabobo, Valencia, Venezuela), even a volume of one-act plays, *An Evening with Hugh Fox* (bilingual). When one of my short stories about this Peace Corps girl I'd met came out, my boss at the Embassy called me in (he was an oldman new-guy; the first year's boss, Bob Cross, had been a super peach), made a big to-do about my writing "salacious literature," at first I was crushed, then found out the mag had been circulated around the whole USIS staff; it was mini-celebrity fame!

You can imagine coming back to shitheaded anonymity in Los Angeles in 1966! But . . . I'd gotten enough push/zest/enthusiasm/confidence to disenable me to ever get put back in THE BOX again!

You can't imagine what the lectures, the invitations to beach-clubs, to embassy parties, having dinner with Maria Tallchief or Lichtenstein, having my family portrait painted by Fantuzzi, official portrait-painter of Pope Pius XII, in retirement in Caracas (incidentally, my parents *destroyed* the 3'x5' family portrait when I got divorced in 1970, although I still have some photos of it), actually going and having a photographer do a portrait-cover for the *40 Poems*, having money for suits and movies and parties . . . you can't imagine what being treated like a Mensch meant to this abused, shat-on, underpaid, ghetto-Catholic, infinitely rejected and unpublished Zero; you create a dead-souls context that's all warheads and budgets, you're going to get THE CLOCKWORK ORANGE.

I mean I'm CRAZY, I've written some 35 novels and I keep writing them, although only a handful have ever been published. But the non-crazy writer confronting our schlockmeister culture, has to inevitably curl up, die, dry up and be blown away. I mean I write a review a day and the only place that ever pays me is *Newsart* and Smith's talking about junking *it* and keeping just *Pulpsmith* which he's determined to make a popular, paid-subscription magazine: THE CURSE OF CAPITALISM! And if you didn't get paid and got *read* . . . . feedback, THERE ISN'T ANY FEEDBACK, YOU'RE SOMEWHERE IN A BASEMENT IN OUTER SPACE BEYOND SATURN, BEYOND PLUTO, YOU'RE CRANKING OUT A LITTLE MAG, WRITING YOUR NOVELS AND POETRY, DOING THESE ENDLESS TREADMILL REVIEWS, AND IT'S BEEN 50 YEARS SINCE ANYONE NOTICED YOU'RE EVEN ALIVE! Absolutely no feedback, no cultural context, supportive milieu, sense of integrated society . . . and now Reaganomics!

When I ran for COSMEP in 1981 I put something in my platform about wanting to get POETRY ON THE TV. I mean you can see what's coming, the total media envelope of 100 channels, TV-computer banking-shopping hookups, PBS hasn't promoted U.S. art and culture, it's re-run BBC! But if you want the literary world to flourish in an electronic culture, you have to go electronic, you've got to have your place ON THE SCREEN. And if you've got boxing on fulltime, chess-matches, gymnastics, programs on Balinese funeral rites, ancient Greek shipmaking, how to garden, how to oil-paint, yoga, silent films, old Marx Brothers, hourly Wall-Street reports, there's no reason we can't have THE JOHN PYROS LITTLE MAG HOUR with guest-reader Hugh Fox, tomorrow Lyn Lifshin, and let's resurrect Doug Blazek for the Friday night show. But (here's the rub) that platform didn't even get me elected to COSMEP!

I mean as a college professor teaching (mainly Freshman) for 25 years, there's no one more aware of THE SPLITS . . . the splits between High and Low Culture, Print Culture and Media Culture, Pop, Schlop, and Deadwood Culture. Yesterday I mentioned Charles Ives in three classes, 90 Michigan 18-year-olders, and NO ONE (even the music majors) HAD EVER REMOTELY HEARD OF CHARLES IVES. And Charles Ives is THE GREAT AMERICAN SUCCESS STORY CULTURE-HERO, and I'm Charles Ives BEFORE; how NOTHING *before* is and even AFTER is nuddings! The wall between The Culture and The People. Either we get pop-schlop-mediafied, or we get buried in oblivion. When I try to read someone like Paul Vangelisti, Jesus Christ, who are you kidding?

70

I mean it's *another* case of the Triumph of the Foreign, Vangelisti getting all enamored with the Open City Bicycle Thief metaphysics of the New Italians. Like Adriano Spatola:

> "Well, let me summarize my studies. I discovered visual
> poetry and the research it entails after having studied, for
> six months, Gestalt psychology ... for me it was decisive,
> for I found that all my 'zeroglyphics' are gestaltic to the
> point of being didactic ..."

You said it, brother!

I mean on one hand you've got the Wool-Brains, all enamored with Post-Modern BULLSHIT, and on the other the Do-It-Yourselfer COMMERCIALISTS, not to mention all the Special-Interest Groups, Serbo-Croatians, The Greeks, Blacks who live in Oyster Bay ... and then Out There beyond The Literary, the real American world watching football and boxing and Hollywood Squares and Welcome Back, Kotter, Laverne and Shirley, Barney Miller, *MASH* re-runs and The Evening News.

We, the Leetle—Leeterary—Magazine Peoples, have become a very special little colony in the middle of Yahooland. How unread, unsung, unbought, unpatronized can you GET? It's a totally new (electronic) ballgame, it's not the 18th-century Court versus Peasants, Artist as Entertainer of The Political Elite, it's the artist become ANTIQUE, a maker of exotic pots and handloomed ponchos. Like Stanley Nelson told me: "Maybe the great art of Our Times will be considered TV ads ...." By whom? Certainly not us as critics, because we're not the tastemakers *either* ... it's *all* out of our hands.

Back when I was doing interviews as a major effort, interviewing Fulton, Duane Locke, Doug Blazek, Morris, etc., the early 1960s kept coming up as KEY TIMES. That was when the avant-garde literary folk "coalesced" out of cosmic dust, became suns and started to shine, when *Dust, Olè, The Poetry Review of the University of Tampa, Camels Coming*, etc., all begin. Of course there was a continuity with earlier time-levels, the Fulton-James Boyer May *Trace-Dust* connection, for example, but the Literary Community for the first time became AWARE OF ITS SELF, LOOKED AROUND, SAW ITS HAIR AND FEELERS AND SMELLED ITS OWN ODOR. Then came COSMEP at the end of the decade, the COSMEP spinoffs like WIP or NESPA. CCLM began to function for THE COMMUNITY and not just for William Phillips (né Wallace Phelps) et Co., NEA money emerged, state art councils began to shell out some cash, we had a kind of GOLDEN AGE during the '60s and into the '70s. The "spiritualization" of the '60s slid inertially into the '70s; and there was cash around, a certain benign sense that we SHALL overcome.

We're very sensitive to political-economic change; that's the nature of the artist-BEAST ... fine feelers, antennae that pick up everything. And the Nixon Era severely wounded our American Artist psyche ... it was the end of bravado, the Good Yankee, and who can say right now what the connection is between the Shame of the Nixon Betrayal and the Ascendency of Haig, the Apocalypsis

71

Now Horror of Vietnam (including the turntail "withdrawal") and the Reagan-omic re-peasantification of The Poor?

Certainly ART is economic spinoff. What Brooklyn Michelangelo has his hands cut off because there's no tools, no plaster, no marble (certainly!), just plenty of nothin'? I know myself when I got back to bankrupting Michigan State U. in 1980 after two years in 100 percent inflation/year Brazil, I had GREAT EXPECTATIONS. And then came the layoff. My wife got bumped, I got cut a day here and there, was forced into bankruptcy, and a year later maybe I can pay my necessities, but *Ghost Dance*, baby, needs a lot of CASH to get up on stage, and yesterday's headlines were $4.1 MILLION MORE CUT FROM MICHIGAN STATE BUDGET, so that's the future! The fat's going, going, gone. Can the Literary Mag Renaissance hang on as part of the lean?

GHOST   DANCE

montana Morrison 1985

Drawing of Norman Moser by Rod Hanks

Illuminations

Norman Moser

Norman Moser was born in 1931 in Durham, NC, and was raised in and around what is now known as the Triangle Area (Durham, Raleigh, Chapel Hill, etc.), graduating from Hugh Morson HS/Raleigh c. 1950, almost at once hitting the road for D.C., NYC, etc., in pursuit of a career as a singer/entertainer. "This idea I got from my Dad who had been a gospel & barbershop quartet singer who had on occasion subbed on the Grand Ole Opry for ailing Lone Star Quartet members. And in fact, was on Raleigh radio & in Raleigh clubs before I left in 1950.

"For a few years, then, I traveled about, mostly as a singer or M.C., landing occasionally in Top Club or theatre in D.C., Pittsburgh, Boston, Blue Angel NYC, e.g., or on Tenn. Ernie Ford's *Local* TV show outa L.A. before Korea hit us. (From '51-'53 was AGVA member & agent was Ledo, Morris, Snyder.) Also was waiter, salesclerk & washed lotta dishes . . . .

"It was not until I ended up in Europe in peacetime military that I started straight acting & a bit of writing. My first finished piece was a musical play for the stage, a collaboration w/2 other dudes about as inexperienced as me, my first published piece was a travel piece in the base newspaper, USAF, Ulm, Germ., & 1 year I got an Hon. Ment. in an international USAF short story contest. About this time I began reading serious (often hilarious too) writers a la Sartre, Camus, Hemingway, O'Neill, Faulkner, Twain, Shakespeare, Tolstoi, Chekhov, Dostoievski et al., in their original languages whenever I could (German, French, etc.). I was intrigued, amazed, excited, inspired, etc. 'Gee,' I thought, 'I could be a writer too if I had their courage of thought and expression.' And, I might've added, their skill & their felicity of expression. By 1957 I ended up at San Francisco State as a Creative Writing major, having begun the slow, painful journey to vision, light and hopefully mastery of craft & art of literature. Now of course, I see my college career as an exercise in futility, but at the time it was a lark, a way of income (GI Bill) & indeed I WAS a very green, inexperienced, ignorant apprentice if ever the world saw one. But I learned quickly, & at first I made quite an impression: in 18 mos. time I was not only the Gater's drama critic, but was also top ed. of the school lit.-mag., *Transfer*.

"Was in metrop. daily *SF Exam.*'s book-section before I had my B.A., & when they told me no drama/arts man had ever won the News award, I took the

News AND Feature awards in 1 year at State, & the next year the (2nd-Pl.) Poetry Prize at *Transfer* as well. But when I proved to be no adept shiteater—they couldn't break me nor make me like them—more & more I was crossed off good lists & added to bad. Exceptions are everywhere, & SF State had its share & more. I did at times have some exacting yet marvelous profs: some of them were Walter van Tilburg Clark, Theodore Roethke, James Schevill. Took M.A., SF State, Jan. '66 (Fall '65 Term).

"That same year I started *Illuminations*. I was a bit tired of the sticky-icky-poo style dominating literature then by the English Dept. syndrome, had been for some time familiar with on-the-rise Beat writers a la Ginsberg, Snyder, Ferlinghetti & others, was already chuckling & grimacing at Bukowski & his protege, Blazek, among many others a la Crews, Wakoski, etc., & was so familiar w/past & curr. Oriental & Latin-Am. & Native-Am. arts/lit. I lectured on all 3 at the old Intersection, the Precarious Vision, c. 1963. Wanting to see MY&/or friends' interests reflected in Lit. for a change instead of, say, Dr. Mark Linenthal's easy choices (of SF St.'s Poetry Center) & being acquainted with a powerful bunch of new writers then a la Bullins, Fowler, Bly, Meltzer, Mike Hannon, Charles Foster, Hadassah & others mostly from either SF State or the Blue Unicorn Coffeehouse/Hashbury, I sent out the invitations & started up my mag & have never regretted it since. Had, incidentally, been working on my 'Shaman Songs' series since c. '63-'64.

"My books are: *Jumpsongs*/Gar Prs, '73; *A Shaman's Songbook*, Thorp Spgs, '75-'76; *Open Season*/Illuminations prs, 80; *I Live in the South of My Heart*, Chango Prs, '80; *The Shorter Plays & Scenarios of N.M.*/Illums. Prs, '81."

Illuminations Press

I 1st learned of li'lmags in the late '50s, in the Bay Area, as GI Bill student. They were all over the area. Doubt if I'd ever read one until then, unless ye count weeklies like the *Village Voice, Manchester Guardian*, et al.

What prompted start own mag? How wore both hats, writer too? I'd always wanted to do one, well for 5+ years, say—in fact, lost me USAF savings in charming weekly tabloid venture called *Bay Window* at first, due to copyright problems w/title, changed to *B. Area Arts Review* (1957-59). Edited litmag, *Transfer*, at SF State, '59-'61, wrote nonf. for everybody on campus & off as Undergrad (in *SF Exam.* book-sect. before I had my B.A.). Thought of a mag. often, friends suggested it, etc. But it was not till 1964 (then Grad stud.) when I saw a bunch of wild but tender & responsible, so-called Avant-garde (or Underground, later term) poets painters musicians actors etc. at the Blue Unicorn Coffeehouse smack in de middle of Haight-Ashbury doing their readings, happenings, etc., myself participating, moderating the weekly B.U. series 1965-66 that Fowler started '64, that I knew the time had come for my mag. & I had the name from earlier projections, proposals of mag. more like *Newsweek* or *News-Art* or maybe *Contact* or *Evergreen*, etc. So having properly, w/due modesty,

76

awaited my turn, I started in like Hell & Brimstone turning to impassioned joy-dance, rich indignation!

Incidentally, some of those in Hashbury & at SF State I printed in earliest editions were Ed Bullins, Charles Foster, Mike Hannon, Dave Meltzer, Hadassah, Tim Holt, Janice Hays, Dave Sandberg, etc. And by 1970 I had also lined up the likes of Judson Crews, Diane Wakoski, Bly, Bukowski, Doug Blazek, Peter Wild & many others from elsewhere.

I have recently begun to wonder at the two-hats dilemma suggested, concentrate almost solely on poetry, fiction & plays now, just doing very occasional article for money usually; but back then I never saw any contradiction between my 2-3 hats as ed., reviewer/nonf. free-lancer or staffwriter/weeklies, etc., & poet/playwright/trickster, talespinner, partly because of the amazingly bountiful energy I had at the time & still have on occasion, in spurts now mostly. I just turned my chair around, so to speak, and Voila! Now, ed., or reviewer, or poet, playwright, talespinner, etc. It was all the same to me. I've always seen myself as simply a professional writer. In Europe they dont make much of these distinctions like poet; talespinner; ed., whatever. I dont either. Should add here perhaps that all my friends and I were since '57 or so immensely excited & influenced by the Beat writers & all they did, stood for.

Did I think of lilmag publshg as way (or prt of way) of making a living? Yes, in the beginning, I did. What's more, in the '60s & on up till early-mid '70s, I either broke even or made some profit on all but one edition, & it was a play by Ed Bullins coming out same year in *New Am. Libr.*/Mentor ed., printed mimeo on cheap 'runny' paper—came just li'l short of breaking even on this one, tho over abt 10-year period made huge 1000% profit (over costs) on Bullins 1st book, *How Do You Do* (1967). Never made anywhere ALL my income from publishing, but at times it was a distinct factor in overall income, & it combined with freelancing & part-time or temporary jobs, was my survival money during certain years in '60s/early '70s. I've never been one to give away an unusually large no. copies of a run, tho usually honor review-requests & have a natural 10-20% exchange/review comps policy.

Illuminations 1 came out Summer 1965. Have done 20 editions total of all sorts, mags, books, tabloids, broadsides. I'm doing books now, just started in. Found that a mag. was no longer rewarding financially or re one's total emotional/artistic (or esthetic?) investment: Too much work for too little income. Did exactly 11 editions of the mag. + 4 editions of (then) UPS-tabloid *Pulse*. If had shitloads of $$$ from rich Aunt or etc., might continue it as specials of fiction &/or an annual along lines of *New Directions, Discovery, New World Writing, New American Review*, et al., very very occasional colls. of poetry perhaps. I dont regret anything I ever did of course, personal or professional. My littlemag experience was invaluable to me. But I wouldn't start up a new mag or new series of *Illuminations* unless I had a livable income + publ.-funds ahead for about 8-10 years. I am not well off. As I sd in No. 10 mag, "Paupers should not be publishers." The market is just too saturated now for a quality litmag to sell easily & well as it did in '60s/early '70s.

Illuminations 1 & 2 were in the loose, large (10x15) Folio Format & all since then have been in mag, book or tabloid format, mostly offset runs, very few mimeo eds. Until last year my runs averaged 1,000 or more, high run was 2,000 for Bullins' *How Do You Do* & coupla limited eds. running in the 300-500 range. Am now averaging 300-700 for my books, down by half or more from '60s & this is based on what I & 1-2 friends can distribute here & nationally. I.e., I don't print huge over-runs like some do. (% for comps is always figured in . . . .)

I dont believe in giving away copies except to close friends, lovers, or respected pros & felt that way at the outset & still do. Anyone will make exceptions at times because it feels right to do so & is good for business, too, as recently did at 2 Seattle bookstores to quite warm human (female) beings who were about as broke as we were & who'd just bought what they could . . . (afford + sell).

All mastheads/All editions, have stated our purpose: "to help bring poetry back into the marketplace (& to) faithfully record the work of professional & apprentice writers, poets, painters, dramatists, philosophers of any persuasion or nationality."

I also like a lot of variety & am particularly partial to the work of budding or pro writers/painters etc. of what we now call the 3rd World or Minority folks. Always been an eclectic. I'll deliberately put lyrics & visionary or nature poems or fictions right next to political or conventionally structured or stylized (quality) pieces to get that excitement & contrast of differing styles, constructs, views, etc. In fact, the mags that amaze me the most are those, like *Black Mntn. Review, Wild Dog*, both long gone, that do exactly the opposite: publish just one type of narrowly-conceived, perhaps even academically-oriented, piece. How the hell do they do it? Do a quality mag, I mean? The 2 named were definitely quality mags & am proud to say was in one of em meself.

I think I succeeded handsomely at what I set out to do, gave more than one writer a beeg boost to his "career" to boot, & judging from letters, reviews, etc., I did not merely imagine I did a quality mag, I did a quality mag & a fuckin half r more. But as I sd, there's absolutely nil market for such a mag in today's confused chaotic anti-art anti-literature cluttered sloppy shitass fuckedup market/ world.

Yeh, I've lost my cherry fer sure. My ideas have changed some but not much, my writing is much better, am unqualifiedly a pro, no longer an apprentice. But the market's tangled, hopelessly cluttered & confused & the trade houses & popmags been so demeaningly forced into airing pablum w/1-2 exceptions, a la *Harper's* & *Atlantic, N-Yrker* at times, that I do not see a place there (in the market) for my mag, & sometimes I wonder if, after all this work to build up this mag & learn my craft as a writer, there's a place anywhere on the world publishing scene for myself & sev. of my friends. In this respect I haven't changed as much as the world has. Can't resist adding that me & my 6-8 unpublished books & li'lmag eds. that dont answer letters or keep obligations cause me to see the world these days as a very dismal place for a writer not in a clique nor commercially established or famous. One thing puzzles me a great deal: you'd think mags or presses would follow up with books by writers they'd featured in '60s/'70s, and I have with extremely limited funds located 4 poets featured in '60s/'70s eds. of my mag—of them 2 have 1 book out (1 self-publshd), 2 none. Reviewed these 2 books & am currently negotiating to do 2 or more books by these neglected writers. But in my case only 2 mag/presses who featured me in '60s/'70s have reviewed my books or have published books: Gar Press & Thorp Springs. That leaves *Small Press Review, Grande Ronde Review, December* & *Vagabond* among others who featured me in '60s/'70s mags but never thought to even ask after my many unpublished books not to mention publish 1-2 of em (tho 2 did, I admit, review a book of mine, 1st & last). Wha' gives here, Mose (r worl)?

I'd say if the tremendous volume of mss., letters & cards received since '65 were 90-95% positive and if such a mag. received 20-25 reviews, all but one favorable, & was 9 or more times reprinted in anthologies, the response was overwhelmingly gratifying. *Illuminations* has been mentioned or reviewed in *Life, Small Press Review, Berkeley Gazette, Margins, Nola Express, Durham Herald, Santa Fe New Mexican, San Rafael Independent-Journal* & many others.

Singlehandedly I edited solely Nos. 1, 5 & 11, altho my guiding hand was probably felt in all editions. Other eds. were ex-wife Hadassah, Bryan Daly, John Laue & many others contrb. various ways, including Hal & Carolyn Wylie of Austin as co-publishers 1972-74 for Nos. 6-9, done as Inserts to their GAR APS-tabloid. My own accomplishments? Not sure. A certain authority & confidence, perhaps, driving dynamic energy, finding ways to get things done that looked pretty impossible to others. Determination, tenacity, courage, commitment, and hope this comes across in my own work too. Willingness to try new things, ideas, forms, talent, experiments, etc . . . .

Certainly wanted to print more short stories, plays, essays, novel excerpts, etc. We did air some quality prose, too, but far less than I would've liked if money were there to do it with. Have few regrets, babe, but do feel that as a person I may be at times insensitive to things that to me seem so trivial I wouldn't usually bother, & yet such social & personality diffs. makes the world go round at least as much as luv does. Also, have pretty much given up on it now, but for years somewhat regretted that it was apparently not possible to represent the Beat &/or Black-Mntn. writers as well as the generation that came up w/me early-mid '60s. But however much I desired this, it never came to pass. Apparently there was no more room at the top for us, so that the Beats & us never could sorta meld into one generation, even tho I appeared w/them on occasion in mags like *Wild Dog* & also knew or consorted w/likes of Ginsberg, Snyder, Creeley, Ferlinghetti, Buk., Mailer, Welch & others on occasion. But apparently I didn't know them well enough, since none of em ever published or recommended a book of mine anywhere & only 1 (Buk.) ever sent me poems or stories (all invited to do so). Methinks the problem was I was not a member of their clique(s). Also think I'm a bit feisty & since was a pro c. '63-'64 or so, I come on strong & was never a good shit-eater, likewise most o' me friends in the Biz a la Fowler, Bill Herron, Jim Cody, Paul Foreman, Ben Hiatt, Doug Blazek, Frieda Werden, Jimmy Baca & etc.

It wasn't all pleasant, as ye gather from me last answer, when I started, but as long as ye didn't buck for more (or national) recognition, it was ever so casual & easy-going, everybody knew everybody else. And yet standards were so high too that usually the good work floated to somewhere near the top of the heap & the bad, bland or bullshitty stuff was quickly forgotten. Readings were fewer yet paradoxically not so hard to get, & ye could get on a program or set one up by 1 simple phone call usually (Poetry Center excepted). Very lovely in-spirit-ing, inspiring scene, wide-open, enthusiastic; snobs like Jack Gilbert were few & far between. Irresponsible shiftless lazy skonks existed then too who'd hold yr mss. fer mos. or years without printing them, never correspond or get in touch w/their (potential) contribs., but often we just drummed em out of the Biz. in no time at all if they didn't shape up. Lotsa conflicting views/opinions of healthy invigorating sort of situation (& here, snobs like Creeley were few/far betw.) but lotsa mutual respect too—for most part.

What's it like now by contrast? It sucks. Stinks like a pile o' shit! A new generation of pampered spoiled brats about 80-85% of whom are the unprofes-sional irresponsible lazy skonks referred to above do anything they damn well like w/yr mss. incldn: cut em sans permission, hold em forever (i.e., bury em), print or reprint em sans permission or acceptance letter beforehand, renege on agreements, don't proof well what they do print too often, refuse to take any advice on cuts or format, etc., and refuse to discuss any point involving an opin-ion diff. from theirs, and never stay in touch w/contribs. past, present or future so that ye never have the slightest idea of what to expect. Most o' the time ye send out a mss. these days, kiss that one goodbye: ye'll never see it again, tho of course, occasionally, VERY occasionally, it comes back in print—years later, after was already printed once/twice/thrice in mag, book or anthology. I never hope to see such a goofedup scene again in my lifetime, assuming it'll ever get back to normal. It may not.

Also, there's a HUGE mountain of trash inundating the scene, completely obliterating much of the fine work still coming out in small presses, where most of the real literature of the '70s/'80s is issuing (try scanning trade lists for qua-lity literature these days). If this is what has come of the Hippie development or the first almost totally college-educated eds./writers generation, can't say as how I like it. Too sloppy, too much 3rd-rate/4th-5th-rate work praised to the skies, eds. who cant read, writers who cant write, all of whom think they're Hot Shit— which they ARE, of course. Hot shit melts! I bet there aren't 10 really sharp 1st-rate eds. in America today—most have gone elsewhere for a living. And most o' these younger poets n talespinners who have 17 chapbooks out before they're 27 are just imitating the Beats or even more academic established writers; conse-quently, we have yet to hear what they REALLY think, feel, so don't yet know who they REALLY are. How sad, how fuckin sad! Why must everyone's apprenticeship be conducted in public now? You tell me, Reggie! Has no one ever heard of modesty or integrity before? Poetry, or good drama or fiction either, just doesnt usually go at 80 mph in the Fast Lane oblivious to everything, son!

Little mags were traditionally primarily literary in content & scope, or per-haps represented 1 or another minority political view, traditionally leftist or

Black-intellectual or -politics, e.g. Now every community or feminist group has a newsletter, tabloid or mag, a few of em quite good; but these comm. or feminist groups' publications, when they pretend to literary merit, more often than not fall short, I'm afraid. Sometimes I think these comm.-group publications should by law be kept out of bookstores, as professionals are having a hard enough time as it is selling their (usually quality) works. I'll not get my way, of course, anytime soon. Was just a thought.

The small press world is increasingly the only place with a serious abiding interest in what we used to call 'serious literature' (of which humor is 1 genre). Trade house & popslickmags increasingly simply cannot compete w/TV except by airing very questionable stuff, nonBooks, CoffeeTable books & the like.

Since the entrance of so many MANY political, feminist & comm. publications into the small-press world, littlemags have gotten increasingly politicized, if one may so put it. This is probably to the good. Even many literary mags are now avowedly Marxist, where before this was for most not quite a possibility . . . as yet. And all this has jazzed up the commercial press to the extent that, on occasion, things which formerly NEVER would've seen print in commercial pages, all of a sudden turn up in books by reputable houses or in likes of *New Yorker, Harper's, Atlantic*. (The same could be said of the current meditation & 'Mystical' craze.)

All thru the late '50s & the '60s/early '70s, life for most of was just a lark, one's living could be a part-time job, had a pad San Fran early '60s fer $35. mo., e.g. Easy as pie. One could publish & still have loot left over for traveling—just try that now! Psychically, spiritually, artistically: very much rewarded me. Finally, I started *Illuminations* on savings from 2 fulltime jobs mid-'60s, cab-driving was 1, copyboy/writing/rewriting, *SF Exam.* the other. It pretty much supported itself after that, altho grants & awards did come along with support. At this time, however, I could've done without them. Now that I REALLY need them, cant get a one. of course. Now I teach for a living (at present, Sub., Publ. Schls), & still just barely get by w/very leetle left over for publishing. (Grad. fr. Collg 1965 & since then, worked fulltime abt 8 years of that time . . .)

Until recently editing the mag fitted in very well, easily, even excitingly, stimulated my writing, healthily. Now, sans wife-helpmate (who speaks English), it gets to be a bit of a burden. Originally it altered my life for the better; now, for the worse at times.

I aint in the habit of regretting much the things I do/did. Sure I'd do it again. It was worth it, for sure. I learned a lot about art, writing, editing, literary politics, so on. Oh I mighta used better paper fer No. 5 (Bullins' play, *Gentleman-Caller*); woulda done No. 10 4-5 years sooner if I coulda; woulda done more books earlier if I'da seen the need when/if I had the bread, etc., etc. But I did it all as I did it. Right now I sho' wish I had the sev. thous. needed to do a beeg 300+-pp. anthology, an *Illuminations Reader*. Sev. tries have netted me no grant so far, but may try again. But seriously, I still dig 98% of what I published & that's a damn high average—for anyone.

Ideally what shud background of li'lmag ed.-publshr be? Ideally s/he should not be a poet, playwright or fiction writer—an essayist, perhaps. An excellent example would be Roy Miller of *San Francisco Review*—he never wrote a thing I'm aware of. Why are we having to do this job anyway? If we did not, however, a large % of each generation's writers would either not get published at all or get so discouraged before they did they'd be old & gray & more or less lost to us. Frustrating situation, eh? . . .

When NEA & CCLM started out, no one at the time suspected the effect would be what it is, this mountain of rubbish passing itself off as a really strong viable literature. We saw it at the time as a way for professionals to get help with their mags or with their writing. But of course every 3rd-4th-5th-rate amateur brat in the country who fancies himself a pro has aimed for a grant or 2 r 3 & got 1, 2 r 3 (r more) & lived off the grants (I've done it myself for couple months at a time; my biggest ever was $1,000) with the consequence that we are absolutely weighted down with mediocre stuff clogging bookshelves everywhere, in stores, libraries, etc., so that practically no one except for the literally famous can sell books in any great numbers.

Of course, this great plethora of stuff has some gems in it too, & even if it didn't, would serve a sort of therapeutic purpose, & perhaps all this blooming, a flower out of every tank-nozzle so to speak, may serve some democratic purpose in the way of individual expression of the masses (as it did in China for awhile) that may be good in its way, I'm not yet totally clear or sure on this.

Likewise, COSMEP was a very hopeful thing at first—remember, there were only 75 founding members, of which I was one. But now every newsletter or pamphlet of every comm. or political or feminist or etc. group are members too & it ceases to serve any useful function I can perceive unless it'd be the blind & suffering solacing each other. Hope this is not TOO terribly negative, but dats de way I sees it, folks.

How do li'lmags fit into U.S. society now—not just on litry level? & small presses? Or do they fit in at all? They fit in all right, but their primary purpose now is of a political sort, not literary or artistic, except in very rare cases & I'm hard put to name one. Perhaps certain regional presses/mags serve a primarily literary function now—*Fault, Wood Ibis/Place of Herons, Hyperion/Tawte/ Thorp Springs*, few others like this, etc. In short, mostly we got snowed under by the avalanche of Capitalism & Grantism!

Addendum

Is there in poetry the same Establishment/Hip (or Underground) dichotomy as there is in every other aspect of American life?

There certainly is. As slung mud, it goes: *They* say we don't bathe (and can't write our way out of a bathtub) and *we* say something like, they bring nothing new to poetry, are only holding back social and artistic progress, are actually sad pretenders to poetry, which is, to us, vision or enlightenment—or aspires to it. We add, rather sneakily, "and they can't write their way out of a men's room, when it comes right down to it."

Whether you succumb to my argument or not, it at least gives ample explanation of one simple fact: There is, in this context, a very real rationale for the existence of little magazines. Little mags are almost exclusively the vehicles of all those poets left out of or uncomfortable with the traditional habits of your average university-backed quarterly or review, or most pop-slicks for that matter. Such magazines are literally anathema to most solid, tough, persistent writing poets—and little-maggers are by and large a fairly tough breed. They run away from such magazines like a bear suddenly aghast at being caught with a camp-fire's roasted wiener in his hands—back to the forest, dammit! It's safer there.

Little magazines, then exist primarily for their many maverick poet-editors: companions in banditry, you might say. You'll seldom find one who acts for a single second as though there is actually a public out there. I personally do not like this. But there it is. Fact. One friend of mine prints 300 or 400 copies of a marvelous magazine and it almost immediately disappears. Does this imply a lot of favoritism and in-breeding in the littlemag world? It does. Publishing "friends" may seen natural to anyone at times, but there is far too much of it to suit me—all over the literary world. Also suggested is an almost imperceptible insecurity—as though the last thing in the world my friend wants is for that much-maligned race of general readers to get in their hot little fists a copy of his lil ole mag. Is he protecting them from something?

However, a case can be made that it is precisely the littlemag editor-poets who are the country's, indeed the world's, unsung, unheeded prophets. For that is what poetry at its best surely is—a kind of prophecy or oracle on the state of affairs surrounding us daily. You may not subscribe to this view. I am going to make a case for it. At least you are getting it from the horse's mouth. I edited *Illuminations* 1965-78 & I'm going into books next.

Exposing yourself daily or even weekly to little magazines is a rather differ-ent program from sticking strictly with the daily straight-press, as we call it, TV news, etc., and is in fact proof of a sort for my argument above. It has a distinct-ly visionary cast to it. It's just as though, as you sit with your morning coffee and cigarette, things slowly reverse or invert right there in your coffee-cup, you are no longer in your basement-pad, but are floating up over the buildings and even the planes, perhaps soaring with enchantment or enmeshed with magic of some sort.

Perhaps also I'd better warn you that there are as many different versions of the littlemag situation as there are littlemag editors. My version of little maga-zines is distinctly a West Coast-Southwest version. My collection of magazines, my writing, has a different flavor from a New York poet even of the same rough breed. There are far less buildings and more of spaces, more mountains, more stars to see, out where we live. This colors and enlivens our lives and our poetry. Also we believe in strange things like rain-dances. We believe they have a reality, a validity all their own, quite apart from whether they produce rain. It actually makes sense, though:

> Stomp and dance
> pound the earth for rain
> Stomp and dance
> until the clouds resound
>
> Something trembles.
> Something cracks.
> Something comes down hard.

(Laura Chester and Geoff Young, in "Rain," from *Stooge* 6, which they co-edit.)

Poetry is, I believe, an entirely personal art. Can there still be something valid and meaningful going on here? There certainly can. No one has ever cleared up this matter of standards to everyone's satisfaction. And I can, on reflection, even clear up to my own satisfaction so confusing a matter as why so many little maggers publish themselves and their friends: when you place a new stone in the Zen rock-garden, not only do you understand better the whole situation, you also understand better the origin, source or meaning of your own polished rock, your own contribution to the never-ending process of change, of discovery, of growth, hopefully of enlightenment. You can see clearly, once and for all, that it is a larger thing than oneself, and perhaps at bottom simply corresponds to the bottomless, fathomless mystery of life.

*   *   *   *

It was precisely in this plethora of publications, a swirling kind of hypnotism, that I one day over morning coffee and afternoon meditation conceived of a new kind of television show, to focus on poets and little magazines and to be called, *Poetry in a Rapidly Changing World*, a monthly series to run for at least a whole year and to start off, maybe, as a summer replacement for Dick Cavett or *Star Trek*. Let us assume I planned a show or two on fairly traditional poets like Lorca, Rilke, Dylan Thomas, Hart Crane, Wallace Stevens (but on a show with such prose bards as Lawrence, Faulkner, Henry Miller? . . . uhm, wouldn't wait around for your agent to call, Norm). And likewise, there were separate shows on "traditional little mags" like *Lillabulero, Confrontation, Hanging Loose,* quarterlies like *New York Quarterly, Fiddlehead, Minnesota Review, Massachusetts Review,* and "independent professional" magazines like *Poetry/ Chicago, Choice, Work, Transatlantic Review, Poetry Northwest,* the original *Ramparts,* and many others. Another program was on poetry-book specialists such as City Lights Books, Oyez!, Unicorn Press, Auerhahn Press, Open Skull Press, Something Else Press, Seventies Press, etc. Some of these presses have transformed not only the face but the depths of American poetry. Two entire programs feature Indian and Caucasian shaman-poets: the journeys of both modern and Indian poets, mystics, etc. But even to imagine such a strange TV series as this is to somewhere find a place for the poet as social catalyst or reformer.

It's TeeVee time, sure enough, folks, but it's afternoon now, so switch from coffee to tea. One whole development in recent modern poetry is the poet as the catalyst—not as mere social commentator, but one who stands in direct relation to society and takes a dynamic, challenging stance as poet, man, being, and gladly takes risks. In this connection for precedents there is Neruda's Impure Poetry, Antonio Parra's Anti-Poems and Artaud's Theatre of Cruelty. In America we have the "social surrealism" of Kenneth Patchen, Bob Kaufman, Ferlinghetti, Ginsberg, Walt Lowenfels, some of Robert Bly, even some John Haines. (Shots of City Lights Bookstore now and readings from *El Corno Emplumado, Kayak, Olé!, Poetmeat, City Lights Journal, The Realist,* and many others.)

One step further and you have the poet as reformer, the poet who has a direct stake in reform &/or revolution. With Ginsberg and Ferlinghetti in the wings and with the music of a real revolution of sorts, however sporadic or straggling, in the streets, on-camera strides Charles Bukowski, Doug Blazek, Rich Krech, and others, including most of the black poets in the country. (Shots of Bukowski at the track: "Hello kid. Yew play da horses too?" Krech at a demonstration, draped with sombrero, serape, rifle and crossed cartridge-belts, com-

84

plete with guerrilla-band, towards sundown, sleeping off the wild party of the night before. Sure, the yak's at their expense, but both are farout and Bukowski's something of a genius. Readings here from *Earth, Avalanche, Black Dialog,* the original *Notes from the Underground* and *Evergreen Review*.)

Other editors have been bending or expanding the concept of the magazine by having special editions, special anthologies or series: *Coyote's Journal, Writing, Illuminations, El Corno* again. Others see the magazine as book. *New World Writing* and *Discovery* were among the great annuals of the '50s and '60s, and now there's *American Review, New Directions* and other trade annuals or quarterlies. Others were *Spero, The Outsider, City Lights* again and the one-shot mag-books of *Coyote's J., Writing* and others. Then there's the mag as wild underground newspaper—prophecy, poetry, collage, satire, comix, long rambling journals and letters, lots of hogwash and some offbeat news. Lively, fun-filled, saucy and pert publications—though sometimes the writing is absolutely atrocious. Best of them: *San Francisco Oracle, Open City, Berkeley Barb,* early *Village Voice* and *Los Angeles Free Press, Rolling Stone, The Realist, Boulder Express, Kaleidoscope, East Village Other, Great Speckled Bird* and *The Gar.* It would be impossible to be alive in our time and be a poetry or publishing nut, and not read these papers occasionally, and sometimes more often than that. They certainly provide a unique view of America and occasionally, rather by chance, air some fine poetry.

Another program might be called, *Poetry as Way of Life.* It would show the poetry magazine as the perfect indicator of where these marvelously unruly new editors are at in their lives. I'd use such current mags as *Vagabond, Grande Ronde Review, Greenfield Review, Black Theatre,* etc., and such earlier marvels as *The 8-Pager, Olè!, My Own Mag, Contact, San Francisco Review, City Lights, Genesis West* & others.

Now you see it, now you don't. Can you imagine such a series? Obviously, I can. Many of these magazines have already folded, yet made extremely important contributions to modern literature and life. Of course, in an anti-artistic culture such as ours, a TV series on poetry and little mags is an extremely unlikely possibility. I won't hold my breath till I'm moderating this show, I assure you.

*   *   *   *

The suggestion has already been made that there is a link between the little magazine situation and the overall growth and development of poetry, in the country and to an extent in the world-at-large. What is the littlemag situation indicating about the world then? Well, if there is an oracle here to be found, most of the portents are not good. Our poetry has never been so overwhelmingly negative and full of despair, rife at times with cynicism. And what kind of barometer is the littlemag situation of itself, the world of poetry? On reflection, the biggest general development in American poetry in the last six to eight years seems to be more and more loosening up of the general craft, and less of a tight stranglehold on it by the famous Black Mountain development: I have, not perhaps so happily for my own career as a poet, been something of a leader in breaking up this bottleneck by the Creeley-Olson school of poetry, which was thought at first to be an anti-academic tendency, and perhaps it was at its outset. But Creeley and Olson did not follow through in that vein. Instead, they adeptly joined forces with the academy, and, more avidly than most perhaps, promoted only themselves and their ass-kissers, a genuinely sad state of affairs. Somehow we had, I don't know why, expected more of them. Of course, in all fairness, the times have not demanded a tight-knit art, but a more swinging, loosely-knit art.

Topside now is the broadside slam effect first seen in similar poetry by Ginsberg, Ferlinghetti, Corso, Kaufman, Whalen and others in the definitive Grove Press anthology, *New American Poetry 1945-1960*, also the first anthology to feature the Black Mountain poets. We saw this broad effect at times in Patchen, Neruda, Parra, Yevtushenko and others. It is now taken over by Bukowski, Blazek, Charles Potts, John Bennett, most of the black poets—in fact, by probably well over half the poets in the country. This is a technique usually best used sparingly—such poetry quickly becomes tract. Bukowskis are few and far between, any way you cut it. Everyone tries it nowadays, not always to its advantage. The result? To put it mildly, the Black Mountain movement, though it continues to exercise general influence and is still mostly a quite readable poetry, no longer dominates American poetry.

*　　*　　*　　*

In recent years, though we are not lacking in volumes of quality poetry, no school has emerged, and no single poet with anything like the charisma of Ginsberg, Snyder or Olson. It appears that our poetry is at a standstill. This is untrue. There are new eclectic-mystic boy-wonders aplenty, but we are all such mavericks we do not comprise a school, so the publicity-hounds do not follow us about. And in this situation certain of the older, better-known, poets have probably unintentionally pretended that no new poets have arisen. I would say that Bukowski is the spiritual if not actual father of a whole tough new breed of poets, and that Robert Bly is the same for another, not so wild, group. Who, then, are the new mystic-mavericks? Try a guess? Sure, why not? Fowler, Blazek, Ben Hiatt, Diane Wakoski, Bill Herron, Jimmy 'Santiago' Baca, Art Cuelho for a start. Many others.

If there is one thing that distinguishes this new poetry it is that, though great attention is given to the natural sound of the lines, if there is a choice between a line that is beautiful or obscure and one that is plain-sounding but revealing, clarity and honesty of statement will win out almost every time. This is distinctly different from the Pound-Olson way. To emphasize this point, let me quote from movement 4, "The Radical Papers of Gene Fowler," *Hyperion*, Wint. 1971, Vol. IV. He is waxing angry about "ready-made poetry" for "ready-made audiences." He says:

> Ability as never before, wasted as never before.
> The clear eye and juicy loins,
> The good lungs and firm voice;
>
> Rhythms as never before,
>
> A place to start as never before,
> The rape of the Muse as she'd not been raped before,
> Poems half-birthed, skewered
> And torn apart on the savage teeth.

Needless to say, Fowler has addressed himself with a vengeance to that other, tamed poetry I mentioned earlier, which of course keeps the true poets, those under discussion anyway, from reaching their rightful audience.

*   *   *   *

We are living at present, no matter what the President says, in a severely inflationary period. Naturally, there is little extra to purchase artistic products (rock concerts, "in," poetry *out*). National Foundation on the Arts' awards to writers and (originally only via Coordinating Council of Literary Magazines) to editors quite suddenly burst onto the literary scene, causing much consternation, scurrying about, and many dogfights. In this situation some small-press publishers have changed with the times, some switching to books or to an APS-format, or gotten schlockey-comickey. And as we attempt survival in a rude, greed-deep era, CCLM still will not grant small publishers funds to do books, probably because of a potentially sizable conflict with Eastern trade publishers . . . first novels or collections are sometimes distributed as well or better by small publishers. Reactionary CCLM, however, continues its grants for "one more" issue at a time. Unbelievable! Now National Endowment for Arts belatedly offers grants to do books & magazines as well.

Another way for the littlemag to go in this severely troubled era is to add larger and larger doses of prose and address oneself with a passion to the lost & troubled souls everywhere. Of course, such a program is financially prohibitive anytime, more than ever nowadays. But there are always some who will reach for that ever looming larger audience—3,000 or more. The current trend towards books & prose seems to be well on its way & is almost certainly an omen of the future. The traditional littlemag of poetry may be on its way out—for financial reasons, mainly. Some independent ventures doing very impressive things recently are *Stand, TransAtlantic Review, December, Abyss, The Smith & Grande Ronde Review*. These magazines are at least bucking for the higher circulation figures of such established publications as *Paris Review, Massachusetts Review*, and *Poetry/Chicago*. The most typically littlemag of all the independent prose-poetry publications are probably *December* and *Grande Ronde*. It is probably precisely editors Curt Johnson and Ben Hiatt's natural spunk that will keep them from snaring that elusive higher circulation. Both seem to be feisty, good-humored, immensely gifted and dedicated men. I can only discuss one of them.

The *Grande Ronde Review* had, like *Illuminations*, been in a lapse for a year or two, doing poetry pamphlets in the interim. It has now returned with a flair with a big 160-page edition with an incredible collection of substantial poetry, fiction and non-fiction. *Grande Ronde* #13 has poetry by Norm Russell, Charles Foster, Kell Robertson, Art Cuelho and many others including several Folsom prison poets. This issue has three outstanding stories by Margoshes, Kittredge and Silverman, and several other interesting stories, but it also has a klinker by one of Hiatt's sponsors. That gives you some notion of Ben Hiatt and his magazine. *Grande Ronde* has a feeling for the spaces of the Western states where he and his friends and contributors grew up and still live: Oregon, California, New Mexico, etc. Ben prints 500 of his magazine on an old litho press and sells about half the run.

Most of the fiction has a natural, folksy flavor of nature and farm-life about it, in the best possible sense—not just romanticizing or bending with fashion.

And this is the way Hiatt and contributors actually are. A few of Hiatt's words in a review of a book by his friend Kell Robertson, the folksinger poet, will give you a sense of what I mean:

> . . . our poets come from everywhere but as soon as they become poets they cease being anything else. what we need are poets who can continue to stay in touch with their roots and continue to talk to us. most poets are Poets and move in circles of other poets. they tend to lose contact with the real world and they forget that we must actually share our reality with everyone. just as there are few musicians of any stature who are willing to mingle with the rifraf in the tradition of a woody guthrie so there are few poets who mingle and write to and about anyone other than themselves or other poets.

To my mind the perfect complement to this passage in poetry would be some lines from our new Van Gogh of poetry, Art Cuelho, also from *Grande Ronde* #13.

> I walked into the mountains
> And sat down directly before the sun's light
>
> There was space between the silence . . .

*

> As many days as you sit directly before the sun
> You shall receive these gifts, the heart of this land
> You have named my son, and nakedness is your light.

"Nakedness as My Vision Light" is what he calls that one. The poem on the facing page has the fantastic title, "My Final Copy Is in Blood." It is a strong and heartfelt poem. "When I start cutting into my heart,/ You will know how close I am to you./ When my soul keeps bleeding,/ You'll realize the faith I shared with mercy's dawn." Whether or not Artie actually in literal fact wrote it in blood, one feels he might've, and he is practically the only poet now writing who could give one that feeling and get away with such lines. Cuelho is a marvelous new visionary.

Grande Ronde Review is a fairly typical littlemag—soaring at its best and atrocious at its worst. If this big #13 and smaller nos. 14/15 are any indication, Hiatt has just become a pro, for it is nearly all soaring and passionate material— nine socko pages out of every ten is a pretty damned high batting average *anywhere!* *Grande Ronde* certainly has its own feeling and a certain flair and clarity about it. The magazine is distinct, and clearly reveals the personality of its editor. And as far as I'm concerned, that's where it's at.

*   *   *   *

The wildest of the new Bay Area mimeo/offset periodicals are *Avalanche, Vagabond, Good-bye, Aldebaran Review.* Other publications in the area are *Cloud Marauder, The Second Coming, Hyperion, Shocks, The Fault;* from elsewhere, *2nd Aeon, Prism International Magazine, Phoenix* and *Hearse.* At the

88

moment the Southwest and the Midwest have very active littlemag situations, and there is some evidence that the same thing is slowly happening in the South and other rather provincial areas of the country. Three fine Southern magazines now are *Southern Exposure, St. Andrews Review* and *Truck*, and magazines recently founded in the Southwest are *Quetzal, Changes, Stooge, Esperanza, Advent, Lucille, Austin Pulpwood, Wood Ibis, Ally* and *Oriental Blue Streak*, which flamed out after an issue or two. It may revive. I hate to come on like an old bewhiskered mountain-man with a mouthful of oracle, but it is as though the changes already experienced by many in the heyday of the Beat era, or later, Haight-Ashbury, have only just reached these inland communities. A word of warning, however. In the little magazine business, one's main audience is in one's immediate area, and there are as yet only two or three communities in the Southwest that sell little mags, and they are almost 1,000 miles apart. My own circulation dropped almost by half while I lived in the Southwest (from circa 1,500-1,600 to about 800-900).

If the '70s take on a distinct flavor anywhere, in or out of the literary world, it's not clear what it is. It is clear, though, who the current "darlings" of the little mags are: Blazek, Hugh Fox, Diane di Prima, Lyn Lifshin, Al Masarak, Bob Stout, Peter Wild, Norm Russell and old man Bukowski. You can hardly pick up a magazine without seeing one or more of their poems and tales. And would one of the little maggers himself hazard a guess as to the best little mags currently going? Well, a short list, maybe: *Transition, Alcheringa, Kayak, Choice, Writing, Coyote's Journal, Quetzal, Stand, TransAtlantic Review, The Seventies, December, Grande Ronde Review, Aldebaran Review*, and *The Smith*. And how does this group compare with the most dynamic magazines of a decade or so earlier? Favorably enough, I suppose. However, I find myself still somewhat partial to certain earlier magazines—*The Outsider, San Francisco Review, Contact, Spero, Wild Dog, Synapse, Yugen, Big Table, Metamorphosis*, the first *Second Coming, Botteghe Oscure, Beatitudes, City Lights Journal* and the original *Evergreen Review*. I'm probably wrong. They probably aren't better. But the earlier period unearthed the biggest explosion postwar American poetry has seen, the era when Ginsberg, Snyder, Whalen, Kaufman, Lew Welch, LeRoi Jones, Lenore Kandel and Charles Foster burst wildly and magnificently onto an unsuspecting world. It was when they were much younger and still on their way up and when Gene Fowler, Ed Bullins, Mike Hannon and many, many other others including myself, were just starting out—to climb the mountain, I mean.

But we still have not answered that ever-alluring question, what, after all, *are* poets?—acrobatic clowns, demagogues, madmen, catalysts, stunt-men, egomaniacal moralists or true holy-men? Probably all of them, in part. Naturally, I prefer the holy-man version. Many people will to the end of time stick to the traditional Western view of a poet as a certain kind of communicator, a writer in fact, and I do not deny this view. But the other way gives one's writing a certain grounding in the entire fabric of life and in rather mysterious areas such as ancient culture, prophecy, folklore, ritual dance and song, which is according to some (Suzanne Langer for one) the origin of art in the first place. A poet can be quite validly viewed as a kind of shaman or natural Bodishattva. A Zenman. This curious notion turns up everywhere—*Crazy Horse, Caterpillar, Poems From a Floating World, Illuminations, Origins*, etc. *Alcheringa* announces it will air "songs, chants, prayers, visions, dreams, sacred narratives, origins and namings, magical formulas, proverbs," etc. It calls itself the "First Magazine of the

89

World's Tribal Poetries" and lives up to that name! Perhaps poets are, after all, the mountain-hermits who occasionally, in all eras, appear on the plaza to chant, sing, rap or tell tall tales. In our age they write them down.

Prophecy, poetry and vision *do* sometimes mix. At such times, when we are restored to ourselves, we realize that poetry is among other things a rite of purification. I struggle daily if necessary to keep this sense of it before me. But when we emerge from the dance inside the kiva to peer again at the horrible spectre of contemporary reality, we consider converting the kiva into a fortress and using our art as a battering ram against a demonically evil culture. Sometimes, we do. Other times it's warm fires, warm talk, music and poetry, and we are in the hogan or at a celebration, and then we know the great rites are always before us if we will only seize them, everywhere, anywhere, *all the time. Together.*

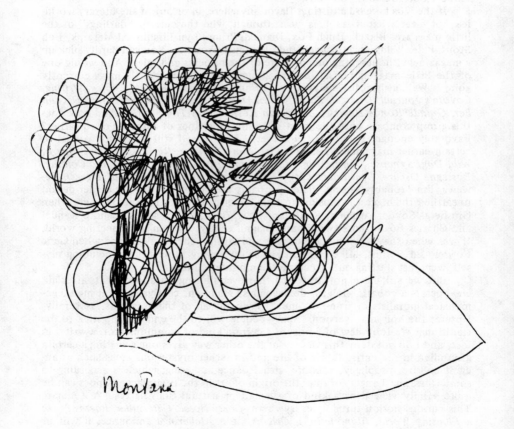

"Slow Bull, Invocation" 49/100 Anna Byerly 1974

A

SHAMAN'S

SONGBOOK

NORMAN MOSER

Gordon Weaver

Mississippi Review

Gordon Weaver

Gordon Weaver was born in Moline, Illinois, February 2, 1937; US Army, 1955-58; married Judith Lynne Gosnell (1961); children: Kristina (born 1967), Anna (born 1968), Jessica (born 1975); education: B.A. (English), U. of Wisconsin-Milwaukee, 1958; M.A. (English), U. of Illinois, 1962; Ph.D. (English), U. of Denver, 1970; current occupation: Professor of English and Department Head, Oklahoma State University; founding editor, *Mississippi Review*, 1972-75; consulting editor for fiction, *Cimarron Review*, 1975 to the present; published three short story collections: *The Entombed Man of Thule* (1972), *Such Waltzing Was Not Easy* (1975), *Getting Serious* (1980); three novels: *Count a Lonely Cadence* (1968), *Give Him a Stone* (1975), *Circling Byzantium* (1980); approximately 70 stories published in various literary and "little" magazines, 1963 to the present; St. Lawrence Award for Fiction (1973), National Endowment for the Arts Fellowship in Creative Writing (1974), O. Henry Award First Prize (1979).

I was introduced to literary ("little") magazines as an undergraduate student at the University of Wisconsin-Milwaukee (1958-61) by my creative writing teacher, Donald Emerson, a great influence on my subsequent career as a teacher and writer. When I had produced what he considered a publishable story, he told me to read some magazines to see where I might submit my work for consideration—thus I found out about the existence of some of the best formats for literary short fiction, *Minnesota Review, Hudson Review, Virginia Quarterly Review, Sewanee Review*, etc. Naturally enough, I was soon introduced by my reading to newer magazines, many of them coming out for the first time in the early 1960s, went on to discover the "network" of magazines (COSMEP, CCLM, etc.) we know today.

I decided to found *Mississippi Review* (which I am pleased to see continues to publish) shortly after I joined the English department at the University of Southern Mississippi. My reasons were two-fold: first, I saw an opportunity—the university administration was encouraging such activity at the time, and, second, I saw two kinds of need for another literary magazine. The state of Mississippi, which has produced so many great writers—because so many people in Mississippi write *and* read good literature—had no magazine of its own. I wanted to create a regional format of sorts to fill that need. Perhaps more important, by

1970-71 I had read enough such magazines to see that too many of them were devoted to what I considered frivolous work, too many were the creatures of narrow ideas as to what constituted good writing, a good number were no more than "self-publishing" vehicles for their editors and those editors' "friends." I wanted to edit and publish a magazine that would be *truly* open to the spectrum of writing flourishing in the country, one that would publish without respect to the writer's proximity, his credits, or his membership in any long- or short-lived "school" of literature.

I had no problem with my editorial activity in conjunction with my own writing; I simply made it a policy never to publish any of my own work in my magazine—and I tried to avoid publishing in any magazines the editors of which appeared ready or willing to "trade off" space with me—this sort of "deal" was and still is rampant. No doubt, to some extent, if one is "known" as a magazine editor, it gets a little easier to publish your work, but avoiding "self-publishing" (a little magazine euphemism for vanity publishing) is the only way I know to keep one's honor relatively intact.

I never saw my editorial work as a means of earning a living. I teach for a living. And I have seen almost no evidence that producing a magazine will create anything by way of "payback" for the professional academic—more often than not, it is considered, at best, "nice," at worst, an irritation.

I began publishing two issues a year of *Mississippi Review*, all I could afford in 1972. In 1974, I was able to support three issues per year. I left the magazine behind when I moved to Oklahoma, but almost immediately was asked to serve as a fiction editor for *Cimarron Review*, in which capacity I read the slush pile and recommend to the editor-in-chief, so I have not stopped, in essence, since I began, though I have not been involved with the mechanics—money, printing, layout, distribution—since I left Mississippi. Literary magazine work is no part of the way I make my living, but continues to be a part of my life.

I was able to print only 500 copies per issue of *MR*. Of this number, I think I reached a "high" of about 350 paid subscribers, mostly academic and public libraries, a lot of individuals in the state of Mississippi, and we exchanged a few copies of each issue with other magazines, exchanged ads, etc. I could not afford to give the magazine away, needing every dime I could scrounge to continue publication. In this I was aided by the university printing plant, which found stock at reduced prices for me, gave me enormous breaks on printing bills, etc.

I do not think my ideas about what such a magazine should be have changed much: literary magazines ought to print what their editors think is the best work available, without respect to fashion or reputation. I do not think magazines should be self-consciously avant-garde or conservative, nor devoted to "causes" (homosexuals, racial minorities, women, etc.). If they exist to provide alternatives to commercial publishing, then they should eschew "causes" like plague— the best of them succeed.

The best thing *Mississippi Review* did was to publish writers of very different styles—I published some "names," a great many got their work in print for the first time, and I cannot think of an instance where we published anyone because

94

he or she was fashionable at the given moment. Beyond that, we devoted relatively more space to fiction than most magazines did or do—one issue contained 13 short stories, for example. At the same time, we featured the work of several poets who were less than fashionable—publishing chapbook-length collections by an individual poet. No doubt I made mistakes, but I can think of no aspect of my work with *MR* that I regret today.

I suspect the birth rate for little magazines is declining, if only because *that* fashion is passing, and will continue to decline as contemporary economics dry up sources of easy funding—NEA, CCLM. I am not at all sure this is to be regretted; an awful lot of trash saw print in the 1960s and 1970s, and maybe magazines will have to have more than a simple grant application form available to continue publishing in the next decade.

I do not see a great distinction between small presses and little magazines—often one is coexistent with the other. Just as such magazines publish more good poetry than commercial magazines, small presses bring a lot of excellent work to an audience, small as that is always going to be. At the same time, they produce more junk, "ego-salve," than the hard economics of commercial publishing will allow.

I cannot begin to estimate the time I spent working on *MR*; I recall countless Sundays with layout spread out on my living room floor, evening after evening reading the slush pile, tense meetings with academic administrators begging funds, discussions with my assistant editors—Walter Everett, Jesse McCartney, Peggy Prenshaw—about the merits of this or that poem or story manuscript. The initial money came from the University of Southern Mississippi, and, later, from some matching grants from CCLM—about $3,500 in all, over three years, I would guess—we paid contributors and expanded the size of our issues.

I guess what I "got out of" editing/publishing, what I still get is "satisfaction" —knowing that I may have given the best sort of encouragement to accomplished authors, that I may have brought an important experience of literature to such audience as I had or have. I also got exposed to the same sort of immature and corrupt personalities one finds in any walk of life. My point here is that I found, and find, "literary" people no better or worse than any other class—and think there is no reason anyone should expect to find it otherwise.

The longer I have been "at this," the more I have come to respect—if not always admire—the magazines that have survived the longest—perhaps I am an elitist: I like *Antioch Review, Georgia Review, Southern Review*, where the quality of work they publish has been as consistent as it can be. I do not like magazines that are self-publishing enterprises, magazines that call themselves "revolutionary," magazines with stupid editorial policies (printing only work by lesbians or Blacks or Marxists or one or another of the avant-garde fashions). There are too many names here to mention, and why be offensive?

I think a literary editor needs to be educated—in literature. And it would be nice if he comes from a monied family. Most of all, it would be best if he had no friends and published his own work under an assumed name.

Government aid, state or federal, has allowed a lot of magazines to survive, even prosper. It has also fertilized an enormous amount of ephemera. There has been only an ordinary amount of corruption in the distribution of this money—magazines that got too much, some that should not have received any, some that received none in a given year because the crowd that awarded the money was unsympathetic, etc. In any case, I think it is clear this sort of aid will diminish greatly, and I do not think it really matters. Good magazines will stay with us because good people are determined that they should. Those that fall among tares probably deserve it.

Literary magazines—literature itself—has no "effect" on our society—at least none that anybody can very tangibly trace; it might be just as well if people seriously involved with literature stop worrying about their "impact" on society. The important thing to remember is that serious, accomplished people have been interested in and involved with literature from the beginnings of our civilization, and it seems pretty clear they always will be. There will also always be some fool with a platform to cry out about the "death" of this or that genre, or to whine that the Philistines do not appreciate what they should. It matters not.

Any activity, but especially "art," is worth doing if you think it is, and as long as nobody can prove what you do is very directly harmful to others, there is no cause for alarm.

MISSISSIPPI REVIEW VOL 12 NO 3 SPRING 1984

MISSISSIPPI REVIEW

C.W. Truesdale

New Rivers Press

C.W. Truesdale

C.W. Truesdale was born in St. Louis in 1929, has lived all over the country, and has a PhD from the Univ. of Washington. He has published 7-$\frac{1}{3}$ volumes of poetry with small presses. He founded New Rivers Press in 1968, and since then, in New York and Minnesota, has published 150 titles.

The Small Press in America: Coming of Age in a Dark Time

A culture without good books is no real culture at all. A country that does not encourage good writing by providing outlets for it cannot possibly have a dynamic and living culture. America is blessed in having an abundance of excellent writers, most of whom have turned to the small presses to get their work out before the reading public, because so many of the commercial houses have abandoned any sense of cultural responsibility they might once have had and have gone for the fast buck and the big numbers game. If a book doesn't make it in those terms in three to six months, it is likely to be remaindered or shredded. That some really fine books, like Judith Guest's *Ordinary People* and Patricia Hampl's *A Romantic Education*, survive that cynical process is wonderful, but I have read two extraordinary novels in manuscript by a fine young writer named Charles Baxter that were turned down by publisher after publisher *because they are too good*. It is not hard to imagine what fate would befall James Joyce's *Ulysses* today, if it were newly written and submitted to an American publishing house. I doubt that even Random House, Joyce's original American publisher, would take a second look at such a book today.

The small press scene in America (and nowhere else in the world) is full of surprises and books of extraordinary quality and originality, many of them beautifully designed and printed in ridiculously small editions. They range from the elegance of handset letterpress books by "fine printers" like Allan Kornblum (Toothpaste Press), Gerald Lange (Bieler Press) and Michael Tarrachow (Penta-

99

gram Press) to the nicely printed and economical chapbooks of Paul Feroe's Ally Press. In between are presses like New Rivers and Holy Cow! that use commercial printers to produce books of professional quality in editing and design. Many small press books, incidentally, have won national awards for design and graphics. In fact, so many good books are published each year by small presses that real choice problems confront even the most discriminating reader, especially since the review situation for literature in America is really terrible. The big Twin Cities' [Minneapolis, St. Paul] dailies, for instance, pay lavish homage to local dance, theatre, and music groups, but very little to regional literature.

The small press scene in America offers a tremendous and eclectic range of good books, probably because it is dominated by writers and not marketing specialists. Each of these publishers has unique interests and taken as a group they come from varied backgrounds and heritages. There is a *sameness* in commercial publishing in this country and a *uniqueness* in small press publishing. America is a *writing* country more than it is a *reading* one. For this reason, many of its best writers, like Herman Melville, have felt ill-used or neglected by the reading public, which tends to be faddish and superficial in its tastes and buying habits. In fact, it is always a surprise and a delight for me to find a non-writer who has read great books and is keenly aware of our literary heritage. That doesn't happen too often, except perhaps in the classroom where a student is sometimes obliged to read a classic or two. A good writer commits himself body, soul, and mind to his work and often spends years of obsessive effort getting it right. Not surprisingly he will probably come to feel that what he is saying is very important and build up an unconscious expectation that everyone else will share that view and treat him and his work with the utmost respect and admiration. When he discovers that only six or seven hundred out of 230,000,000 of his fellow-countrymen share that view, the result can be shattering.

To a certain extent, almost every small press editor/publisher goes through the same experience when he or she is first starting out. Partly this is because most of us editors are also writers and believe passionately that really good writing has got to get out there to an audience that mostly ignores it. It's easy to forget that the really important thing is *to get those books in print* and to do everything possible to see that they are well-received, because a book that isn't published is no book at all. This means that a small press publisher not only has to be a good and responsible editor but is also likely to have to develop sound business and marketing skills—not because he necessarily believes he will make money doing this but because he has an obligation to his authors to spread their words as widely as possible. The most painful thing for me as an editor is to see authors I really believe in virtually neglected no matter what I do.

My personal commitment to quality, excellence, and originality in writing and in book publishing, a commitment shared by most small press editors, has, if anything, deepened over the 15 years I have been doing New Rivers. That conviction has been strengthened by what I perceive as the appalling indifference of commercial publishing houses to new writing of real quality. What few poets some of them publish are either well-established like James Wright and W.S.

Merwin or appeal to faddish interests. There are exceptions, of course. Some New Rivers poets, like Albert Goldbarth, Peter Wild, Siv Cedering, etc. have been picked up by commercial houses for a time and then are dropped because of disappointing sales. Most of those poets return—in disgust—to the small press fold.

Small presses have been around in great numbers for so long now that most people probably take them for granted and assume that they will persevere through these dark, lean times. Historically, of course, the small press phenomenon is of recent origin. Until the late '50s and early '60s, there was only a handful of small presses and literary magazines in this country, and many of these (particularly the magazines) were connected, like the *Kenyon Review, Sewanee Review*, and *Southern Review*, with universities which subsidized them handsomely.

Whether or not the small press movement will continue to flourish or not is a difficult question. Already, a number of presses have folded up their tents and vanished, and the portents don't look very promising. It certainly wouldn't be the first time in American history that political radicalism of the right or civil war have killed off a flourishing literary culture. Right now, public funding for literature has been cut in half, and private foundation support for literature in most areas (with exception of a few states like Minnesota) has been meager. Because so few small presses are truly self-supporting, the drying up of funding sources has forced many of them either to fold or develop enterprising new ways of raising money. Some small presses, like their larger university counterparts, have had to ask their authors to subsidize their own publications (which discriminates against impoverished writers). Others, like New Rivers, have had to cut back severely on any kind of broad national program and have become, in effect, regional publishers, because that's where what little money there is is.

The situation for small presses at this time is tenuous. What would happen to writing in this country if all or most small presses died away is a frightening prospect and an entirely feasible one. Perhaps ten or so books of poetry and a half dozen collections would be brought out by the commercial houses, and almost all of these would be by Establishment authors. Perhaps as many as 20 or so poetry books and a dozen or so short story collections might be published by the university presses. It would be the early '50s revisited when most of the poetry published was academic, sterile, and de-natured. And that was what we all rebelled against—the Beats, the Black Mountain crew, the Deep Imagists, the New York School, and the rest of us who don't fit comfortably into those categories.

The heady, naive days of the Counter-Culture have long been over and we have come into a dark and frightening time. But surely we must have learned *something* from the '60s—that, at the very least, literature is vital and exciting, that it addresses itself in imaginative ways to the real world, and that without it we would all be less human, less intelligent and articulate and more like *victims* of a political madness beyond our control. Many of us, I feel, are coming to believe even more passionately in what we are doing the more we are threatened. Hopefully, we are coming to this realization before it is too late.

Up to now, the publisher has borne most of the responsibility for small press survival, and obviously he will continue to have to be a primary mover. But the writer too must come to be more actively involved in the promotion and dissemination of his/her work, to assume a more active partnership with the publisher. And libraries need to be less concerned with the circulation numbers game and realize that they have a major cultural responsibility to *Living* literature. There is no *good* reason why more libraries—and bookstores—can't carry all the usual bread-and-butter best sellers but also stock a full, rich, and varied collection of small press material, sponsor lots of small press publication readings, and provide a real—and lively—cultural center.

I think that what all of us involved in literature need to realize is just how delicate the network of small press publishing is. All of us—writers, publishers, librarians, and readers—have a stake in seeing that this extraordinary phenomenon continues to flourish.

MORNING WINDOWS

Michael Moos

NEW RIVERS PRESS

Douglas Blazek

Olé

Douglas Blazek

Douglas Blazek was born in Chicago, 1941, St. Elizabeth's Hospital, Polish Northwest side. Father: cost accountant, Arnold Schwinn & Co., manufacturer of bicycles. Mother: housewife. Attended James Monroe Public School in Chicago. Moved to Wood Dale, west of O'Hare Airport, in 1950. Attended local grade school, then Fenton High School in Bensenville. North Central College in Naperville. Worked in grocery stores (mom & pop as well as supermarket), various short-lived jobs, plus six years as a laborer and quality control inspector for James B. Clow, makers of cast iron pipe. Married Alta Judd in 1961. Son Nathan born in 1962. Son Aaron born in 1965. Lived in Elmhurst and in Bensenville. Sold all possessions and moved via car caravan to San Francisco in 1967. Lived on the ocean a few months, then Haight-Ashbury. Settled in Sacramento in 1969. Still there.

BIBLIOGRAPHY AS EDITOR

Olé #1-8, Bensenville & San Francisco, 1964-1967.
Open Skull #1 (all issued), San Francisco, 1967.
Olé Anthology. Poetry X/Change. Glendale. 1967. (Stated 5000 copies but 500 is more realistic.)
A Bukowski Sampler. Quixote Press. Madison. 1969. Approximately 400 copies.
William Wantling: *Down, Off & Out*. Mimeo Press. Bensenville. 1965. Cover by d.a. levy. Approximately 400 copies.
Charles Bukowski: *Confessions of a Man Insane Enough to Live with Beasts*. Mimeo Press. Bensenville. 1965. Cover by Anna Purcell. 500 copies.
Carl Larsen: *The Popular Mechanics Book of Poetry*. Mimeo Press. Bensenville. 1966. Approximately 400 copies.
Charles Bukowski: *All the Assholes in the World & Mine*. Open Skull Press. Bensenville. 1966. Cover by Bukowski. 400 copies.
Brown Miller: *Fertilized Brains*. Open Skull Press. San Francisco. 1968. Cover hand printed by author. 500 copies.

Joel Deutsch: *Space Heaters*. Open Skull Press. San Francisco. 1968. 500 copies.

Robert Nelson Moore, Jr.: *I Was There*. Open Skull Press. San Francisco. 1968. Original silkscreen cover by T.L. Kryss. 250 copies.

Lyn Lifshin: *Why Is the House Dissolving?* Open Skull Press. San Francisco. 1968. Edited by Brown Miller. 500 copies.

d.a. levy: *The Beginning of Sunny Dawn & Red Lady*. Open Skull Press. San Francisco. 1969. Cover by Blazek. 500 copies.

T.L. Kryss: *Nuclear Roses & Quiet Rooms*. Open Skull Press. San Francisco. 1969. Cover by Blazek. 500 copies.

Karen Waring: *A Child's Poem & Poems*. Open Skull Press. Sacramento. 1970. 300 copies.

Douglas Blazek: *Zany Typhoons*. Open Skull Press. Sacramento. 1970. Cover by R. Crumb. 200 copies.

SELECTED BIBLIOGRAPHY AS AUTHOR

Skull Juices. Twowindows Press. San Francisco. 1970. 1000 copies.

Flux & Reflux. Oyez Press. Berkeley. 1970. 1000 copies.

I Am the One. (w/Don Cauble & T.L. Kryss). Dead Angel Press. Portland. 1972. 175 copies.

Lethal Paper. The Stone Press. Norwich. 1974. Cover by Stephen Homsy. Approximately 300 copies.

Exercises in Memorizing Myself. Twowindows Press. Berkeley. 1976. 500 copies.

I Am a Weapon. Ox Head Press. Marshall. 1975. 400 copies.

Edible Fire. Morgan Press. Milwaukee. 1978. 500 copies.

I was living in Huckleberry's town. Not Hannibal, Mo., but Bensenville, Ill. Interchangeable as far as innocence goes. The year was 1963 and I was trying to enter the backdoor of literature by writing Hemingway truth with Kerouac vigor. Nothing was getting finished but poems, and they were all yapping barbarically like Ginsberg, Corso, Ferlinghetti and the whole gang in Don Allen's *New American Poetry*. I had left college two years earlier because of an archtypal romance with my highschool sweetheart and because of the fetus humming in her belly. An iron foundry owned my soul but bought the bread. Huckleberry was traded for a group of jazz musicians who initiated me into Chicago's subculture. At the time such knowledge surpassed anything the Old Greeks and Romans had to offer. It was becoming quite clear that I had to opt for Looney Tune Exile rather than drink the spiritual hemlock offered by society. More and more I considered myself a writer, one who could live and speak only outside the boundaries of bomb doom and bonsai intellect.

I knew nothing of littlemags, only that I needed to release my caged voice, to make it count equal to any Vietnam War protester's or any Southern Freedom Rider's—there was great despair at The System, a revolution of conscience and consciousness taking place and I thought the arts was where I should engage it. Little did I know that dozens of other writers, mainly poets, scattered around the country had simultaneously chosen to do the same thing for virtually the same reasons. Boldly, I sold the Gretch drums onto which I had been tattooing my demons and purchased a Sears mimeograph.

In college I had published, by means of spirit duplicator, a literary-ish magazine called *The Crib*, an alternative to the tedious official publications, for which the president contemplated expelling me. My inspiration for this went back to when I edited, and wrote most of, the grade school newspaper; even farther to when I created my own three-page newspapers via rubber stamps and carbon paper and sold them to my parents. I reasoned that if I could project my inner world to my parents and to the student body, I could project it to the world at large, which wouldn't, I had likewise reasoned, expel me, though I did get investigated by J. Edgar Hoover's boys. At that time I was cursed with a personality that needed to influence, to shape the world. My parents allowed me immense freedom to introspect and to live by my own design. I had a gloriously unstructured, undisciplined life by which I would test multiple levels of experience without guilt or criticism, questioning everything, especially religious, social, political and artistic conventions. This weened an assertive ego, the impertinence that assails history. Writing seemed the natural outlet for my questioning, the searching for and re-establishing of a new system of values.

At this time a copy of *The Chicago Literary Times* fell into my hands. In it was an article mentioning various upstart poetry journals, to which I immediately submitted my own upstart work, one being the CLT itself. Ron Offen, its poetry editor, accepted a poem and in conversing by letter I discovered he was almost a neighbor. We met and he filled my arsenal with information and addresses. My own littlemag, a homegrown rogue variant of *Evergreen Review*, was launched. I suppose this illustrates little more than growth by imitation, assertion by rebellion, but I had a vision of life as I had learned to love it that was being destroyed by men who lost their ability to love, who were sick with greed and power, and I had to do something about this. My typer and mimeo were weapons of enlightenment, O glory to heaven!

The first issue was a horror. I had never cut a stencil or cranked a mimeo, and by the results one could conclude that I also typed with my feet. I was so embarrassed by the horde of errors, that I hand-corrected all the contributor copies, thus adding to the mess. Excluding the price of the machine, if I remember right, postage, paper and supplies for each of the first few issues cost between $50-75, a figure that, considering the wages I was earning, was barely affordable. Offset printing (estimates then were $150-200) was as out of the question as buying a stupa in Tibet.

Subsequent issues became more readable due to my learning the witchcraft of typing stencils and my relinquishing the presswork to the talents of my wife. I recruited who I could for that initial issue, surprised, actually, that a nobody like me, offering only the crudest scratchings on the wall for publication, was awarded work as substantial as what it was. Those poor contributors never knew what they were getting into!

Later, by reading other littlemags I located and corralled many of the poets

I desired for the *Olé* "stable," though I would estimate that most found *Olé* by word of mouth. Other poets, such as Al Purdy and Harold Norse, were steered my way by Bukowski; or T.L. Kryss and D.R. Wagner by d.a. levy; or somebody by somebody.

As the fantasy to continue publishing *Olé* snowballed, I noticed a compulsion to search out my immediate predecessors as well as my to-the-moment contemporaries. Through Gotham Book Mart and Phoenix Books in New York and Asphodel Books in Cleveland I ordered copies of *Yugen, Floating Bear, Kulchur, Black Mountain Review*, etc. I wanted one big glorious Dagwood sandwich of the famous avant-garde journals, something I could use as internal traffic control for the endless meal of oncoming littlemags.

I was soon to realize company in my venture from nearly every city, town, hamlet and last-stop gas station in the nation. Kids in high school, convicts in the calaboose, monks in abbeys, were all getting into the act. Mostly it was the world war baby boom that was exploding into print. College drop-outs as well as creative writing majors (who, in earlier generations, would have simply become the teachers who supervised the campus-circulated literary rag) businessmen and basketball players, physicists and journalists, pharmacologists and short order cooks were all editing littlemags.

Maybe James Callahan of Hors Commerce Press or Kirby Congdon of Crank Press would send me addresses of conspirators and I would post a heap of *Olé*s their way. Other littlemags like *Wormwood Review* and *Trace* published invaluable exchange lists. Maybe John Bennett of *Vagabond* or Gene Bloom of *Entrails* would write me of a new mag in the incubator and I'd pop an *Olé* in its direction. When D.R. Wagner of *Runcible Spoon* left Niagara Falls for California I sent him a bundle to distribute gratis. Handfuls were customarily sent to d.a. levy in Cleveland to hand out on the streets. When Steve Richmond of *Earth Rose* opened a bookstore of the same name, I sent copies as I would to any store, headshop or trading post that gave indication it was sympathetic to littlemags. Word transmissions of often ungodly length were returned to virtually anyone who contacted *Olé*. Communication flowed by mail as freely as beer at the pub.

My job at the foundry was exhausting: hot, dirty and dangerous. Many of the old timers were missing fingers, walked uneven or had scars like lizard tails implanted in their flesh. Summers we would work extended shifts: 10-hour days, 6-day weeks. Sometimes overtime. Sometimes double shift: 16 hours straight. Winters were a little better; as orders slowed, our work hours would revert to normal, eventually reverse polarity to where we'd work only 4-day weeks. To make ends meet I'd sometimes take on a weekend job moving furniture. Usually it would be a downtown Chicago firm that was moving to another office. Such jobs would start around 6 p.m. and last until daylight. I'd always come home feeling as if I had just been crushed between two planets.

Frequently I was ill. If it wasn't bronchitis or a virus it was something psychomatic affecting my heart, stomach or colon. I lived as much on medicine as I did food. No wonder, when you consider how greatly I desired to be a writer! After an average day's work throwing around tons of iron pipe, I would come home, change, eat, then plunk myself in bed, pull my typer-on-a-writing-board across my lap and conduct the business of editing *Olé*. Weekends I would spend typing stencils, writing poems and working around the house—that is, after a good Friday night bash in the jazz joints. Sometimes I would take Saturday off and spend the day with my friends doing something bizarre. On Sundays I'd compensate by working 12-16 hours editing, etc. I was a madman, of sorts, possessed of literature; or, if you will, anti-literature. I was destroying myself. The more I edited *Olé* the more I realized that there was nothing in the world I wanted to do except write. Nothing. Absolutely nothing. When the family physician told me in extreme frankness that he'd be surprised if I would live to be 30, I knew changes were in order. It would either be writing or that six-foot abyss.

I proposed moving to San Francisco where the weather behaved itself, the pace allowed for deep breathing, a literary community thrived and where I had a friend who was willing to temporarily house the family. I also proposed that my wife become the principal breadwinner; and, out of a munificence and love that astonished me, she agreed. Naively I expected *Olé* would thrive out west, that I would be able to coax its future out of nothing more than fond desires. In an old-fashioned way I learned that literature doesn't thrive without money.

I couldn't conceive of making a living from editing littlemags except to engender enough cash for the next issue. If writing was an organic thrust outward from my life, editing was a synthesizing of externals into it. Expecting a glut of greenbacks might have endangered the purity of my concern, allowing the Darwinian mind to make compromises in favor of popular taste; and popular taste, I have found, nearly always disappoints with its lethargic perceptivity, its unwillingness to purge layers of complacent notion. Art has always meant a pursuit of lasting truths framed in a language that doesn't fatigue. Popular taste has little use for art; and to me, editing is, at least ideally, a kind of art.

I had been dissatisfied with most of the poetry I had read up until the Beats. I considered much of it overwritten, passive, pretentious—speaking not from the world that rubs so fiercely against the depths of our flesh, but from an artificial atmosphere of erudition, a tradition of elitist contrivance. Court music. Presidential portraits. Of course, Baudelaire, Rimbaud, Whitman were some of the first to contest this dullness. I embraced them. The discrepancy between the life I was living and what I was reading had been in the process of being mediated before the first issue of *Olé*. It was a time to slay dragons. A healthy arrogance is needed to assert oneself at right angles to tradition, to hook onto that straight line, heat it white hot and bend it a few degrees. God knows I had such arrogance and, in a small way, tried to change the direction of literature. I was impatient, and not a careful reader—though I gave myself entirely to my causes.

"Every inch of planet Earth, every curse word, every thimble, every spot of dirt, every slam, bang, jing, every chug in the harbor is poetry. Add the thumbscrews to the raspberries and you have it." This is from an editorial in an early issue. Doom was immanent, it was in the clothes I wore, in my hair shampoo. I needed a poetry that was for the living not the merely existing, a poetry that sparked one to a greater realization of his life—something powerful enough to compete with television and bold print headlines.

Great poets will no longer appear from an upper-middle class. Poetry is no longer a luxury, it is a necessity! Shun the world "literary," it is the key to tea and donuts on Saturday afternoons. There is no need for parlor poetry that reinforces old ideas and comforting philosophies. As Kirby Congdon once said: "Poetry must disturb and upset; otherwise it is merely schoolwork industriously taken home and worked on after class. Poetry is an art which the public should actively seek out, talk about, buy and read, instead of study or listen to in dim auditoriums."

Here was my call for a poetry that is dangerous, that will take risks, that can initiate a transformation in consciousness which would, in turn, animate positive change in the outer world. Not poetry as logistics or pragmatics, but a poetry that is nearly visceral in its implications, that eats and exhales the smoke of the earth and makes us all do the same. Let me quote at length.

Literature is . . . emaciating into a sweet nothingness of whipped-cream —all lather and gauze and belongs in the catacombs with the mummies unless we resuscitate it. Put your hands into your gooey protoplasm and smear a little of it on paper. Blow a little fire into this fetid, stale, miasmic, pallid, castrated, stifled, unwholesome thing called communication. Let's not *pretend* anymore that we are alive.

To hell with pretentiousness and artiness. To hell with polite dictums and decorums. Civilization . . . has done little but slaughter . . . in war, . . . in the name of Christ, in the name of the state, in the name of some "ism." It has created one mass lie that is reiterated every second on TV, in the newspapers and *Time* magazine. It has made us . . . monomaniacs for artifacts and the holy greenback dollar. We are . . . confused, lost and willing to obey the ringing of any master's bell . . . . We are the creators and the victims of a society that controls us. Oh, this diatribe is trite and endless, but I needn't go any farther for I have accomplished my mission of articulating the feeling of *Olé*. But remember, there are still things to celebrate and the best celebration is expressed in song and the logical extension of song is a shout. So, don't be timid. If you still care . . . THEN SHOUT! Put teeth into your words. Lift some hearty weights. Get that blood to cooking. Sneak a peek between your crotch and see if you still have hair there. If there *is* hair, *say* there is hair. Don't hide the balls either. If there are balls, then include the balls and make them look like balls, know they are balls. POETRY WITH BALLS! POETRY THAT IS DANGEROUS! MEATY POETRY! Juice to make the ears jump . . . SOMETHING!

Art has tendency to detach itself from life. Blood becomes water and beads up on the page—bones don't break, they mellow and turn to rubber. We need a new audience to read these new poets. An audience with guts and imagination. An audience that loves the future because it is the key to its shackles and blindfolds. An audience that understands that "major" poets begin as "minor" poets, that in-groups are a society of morticians building their own coffins. An audience that is not so narrow-minded as to believe the foible that good poetry is necessarily decent.

We need an audience that will grow with the poet and an audience that will let the poet grow. Today's audiences expect an artist . . . to give them his life's work for nix as if it were a quick vibration in the mind-crotch. WHAT NERVE! It's about time those confessed lovers of poetry paid for it—a few bucks here and there will do fine. It's these few measly bucks that keep the poet creating and the little magazine editors publishing. As Kenneth Patchen puts it: *"People who say they love poetry but don't buy any are a pack of cheap sons of bitches."* The poets of America are not an organization; they don't go from door to door asking for your dimes and quarters. They don't have their hands in your paycheck before you get it. There are no poetry telethons.

Why isn't poetry more in demand? Maybe if it were more celebrated we wouldn't be scrounging and hustling for $$. Kirby Congdon knows why it isn't in demand: "It simply isn't that interesting . . . . Instead of having things that *must* be said in one way or another poets search around for lovely or clever things to write poems about. [They] don't speak the language which the rest of us speak . . . and why bother to learn theirs? It is usually only a means, anyway, to impress the juries on the Guggenheim, Ford, etc. gravy trains."

New York and San Francisco are no longer the only centers for literary explosions. It is happening everywhere! There are subversive way-stations, parts of an underground railway that link all cities in a huge reticular mass of ganglia, being born every day. This is a new, more serious, more responsible generation than the last. We are not here to pull down our pants but to roll up our sleeves and do the work that has been let go for a long, long time. We are not going to let poetry get away with being uninteresting gibberish written in a mysterious language.

Olé is concerned with poems that are written the way we . . . live; *not* poems that are kneaded, hammered, tooled over with all sorts of theories, then passed off as something that is supposed to resemble life. They simply don't. They are a manufactured item—another artifact *in life.*

There is no one in particular to whom we are speaking. We speak, that is enough! We speak to the universe, to ourselves, to America, to the college professors, the mothers, the mechanics—we are here to bring ourselves, you, everyone closer to life—we are here to communicate—noncommercially, with scars on our bodies. Poetry is a method of finding new answers within ourselves. It is time for a change in diet! Here it is: *Olé!*

Gulp! Arrogance all right. But it was such a complete conviction, so attrac-

tive a romance. Even now, looking back 20 years, I am amazed at the forceful-
ness and strength of the vision. After an issue or two I began to locate poets
who were writing what I was looking for though I really couldn't fill an entire
issue with it. At the time I considered it a most genuine writing engendered
from a most genuine living. Common experience belonged to art more than
intellectualization did. Emotion is the fuel of meaningful poetry; but I believe
I confused suffering with genuineness. If I condemned other writers in other
ages for being affected by a romance of Art, then I was likewise caught-up in a
romance of suffering and disillusion. Bukowski's influence can partially be
blamed for this; but so can my coming of age, possessed with a poet's sensibility
and sensitivity, in a No-Exit post-Hiroshima iron foundry. In fact, it was this
employment, my microscopic paychecks and my chronic poor health that set
the ground work for my walking in Buk's neighborhood.

After eight issues of *Olé* I called it quits. Why? Burn-out is one answer.
After the full-time job at the foundry there was the second full-time job on the
magazine. Wife/family/house were a third full-time that was dwindling to part-
time. I stole from the clock to see my friends, read books and write for myself.

Another answer is that deserting Chicago for San Francisco took all my savings. Prior to moving, support money came exclusively from my wages, with
additional aid from my father and a few friends—those blessed few—plus bookstore and library sales. For the first two years on the coast we existed on an income that even a bum would be ashamed to admit. I kept putting mimeo paper
into the grocery cart but upon returning home from the store the paper had
transformed into wheat bread and swiss cheese. We ate sandwiches and the
press died. The unbelievably stingy CCLM grant for $250 was too little too late
to make a difference.

But really, beyond this, the end was voluntary. *Olé* had approximated its
intentions. To my satisfaction the mag demonstrated that life and art were
inseparable. It wasn't as if, say, Langston Hughes or William Carlos Williams had
never written, or that I hadn't read them, but that a less poetic, less "precious"
poetry than even theirs announce itself. A poetry alive *right there*, at the front,
where it jumps off the page against the reader's eyes and battles his consciousness for eternal placement. A poetry that wouldn't lie for Art, wouldn't do
tricks for publication; that was virtually ruthless in exposing truth and prying
open the vault of human emotions. An irreverent poetry that freely chose its
targets, concentric aim starting at the heart working stark naked into the last
half of the 20th century. *Olé* accomplished this more in spirit than in fact but
gave evidence to what had previously been pretty much a drawing board concept. I reckoned then that I would have to pursue this poetry myself to amplify
its texture, which I did for perhaps a year or two longer until surfeit. *Olé*, as I
look back on it now, was a healthy and necessary response to the oppressive
elements that existed prior to the 1960s. It contributed to opening things up so
one could write the way one wanted. After all, another generation's language
is someone else's perception of the world. Much of the poetry published, especially the poetry I wrote, was characteristic of youthful rebelliousness, post-
adolescent anger and disillusionment, a searching for a Holden Caulfield genuine

identity, a testing of limits, an insurgence against the false. However, it was a posture that could be sustained only by cauterizing the mind's growth.

I was beginning to detect that too much of *Olé*'s poetry was strong in statement but inconsistent in execution, untamed as a drunk rhinoceros taking a bath singing a song of revolution. And not just *Olé*'s but poetry as published in many other littlemags. It had the taint of juvenile wall spurts, of deep-sea divers suffering rapture of the ego-depth, of giddy boys flinging fresh horse pucky. If not that, then it was simply third-rate, a so-what yawn after the late night news.

Why should I have dawdled there just because my hand cranked the press? The danger in littlemags especially at this time was that they could be a thin disguise for quasi-vanity publishing. Not all of them, certainly. And not all that were suffered mediocrity. The worst offenders, though, were the so-called New York School of Poets and poetry club types and their cheerleaders. Anyone, literally anyone, who could afford a TV could afford a mimeo and publish his own version of the world. It seemed for a moment that this was happening; I could feel the claustrophobia of the crowd. All of us were testing the air waves. Yet, it *was* exciting. Not monkeys doing Shakespeare-past but monkeys trying to do Shakespeare-future. I was one of those monkeys who wanted to grow to be a Great Ape doing best what Great Apes do.

The years spent publishing were years in which I worked persistently at nourishing the tentacles young writers from everywhere were beginning to send out. Prolifically, I wrote letters to help widen the base of action, to engage others in a dialogue of poetic reconsideration.

Half of each run of an issue (i.e., 200-250) would be given away gratis in hopes of promoting the cause of poetry. Later, as a board member of COSMEP, I participated in refining littlemag direction, especially by initiating the first bookstore survey in hopes of informing editors which stores were sympathetic to alternative publishing and in hopes of enlightening the stores to their responsibility to living literature. It was a marvelous time of self-discovery and discovery of a common cause. Yet the press was becoming an identity, a key to a special fraternity, something like sports clothes to a jock. It told me who I was. *Olé* was on index cards across the country. I was *Olé*. I wore an invisible word tuxedo. The danger as I recognized it was of clipping my wings to remain in the nest. My natural instincts told me I wanted out, to return to the No Man's Land from which I came so that I couldn't be defined by anything too cramped to contain me. Moving to Sacramento from the culture hive of San Francisco was symbolically, if not literally, that return. I knew I was back to nowhere when I attended an editor's conference several years later and saw how the other still-active editors in self-made limelight cock-walked and quick-warmed their embrace of fellow editors in hopes of making some nebulous alliance that would advance their publication, their identity; and at the opportunity of netting more grant money they would dance the hula on top the Goodyear blimp. All this was rather subtle, but I sensed it just as I sensed I was not really of the cloth any longer. I had been snipped out and another editor was sewn in.

Back in the '60s it was too damn easy, at least for me, to get published. The temptation, unless principled against it, is to leap at the opportunity to see one's name in print. Editing a magazine offers visibility as well as "club member advantage." Much of what I wrote was too negative, too roughhewn. It was cursed with didactic obligation, a spot-lit ego and unruly imagination. A wiser poet would have suffered anonymity longer, wrote this stuff and crammed it under the bed. But then, admittedly, I needed the encouragement of being published and the "extended university" of the editor's desk. Not having had the fortune to be able to go to poetry finishing school, I was left with the alternative of becoming a writer solely by writing, by acquiring useful feedback from my everyday experiences. I did too much growing up in-print much to my detriment, a hard-to-reconcile fact for those who have come to know me by my later work. Unfortunately there are also those who remember me *only* from the early work and consider that representative.

Originally my intention was to transform *Olè* into *Open Skull*, a magazine devoted exclusively to correspondence between poets, to demonstrate the inevitable spill-over of poetic temperament into an informal bath of prose. Letters, I had determined, could be an art form in and of themselves, especially when the poet would be in an impassioned state of mind, unloading his soul, unconscious of the possibility of his words ever burning beyond his correspondent. I was convinced that letters had the potential to penetrate our masks and costumes in a way that no other form of written communication could. Editing *Olè* gave evidence of this and I wanted to give my supposition a chance to ignite the imagination of others. I calculated that I had already accumulated enough for a dozen issues, the last six being devoted to letters from Bukowski. After that . . .?

Open Skull perished after a single issue for the same reasons as *Olè*. In 1970 the last chapbook was published and my hands were finally wiped clean of ink. This 12th chapbook ended a series I had begun in '65 as something of an augmentation and clarification of editorial objective. Not every poet deserving of participation was included; but, as stated before, it was time to take down the shingle, to pack up and leave, to turn my back on whatever I had accomplished, on friends who couldn't follow; to deposit this episode in the bank of experience as something peculiar to my fate, to withdraw only what would sustain as the future dictated.

Asceticism is almost the word to describe my existence these last years. I've committed myself to learning, certainly from books but primarily through introspection; through careful and repeated examination of the details of my life. I live quietly with few contacts to the outer world. I have chosen not to be a teacher, as imperative as this status appears today in order to legitimize being a poet and to facilitate the grab for laurels, primarily by reason of temperament but also because I suspect that an overly cozy household leads to incest and I wouldn't want my writing to suffer this. Reading work of the young university-trained poets of the last decade or so gives me the uncanny and chilling impression that so very many of them come off the assembly line identical under the hood, a little stylized bodywork making the only difference. As wonderful as the classroom often is, and as helpful as I'm sure it would have been in guiding me through the minefield of writing poetry, when Art is institutionalized it risks being placed in a zoo: teachers reluctantly becoming zookeepers, students

114

learning how to administer tranquilizers, techniques of de-horning . . . . Art breeds at a bullish rate in this sanctuary, lives well off the royal family's table droppings, but its offspring tend to approximate trophies in a game room rather than the beast itself enlarging the wilds. I desired only to be my own protegé.

The dollar doesn't linger around the house. As soon as it walks in the door I chop it up, send the bulk of it back to rich people and keep a torn corner for postage stamps and books. The wife dances all day with numbers for a woman's salad and I work in a shop that peddles fancy-priced words for the dressing. Both my sons are full-time college jockeys studying art and philosophy and work part-time with tropical fish and native plants—I hardly see them anymore. I've had time to settle deep within the heart of the source of my poetry: the family cauldron, the psychic soup pot and how the outside world clangs with its iron spoon against it. As my physical environment has changed so has my poetic environment, mind reacting to external suggestion. I'm careful to sustain neutral grounds so my poems have less chance of being kidnapped by what surrounds me and instead grow from their own uncontaminated soil.

I find little resemblance between what I am now and that young man in his twenties who was so wild with his language, so headstrong and hard-toned, who berated the world with his poetry and willingly devoured such overloads of suffering, spasming in reaction into zany hyperbole. He could write two or three poems a sitting and impatiently submit them for publication the next day. He was compulsive about compiling his poems into chapbooks, like recipes as soon as he had enough ingredients: "Get 'em out of the way an' move on," I can still hear him cry. It was impetuosity rather than lack of caring, but mostly it was a need to constantly crawl into words on the page and increase their voltage until transformed into a sharper, more heightened, *more real* life. Words, for him, were no longer symbols but the place where life was lived after it was lived elsewhere. Or, at least, that's what he romanticized.

Over the years I've worked for a balance between "writing poems" and having "poems write me," at taming my language, eliminating self-indulgence, clarifying motive, tightening mainsprings—encouraging each poem to climb to the farther peaks of my consciousness. I've learned, to a degree, what kind of truth makes for good poetry and what kind for bad. My pen is now filled most generously with re-write ink. Poems sit around the house for months while I try them on over and over like a pair of hiking boots before they tread terra firma. There have been fewer and fewer books and chapbooks—I wait, I consider and reconsider, assemble and tear apart, rewrite, consider again, not wanting to be embarrassed by work that had the heart but not the head.

In "exile" I have been successful at overthrowing the Beat/Bukowski influence and assimilating other quite different tones, hearing the emergence of something *individual* within a symphony. I took the risk of allocating letters *a* and *b* to see if there was a larger alphabet to use.

I would rather my poetry be less a summation of all that I've read than creatures of profound feeling and imagination pulled from the mainstream of my life. I'm trying to inform my poems of things difficult to know, the knowledge of intricate existence, several steps removed from the obvious, a view that sees

115

what nothing in life prepared me to see. Previously, my writing had been primarily on a single level, a reaction to the discovery of unfairness and brutality in the world—emotional realism, if you will—but as I approached the age border of 30 I became aware of many other levels and sought to write a poetry of discovery.

I write every day from an evolving consciousness. Early morning finds me finally exhausted from grinding my bones against the whetstone of words. A cellular chorus renders a blessing for all that makes this possible. When I arise the next day I'm always eager to re-read what I've accomplished—it gives me that sense of having traveled in my sleep, of finding myself somewhere other than where I was. Writing is my life's work and I am faithful to it despite the enormous difficulty this decision has meant.

It is clear to me that editing *Olé* altered my entire life, supplied impetus, orientation and practical application to the notion I had that I was indeed a writer. The premeditation of an editorial concept helped build the infrastructure upon which my poetry has thrived. It was the machinery in which my necktie got caught, pulling me, so to speak, down the wonderland rabbit hole. Some old general might say it was the battlefield that made me a soldier. Having survived the "littlemag wars," I feel I'm privy to a more intimate perspective of publishing than if I had only read about them in revisionist memoirs.

Editing opened many doors, provided many endearing friendships. Exchange policies sent dozens upon dozens of other littlemags knocking on my door—a robust fraternity which I studied and borrowed from and grew. My life had a larger focus of activity while editing than it does now. I was contributing energy not only through my writing but by taking the writing of others and placing it in a context that expanded each individual piece—the feedback from other poets and editors, in turn, expanded the context. I felt as if I were touching greater areas of living than I could singularly. The whole experience was exhilarating. Joy. Another way to love.

Most of the littlemags in the '60s had distinct personalities, probably acquired from the rapscallion nature of their editor and his divergent means of loading the larder. The best editors were impassioned true believers, crusaders to reassert the value of such societal discards as truth and vision. They opened outward toward possibility, scoffed at the idea of publishing merely competent writing, writing that was a summation of standard influences. They incited meaningful dialogue not only by choice of oar but by navigational bearing. The idea was to test and to challenge, to open doors by tearing down buildings, to expand barriers by repossessing control of language. Art-sensibility superimposed upon life-sensibility was polemic and they were fearless in being called to this higher order of confrontation. A newer and larger audience for poetry was being cultivated. If it wasn't for the vitality of the littlemag in the '50s/'60s, I don't believe poetry and short prose would be prospering as it is currently.

Today the littlemag scene is stable. No groundbreaking or taboo breaking. No need to go underground to avoid censorship. Less spirit, less individuality. Respectability. Not that it's necessary to have controversy buzzing in one's face all the time, nor is it necessary to constantly be taking risks. This is a time to evaluate, to utilize advancements, to evolve in a surefooted manner from the quake of the transitional '60s. Some magazines are grounding themselves, others are academizing. When a magazine is rallying against something, its vigor is usually more interesting than publications that have modulated their standards to the point of entrenchment. Certain writers have emerged and matured far beyond the capacity of the crowd. This is how it always works. These writers are a product of their age but continue to grow, surpass it, carrying forward its consciousness. They carry the vitality, not the crowd, the movement. Crowds go home. Movements gyrate and collapse. A birth process. The age of the '70s/ '80s is busy assimilating the generations before it. It can't move on while eating, passing its food to its young. Building an empire. It will be a while before enough free spirits find the empire too repressive and fling a Ginsberg cocktail into its parlor.

If littlemags 20 years ago erred in the direction of crackpot chemistry experiments, it was because of their enthusiasm to give a horse wings. If the littlemags of today err in the direction of uniform tone, of closed family experience, it is because they have over-learned their Sunday School lessons and have closed their eyes to await a kiss on the forehead from Billy Graham himself.

The '50s/'60s magazines that I cut my teeth on, besides those previously mentioned, were, at first, more-or-less the outlandish ones: *Evergreen Review, Big Table, City Lights Journal, Beatitude Anthology, Wild Dog, Camels Coming, Grist, December, The Outsider.* The pivotal point when I began to expand my reading came in 1969; recently retired from editing, newly anchored in No Man's Land, I was beginning to seriously consume the poets Simic, Kinnell, Ammons, Bly, Edson, Merwin, Hugo, Plath as well as such exotic treats as Holub, Popa, Herbert, Ritsos, Seferis, Transtromer, Mandelstam, Ponge, Borges, Paz, Amichai. In addition I was re-reading writers I hadn't paid enough attention to earlier: Rilke, Vallejo, Neruda, Milosz; even Eliot and Stevens. These discoveries led to others, and my reading sensibility evolved to *Lillabulero, Kayak, The Sixties, Dragonfly, Stinktree, Skywriting, Choice, Granite, Hearse, Invisible City, The Falcon, The Stone, Some, Crazyhorse.*

In the '70s some very good littlemags were born, many still highly alive today: *Ironwood, Field, Antaeus, Ploughshares, Cutbank, Durak, Sumac, Unmuzzled Ox, Alcatraz.* I have counted these among my personal favorites.

University quarterlies were anathema to me back when I was editing. I distrusted them on principle for the same reasons I eschewed Auden and Lowell: they seemed almost personally responsible for the clenched mind that prohibited literature from being responsive to young writers who weren't East Coast intelligentsia. As unfair as this prejudice might have been, I thought that only dead writing was interred in such tombs.

TriQuarterly, New American Review, Iowa Review, Chicago Review, Ohio Review, Paris Review were and still are surprising exceptions, though I have yet to find vitality in such as *Partisan Review, Sewanee Review, Southern Review, Quarterly Review of Literature, Poetry* (Chicago). Their primary function will always be to encase this year's fecal forgeries next to the shamanic coprolites of yore: dissect and classify, preserve and endlessly duplicate.

117

I suspect many editors of littlemags, especially those sponsored by or associated with colleges, are too narrowly exposed (perhaps because of their youth) to give their editing depth. They are too responsive to the breed of poetry with which they have most recently been sleeping, and to the sensibility of their latest instructors. Their *eyes* are trained to recognize familiarity of execution, promise of talent, but their *hearts* are unable to sense authenticity of persuasion. Apparently they regard the poems submitted with a correcting stencil: those that show up in the windows are publishable, those covered by the stencil are not. As yet they are still artificially sophisticated; they have gone only *so far*, this distance being enough to know "brand name" poetry but not far enough to be able to identify the subtler guises of genius. They are simply too tied to the process of being taught rather than to the process of learning experientially. They don't trust themselves enough and are too orientated toward success as conventionally defined. I tend to liken these young editors, and most other products of creative writing classes, to foreign enthusiasts of American jazz. They imitate out of love, often brilliantly; they can improvise a technically flawless bird (pun allowable), but it doesn't fly. It lacks that certain something, and they simply have no choice but to keep playing until one day, if fortunate, it is airborne. But at this moment that music is no longer American. It has become intrinsically their own. In the meantime, we endure a hell of a lot of competent mediocrity, prize-winning mediocrity, to the point where we run the danger of acquiring a taste for mediocrity—if this hasn't already happened, or is this a historical given?

By temperament I've had difficulty with such littlemags as *Caterpillar, Angel Hair, Burning Deck, L-A-N-G-U-A-G-E, Truck, Elizabeth, Coyote's Journal* and *Io* but not for lack of trying and not to the point of sustained inflated emotion. Poetry, by its very nature, is a positive force—a force deserving of the chance to find and affect its audience; whether such poetry is pedigree or mongrel, theoretical or indigenous, exposure to its fragments is bound to radiate a few. That poetry should be free to consort on all levels, exercising its multifarious nature, only strengthens it. That the distinction poetry secures in history be decided by era, geography, nationality, race, sex, politics, social position, wealth, trophy count, rhetorical bigotry or clannish autocracy is inevitable but repugnant and is, as far as I'm concerned, the only foe worth entertaining within the world of literature.

Now that there is government aid to littlemags, editors can, if they get the hang of the ropes, perpetuate their function indefinitely. By this I mean that editing can get to be a second suit of skin—we step into this other personality and without recourse behave accordingly. Our central personality identifies with this role, inflates itself into a persona and functions in a world whose laws often overflow and define our central, or true, selves. This is the beginning of a bureaucracy. Whether editors or critics or professors, whether administrators in arts programs or poets who have engineered a career, as long as one believes he is his job rather than his job being something he does, he will maneuver, manipulate and maim (well, maybe not maim) to maintain it. There is too much invested in this romanticized version of ourselves. We are the title and the title is us; take that away and we are nothing. Hence, elaborate mechanisms are soldered into

118

the system to safeguard the position we've achieved. These safeguards in conjunction with the political maneuvers of the persona tend to keep power in the hands of those who have it.

Certainly an old story, but this is primarily what I see happening with littlemags. Government aid (and college funding) have made it possible for many mags to survive which would have otherwise sunk into bogs. This is not to pass judgment on whether they should or shouldn't survive; nonetheless, there is a greater ratio of mediocrity to vitality in those that do. But even mediocrity is preferable if the alternative means that smaller communities go without an active arts consciousness and we revert back to New York City and San Francisco being the only two places where one can hear Chopin, everywhere else it's Liberace. Because poetry is a humanizing and consciousness-ripening agent, it is important to keep the wafer in the mouths of the cognoscenti and to Socratize the uninitiated.

Littlemags are in a sense missionaries for poetry. They are psychic guerrillas that can enter common households on ordinary streets in Quotidian, U.S.A., and reach into the gearbox of any ageless hero to engage the poetry gear before a common tool realigns it to turn only for The Company.

But they are also much more. I posit that they serve at least seven functions that few if any other publishing outlets serve: (1) as rites-of-passage from ungelled artistic incipience to maturity (or at least conception of purpose); (2) as laboratory, the place where ideas become clay models, where new moves are choreographed, where the shaping of new lungs finds a new blend of oxygen; (3) as extended epistle passed between like minds and to heathens in a proselytizing gesture; (4) as political statement; art as opposed to civilizational nihilism or inanition; (5) as weapon, a source of power to assert one's influence against the tyrannies of governments, police, bureaucracies and institutions; (6) as personal mandala, housing life-force energies—a focal point from which one functions, beatitudes at the back, a religion with no central figurehead, just the doing of spirit for the cause of goodness—all returns measured by increments in consciousness; (7) as justification for an existence that is best justified by commercial publishers (old thinking) when such publishers have either rejected an editor (writer) or rejection is presumed imminent.

I don't see that government money has corrupted editorial decisions any more than persona-bureaucracy has. Littlemag editors, as I've known them, are a pretty independent bunch who have exhibited integrity when it comes to eating only foods that distinguish their epicurean palate. It's when their taste buds suffer dwarfism or pop culture pollution that embarrassing concessions are made, or the magazine becomes a flabby tourist with travel decals covering the Dodge's windshield, obliterating vision.

As for COSMEP, I was winding down as it was tuning up, so I haven't personally been much affected by it, except that at its conception back in Berkeley in '68 I had a splendid time. With *Olé* I learned everything trial-and-error. It was fun that way, more soul-nourishing than reading *The Joy of Operating a Littlemag*. Editors who read such publications are probably better organized: they press the right buttons and the mag, all 500 copies, pops onto their laps;

but all they have are 500 copies begging justification. If COSMEP helped, and I believe it did, I would estimate that that help was in gathering the chiefs to orgy-out their problems, to clear the runways in every direction and mastermind a flight plan that would allow the tribes to reclaim some of their land.

I would think that alternative distributing agencies, publishing co-operatives, print centers and writer's organizations have all helped poetry to survive in a society that has turned its serious artists to figureheads, tokens of spiritual wealth rather than actual living sources to be experienced. *The Best-Loved One Hundred Poems* is a terrific seller at shopping mall paperback emporiums. Copies are gift-wrapped and given at birthdays, weddings and graduations as a symbol of something esteemed by tradition to be one of the highest achievements of mankind. Yet those who give and receive these gifts would never carry poetry in their back pockets. They genuflect by conditioned reflex. They like the *idea* of poetry but have learned no use for it. In fact, they can't fathom it because they are unable to apply their minds to its codification of language. They went to school it seems only to get a job and once employed all they crave are ego-boosts, artifacts and diversions.

Governments are reluctant to grant money to individual writers because they, the writers, are not diversions, and can't be held accountable to what they produce. Organizations fare much better because they can be audited and monitored and because the result of their effort usually qualifies as more diversion for society. Governments, so to speak, sponsor productions of *The Best-Loved One Hundred Poems* but not the best-loved 100 poets.

Bureaucracies adore figurehead culture systems. The symbolic poet is easily assimilated into society without causing harm, allowing society to feel it has fulfilled its cultural obligation. All the outpourings of poetry won't endanger it because it will all be cloth for the royal tailor to assimilate into a robe for the king.

On one hand, the rise of writing organizations, government aid and the entrenchment of creative writing in the universities has offered a wildlife sanctuary in which the creative artist can thrive. On the other hand, it has made it easier for the less-talented artist to receive much more "air-space" than was previously possible, but has also co-opted the energy of truly talented writers into pedagogic and/or academic subservience. Teaching provides a fair amount of happy paychecks, adequate writing time, opportunity for making many alliances with those who share a mutual interest, all while working at what one loves best. It sounds absolutely ideal (most likely why such a protective bureaucracy has been created around it) as long as one can avoid being compromised. The philosophical dilemma seems to be whether an artist can remain his own "beast" in such an environment or whether he must leap the fence and become a maverick.

Richard Hugo once said in an interview that "what a poet did for a living wasn't very important." That seems to be the farthest from the truth when it comes to having a chance at being inducted into the "elite 40"—virtually all professors. The first question I'm inevitably asked when a visiting poet, a professor, naturally, at some university, comes to town for a reading, after I introduce myself, is "Where do you teach?" When I answer that I don't, the visiting poet

120

turns to the local professors for conversation, with whom he is apparently more comfortable and considers more legitimate.

As I suggest earlier, the world of poetry, of virtually all creative writing, is determined in large part by a power complex that works through the universities. Poets today want careers as poets (what a relief it must be for a parent to know their once peculiar child is now carrying a briefcase) and bureaucracies are the most legitimate dispensers of careers, and universities are splendid facilitators of bureaucracies. So just about every poet gravitates in a trance toward mecca and swaps a mythology of identity for an M.F.A. I don't mean to say that many poets who have levitated into the hierarchy don't deserve their reputations or the leverage that accompanies their position. If they are masters they deserve everything, I suppose. The quality of teachers over the years has been so great that it couldn't help but to produce many astounding talents. These talents have, almost unanimously, likewise become influential teachers. But in the formation of a protective bureaucracy it is perhaps inevitable that published poetry has degenerated through progressive imitation. Occasionally distinct and authentic voices emerge *after* having assimilated influence, but the vast majority simply succumb to over-influence, remaining a crusoe parrot to Crusoe.

Apparently the young poet reaches a high level of sophistication early. In the emphasizing of previously known methods of composition he finds that learning formulas helps him "re-voice" what is being taught, permitting him to write up to expectation. Being taught how to recognize and imitate "good writing" sometimes succeeds too well, creating a facility of clever disguises that seldom transcend initial ambitions. So many poems down the road, the formula becomes just "another day at the office."

Academics in the past were readily spotted because they wrote by formula incestuously from literature. The current generation has its neo-academics, some who have been taught to turn away from literature and write out of their own life experiences; but their instruction bred a reliance on tell-tale linguistic mannerisms and imagistic techniques that now belie their true nature. Oh, for sure, some rebel against their own early work, as I did, as Bly, Wright, Merwin, even Lowell did; but this is the exception.

A printed schematic of this bureaucracy is rather elementary, both unconsciously corrupting and consciously benign; certainly goodly-intentioned but best serving to those most competitive. Anyway, I see it structured something like this. Creative writing instructors give recommendations for Breadloaf, Yaddo, et al., and to post-graduate workshops, recommend graduates to teaching positions, recommend for Guggenheims and other grants, serve as judges in contests, help select editors for school literary publications and exert influence as to who gets published, also to book publishers when a student is ready with his thesis (usually a ms. of poems) and are usually the critics who do the reviewing. Each instructor has at any given time at least one "favorite son" student whom he promotes to the writing world—the success of this student being a direct reflection upon the worth of the instructor's teaching abilities and his greatness as a poet—sort of like a king preparing heirs to the throne who will maintain the empire in the best of tradition.

121

In order to advance their careers, the students choose teachers and/or workshops as carefully as Young Democrats choose a candidate to support, attend Breadloaf/Yaddo, edit the school literary magazine making sure they publish those with Big Name Pull, get their M.F.A. and their thesis of verse published, secure a teaching position, enter contests—as many (if not all) as possible—apply for grants, submit poems to all the prestigious journals, especially those whose editors they published as a student, get another book published smothered with blurbs from teachers they studied under or ex-classmates who are now brilliant poets themselves, invite professor poets to read at their school so as to be invited to read at theirs, edit a Big Time Journal that, naturally, publishes past teachers, ex-classmates, hierarchical poets whose favor is worth courting as well as favorite son students, review fellow poets (favorably with quotable lines that easily convert to blurbs) so they will return the favor, and, like 19th/20th-century enterprising over-achievers, amass credentials, amass credentials, amass credentials.

Little of this is new, nor is it intrinsically odious, nor are the writers who run the machinery, who, in time, become cogs. It's simply banal. Wanting? Yes. Unfair? Yes. But mostly banal. A successful career in and of itself has usually been improperly equated with greatness, just as financial wealth has; and even, in a perverted sense, mere notoriety. Bureaucracy has usually been a prerequisite in order for middling talents to have prosperous careers; true giants ride the tide of this game, but would thrive in spite of it. If there is an intolerable deficiency it is the consequential segmenting of the poetry community into hierarchies, the dominance of an older consciousness based on competitiveness over a new age consciousness based on co-operativeness, the condescension toward poetry activity outside the swelling academy, and the writing of serious poetry geared to do little more than win acclaim from the academy, the *new* academy.

And somewhere outside this bureaucracy looking in, perhaps a bit envious, but well-stocked with healthy skepticism if not historical pessimism is the true littlemag: guardian of free spirits, sacred ground for experimentation and rebellion, launching pad into the unknown. The art that lasts has always been done by free spirits.

seven

George Plimpton

The Paris Review

George Plimpton

George Ames Plimpton was born in 1927 in New York City, studied at Phillips Exeter Academy, and received a BA from Harvard University in 1948, an MA from Cambridge (England) in 1950. He has been editor-in-chief of *Paris Review* since 1953, was director of the American Literary Anthology program from 1967 through 1971, and a member of the advisory board of the Coordinating Council of Literary Magazines in 1979. Among his books are *Out of My League, Paper Lion, Shadow-Box, A Sports Bestiary*, and *Fireworks*. He is editor of the Writers at Work volumes—and a member of the NFL Alumni Association. His U.S. clubs include Century Association, Racquet and Tennis, Brook, Piping Rock, Dutch Treat, Devon Yacht, and Coffee House.

The following article is excerpted from "The Paris Review Sketchbook," with permission of the editor, George Plimpton, given thus and so: "Dear Diane Kruchkow: Everything I've ever wanted to write about the Paris Review can be found in the 25th Anniversary issue which I've taken the liberty of sending you under separate cover. I hope that will suffice. The material is accurate, which is more than I can say about some of the stuff I've read of your co-editor's that I happen to know something about. It was a long time ago, but not long enough to forget . . . . George Plimpton."

("The Paris Review Sketchbook" originally appeared in *The Paris Review* no. 79, 1981, the 25th anniversary issue of the magazine, which appeared in its 27th year of publication.)

. . . The first *Paris Review* office was in a small room in Les Editions de la Table Ronde, a publishing subsidiary of the house of Plon, a solemn, conservative, very austere publishing concern with offices around a great enclosed courtyard at 8 Rue Garancière opposite the walls of the Garde Republicaine . . . .

Every evening at six the concierge locked the door from Les Editions de la Table Ronde to the courtyard. Keys were not entrusted to *Review* personnel, so the procedure for editors working late was to leave by the windows—hanging from the sill by the fingertips and then dropping into the Rue Garancière below . . .

The Café de Tournon was around the corner. It was not only the hangout of convenience for the *Review* people, who would drop down from the office window after dusk to meet there for a drink, but it was removed enough from St. Germain-des-Prés, where the tourists sat in the cafés and craned their necks looking for Jean-Paul Sartre and Simone de Beauvoir, and from Montparnasse, where the older tourists sat in the Dôme or the Rotonde and chatted about *that* generation, so that it had a comfortable, private, and rather drowsy ambiance of its own. Regulars did not talk about the Café de Tournon too much . . . for fear it would be overrun and "spoiled." Those who went there had an almost proprietary attitude about it.

One of the regulars was Eugene Walter. He lived across the street in the Hotel Helvétia. He was known by many in the Café de Tournon as "Tum-te-Tum," from the first words the editors of the *Paris Review* ever heard him say. He had pronounced them upon hearing that a story of his, "Troubador," had been accepted for the first number of the magazine: dressed in a faded, linen suit he stood in the doorway of the board room of La Table Ronde, and upon the news of the acceptance from the editors, he announced, dragging it out, "Ah, Tum-te-Tum!" . . . providing a name which stuck, though he preferred to be known as Professor James B. Willoughby. That was how he signed his letters, under the salutation "mille fleurs." He came originally from Mobile, Alabama. . . .

The first publisher of the *Paris Review* was Prince Sadruddin Aga Khan, half-brother to Aly Khan, and the second son of the famous potentate H.R.H. Aga Khan, who occasionally put himself on a pair of scales and was paid his weight in various forms of tender, as a kind of tribute by his Ismaili Muslim followers. Sadri—as everyone knew him—was Harvard-educated, on the *Lampoon* there, and interested in arts and letters and those of his contemporaries who practiced them. He was persuaded to take on the role of publisher in 1954 during the running of the bulls in the summer of that year in Pamplona—being asked by the Editor as the two stood in the cobblestoned streets, waiting for the rocket to go up down by the pens signifying that the bulls had been let loose. It was an unfair time to ask anything of anybody . . . since what one wanted to do was rid the mind of everything except the thought of what was in the street and coming up behind. So Sadri said yes quickly ("Oh, for God's sake, yes!") and then concentrated on his running technique.

His name appeared at the top of the masthead in the *Paris Review #8.* He rarely came to the offices. He was busy representing his father in their constituencies around the world. But if it had not been for a financial commitment, the *Review* could not have continued . . .

In 1956 he married an astonishingly beautiful girl, Nina Dyer, the former Baroness Von Thyssen. She had a black panther that she walked at the end of a leash. . . .

126

Their lives changed, Sadri's father died. The marriage fell apart. Sadri's responsibilities, and his sense of them, increased. His wide knowledge of global problems was recognized with his appointment by U Thant, then Secretary General of the U.N., as High Commissioner for Refugees. But despite his great responsibilities, the *Review* always seemed to remain an involvement. When Sadri gave his first speech to the General Assembly a press release placed on the desk of each delegate made special mention of his publishing position with the *Paris Review*.

When the new publisher took on the financial obligations of the *Review*, they were in truth small—not more than $500 owed to the printer on the Rue Sablière—but his presence on the masthead gave a great sense of stability to the magazine. Also of considerable importance was that he persuaded his father, the Aga Khan, to establish an annual fiction prize. His father not only set up the prize but entered the competition with two entries of his own. They arrived in white vellum folders—short stories of considerable if somewhat antique charm, both markedly influenced by his close friend and neighbor in the South of France, Somerset Maugham. The Aga Khan was not discouraged that the judges (Brendan Gill, Hiram Haydn, and Saul Bellow) passed over his stories. . . .

The Quat'zarts Ball is held in early July. Members of the *Paris Review* staff were occasionally invited by the French art students who give the affair. The march to the site of the Ball started in the early evening. Just about any kind of excessive behavior was condoned that day. There was always a motif . . . with a costume to suit it, which very often came off during the march. The paraders, semi-nude, would break way and help themselves to food and drink from people sitting in the streetside cafés. All of this was treated with resigned amusement by the Paris populace. They gave up their glasses of wine with a shrug. The police behaved. It only lasted for 24 hours—from noon to noon the next day. A college friend of the Editor's went up to Montmartre after the Quat'zarts one year and sat naked on a bar stool, chatting merrily with people coming in for breakfast or an aperitif, until at noon a *flic* sauntered in and told him politely that the twenty-four hours of the Quat'zarts were over: it was time to get dressed. He took a taxi, which the doorman at his hotel paid for, and he went naked through the lobby up to his room. Everyone knew that on that day it was nothing out of the ordinary. . . .

One summer the Editor went with a group which included some of the *Merlin* crowd—its editor, Alex Trocchi, his girl, Jane Lougee, Christopher Logue, and some others. The theme that year was Greek. Everyone wore sheets cut to tunic length.

It was at the Wagram. At ten, after the march was over, the doors were shut, locked, and they would not be opened again until dawn. The crowd milled around the dimly-lit hall. Those who wished to remove themselves from the hectic goings-on that would begin below peered down from the boxes and balcony-seats. . . .

The music for the dancing was provided by a military band that sat safely out of harm's way up in the second balcony. The music blatted down—much of it from tubas and other horns . . . a kind of military stomp. The dancing was indecorous, and often disintegrated into long crack-the-whip lines . . . a file of half-naked dancers and *snap*! the two or three at the end would sail off on the fly into the straw heaps set about around the circumference of the hall.

At one point in the evening, each of the ateliers performed a "spectacle" up in one of the boxes or, for the larger effects, on scaffolding constructed in the balcony. Invariably, what was illuminated in the beam of a searchlight was a kind of "living statue" tableau. A grand prize was offered for the most spectacular. . . .

The Editor's hosts, the smallest of the ateliers, did not have a tableau prepared. The students were embarrassed about it. Alex Trocchi told them rather grandly, with only fifteen minutes or so to go before the searchlight picked out their box, that his group would put on a living tableau on their behalf that no one in the hall would forget, and which, to boot, would probably win first prize. The tableau would feature Alex himself and Jane, the beautiful young publisher of *Merlin*, copulating on the velvet balustrade of the box, visible to the crowds below, their bodies glowing in the searchlight glare while the rest of his group stood in the shadows of the box with long palm fronds and fanned them.

All of this came as somewhat of a surprise to the French student-hosts, and also to Alex's friends, especially Jane. But such was the excitement of the moment—the booming from the military bands, the frenzied movement of the dancers, the searchlight in the darkness—that the scheme seemed inspired. Jane rushed up the little circular staircase to the box above to prepare herself. Sheafs of hay were collected to act as palm fronds. Alex reached for a tin cup hanging from a friend's neck and had himself a drink.

When shouts from above indicated that it was time for him to get into position, Alex started quickly up the circular staircase to where Jane, lying naked on the box-railing was waiting for him; in the darkness and in his hurry he conked his head on an overhang just at the entrance to the box and knocked himself out cold. He tumbled back down the stairs. While he was being ministered to, laid on a bed of straw, shouts drifted down the stairwell inquiring what was going on . . . it was just seconds away from the searchlight . . . where was Alex?

When the searchlight reached the "tableau" it illuminated the back of a naked girl half-reclining on the balustrade, her head turned away looking back, as if expecting someone, into the recesses of the box where in the shadows, a single figure (the Editor) was discernible waving a stalk-like sheaf of straw. No one knew what to make of it. The searchlight gazed on the scene for an interminable fifteen seconds or so and then moved on. Afterwards, there was a rumor that the atelier had won a prize for "symbolic effect."

Alex was furious. "Why didn't one of you take my place?" he asked. Nobody was quite sure how to answer that.

Joan Dillon was the daughter of Douglas Dillon, the Secretary of the Treasury in the Kennedy administration, a graduate of Foxcroft, subsequently Princess of Luxembourg and now Duchesse de Mouchy. . . . A charming and practical person, the artistic side of things interested her less than the magazine appearing on time and that the office should bear some semblance of order . . . a concern which lends a certain poignancy to a reminiscence of an evening when the magazine had its office in the Rue Vernet on the Right Bank. "I was working alone in the office," she wrote.

> Nelson Aldrich, who was the Paris Editor then, was out delivering. He was due back about 5 p.m. Suddenly a couple of *horrors* pushed through the door speaking a language incomprehensible to me. I recognized at once that my intruders were Allen Ginsberg and Peter Orlovsky. They were doped to the hilt. They had an idea that we had the original correspondence with Ezra Pound and wanted to go see it. I told them this was not true and asked them to leave. They tried to get at my files (the first existent in the Paris office . . . Robert Silvers just stacked his papers on the floor). I defended the files physically, behaving abominably, as I had no wish to clean up the mess they were sure to make. They remained, talking their strange language—"Mother-this . . . Mother-that." I began to stamp envelopes for a future mailing drive so as to look busy. Then they decided to take another tack; they lay down on the floor to make love. I was just about 5 p.m. then—the hour when friends usually popped in to ask one for a drink up at the Stockholm, which was the neighboring cafe, after work. At least five people looked in and fled without doing a thing!
>
> Then the telephone rang. It was Nelson. I politely told him that we had guests and who they were. Nelson's reaction was, "Oh, my God, do you think they can tell I have a tuxedo on? I've been asked to a fancy dinner. I was going to stop by but now I can't. You cope."
>
> The situation was solved by a slight, well-dressed English friend who worked for the Ogilvy advertising agency. He appeared at the door and flew at the tangle of whatever and booted them out with inimitable English scorn and ridicule. I saw the two of them a few years later at a party. They had become successful. They were surrounded by lawyers and business people. Both were wearing ties and ill-fitting blue suits. It seemed a change.

A feature of the magazine from the start has been the interviews on the craft of writing. One of the early ideas was that while it would be difficult to elicit original material from established authors—the magazine could hardly afford their work—it might be possible to get them to talk about writing in an interview. Their names would appear on the cover. That would help sales and subscriptions.

The magazine was fortunate that in 1953 the Editor was studying at King's College, Cambridge, where a great literary personage resided . . . E.M. Forster, "Morgan" as everyone, both students and faculty, called him—a somewhat rumpled, very shy personage who lived in rooms overlooking the Great Lawn of the college and was then considered the greatest living novelist in the English language (*Passage to India, Howard's End*, and so forth) though in fact he had not published a novel since 1924. Forster was seventy-four in 1953, the year the *Paris Review* began in Paris. At the time he was writing an opera with Benjamin Britten (*Billy Budd*) and he would ask undergraduates, "What . . . um . . . do you know about writing operas?"

That was very much in the tradition of the college—that intellectual curiosity was shared among those within its walls, whatever their reputation or age. Typically, Forster took an interest in the *Paris Review*. The Editor had come back from Easter vacation in Paris that year and told him of the plans to start up the publication. There had been talk of limiting criticism in the magazine, and if a contemporary author was to be the subject, the hope was to interview him first-hand rather than relying on an interpretive study. In fact, would Forster agree to be the first interviewee?

He agreed and the interview, which was conducted by P.N. Furbank and F.J.H. Haskell, one writing down the answers in pencil while the other concentrated on the questions (tape recorders were still a few years away) was a feature in the first issue of the *Review*. In it Forster talked about the problems that made it difficult for him to write fiction, namely, what he called "fiction technicalities." The form of the interview established that of subsequent interviews, over a hundred conducted to date, many of them compiled in the five volumes of *Writers at Work*, published by the Viking Press.

The novelist, Irwin Shaw, was always very much on hand in various places on the Continent while the magazine had its Paris offices. . . . Klösters in Switzerland where he skied ("looking very much like a boulder coming down a mountain" as an observer described him), St. Jean de Luz, Rome, the South of France, Paris itself. . . . Wherever he settled, Shaw was hospitable to those associated in any way with the magazine. Indeed, the practice for many editors leaving Paris for a week's vacation was to find out Shaw's whereabouts and then take lodgings or rooms somewhere nearby, the more inexpensive and rundown the better, because Shaw, as a host, would provide every contingency of food, drink, or entertainment. His houses were focal points for Americans from the literary, and also the movie world, when they arrived in Europe. In later years, James Jones and his wife, Gloria, provided the same kind of gathering-place at their home on the Ile St. Louis.

Here is what Irwin Shaw remembers of his *Paris Review* friends:

When, in an article in the New York *Sunday Times Magazine*, Gay Talese described the group of young Americans who frequented my apartment in the 1950's and 60's and went on to found the *Paris Review*, Talese wrote that they were looking for a Hemingway. At the end of his piece, as I remember it, he declared that I was not Hemingway. Whether he meant this as a compliment or not only time will tell, but it seemed to me that what the young men were really looking for were all the pleasures and educational opportunities the city could offer them. As far as I could see, they found them in abundance.

As a group they differed greatly from the aspiring writers I had known in Brooklyn and Greenwich Village when I was their age. My contemporaries, growing up in the depression, were ferociously competitive, honest in their opinions of their friends' work to the point of snarling hostility, fanatically and openly ambitious, poor, and out of grim necessity ready to do any kind of writing that promised to support them and their families. This included writing soap operas, advertising copy, newspaper fillers, and in some cases lurid pornographic novels to order, under a variety of assumed names. They could be seen after night school arguing in downtown cafeterias in the unmusical accents of the streets of New York about the merits of Proust and Hemingway as they sat hunched over thirty-five cent blue plates and nickel cups of coffee. Their idea of a vacation was a ride on the subway to Coney Island with drab but insanely virginal girls who condemned them to nights of desperate celibacy or desolate marriages; and behind them you could almost hear endless bitter debates in their homes during which they were branded by their parents as loafers who refused honest jobs to pursue the chimera of The Great American Novel.

In contrast, the literary hopefuls of the Paris contingent spoke in the casual tones of the good schools and could be found, surrounded by flocks of pretty and nobly acquiescent girls, in chic places like Lipp's on the Boulevard St. Germain or on the roads to Deauville or Biarritz for month-long holidays. They were mild-mannered, beautifully polite, recoiled from the appearance of seeming ambitious and were ready at all times to drop whatever they were almost secretly composing to play tennis (usually very well), drive down to Spain for a bullfight, fly to Rome for a wedding or sit around most of the night drinking. As far as I could see, none of them had a job and although they all lived frugally in cheap rooms they gave the impression that they were going through a period of Gallic slumming for the fun of it. One guessed that there were wealthy and benevolent parents on the other side of the Atlantic.

They were invigorating to be with and voiced what opinions they had softly and I was happy to have them drop in and drink my booze, both in Paris and in St.-Jean-de-Luz, where I spent my summers in a big barn of a house, overlooking the valley of the Nivelle. There they appeared, ready for long nights at the Café Basque and picnics on the beach, to which Ben Bradlee, less powerful then than now, and I would ride through the sun-tanned traffic in an open car holding a huge flower vase of ice-cold daiquiris on the way to the elegant bodies sprawled on the expensive sand along the edge of the blue sea.

Perhaps with a tinge of my youthful jealousy of young men like that I did not let them off wholly unscathed. Using an innocent anecdote about a near-drowning I had heard from three of them, in writing a story about the incident, I had, for the purposes of art, shamelessly transmuted the three characters, making one boy a coward, crafty and

131

disloyal, the other betrayed and simple-minded, the girl immoral and a tease. The principals recognized themselves immediately when the story was published and laughed, amused, at whatever malice the story contained.

In those sweet summers laughter came easily.

It was that comparatively serene time when America, at least, was not engaged in any war and the phrase, The Silent Generation, was used to describe the young men and women of the era. While my friends talked a great deal and were unaggressively in favor of Adlai Stevenson, they bore President Eisenhower no malice and the description, unfair as it was, was perhaps as fitting for them as any other. They went off on no crusades, they did not seem to be tempted by the Left, either French, American or Russian, and if, for want of a better word, they might have been termed capitalists, they were not intense about the system which cradled them. The political turmoil in France over Algeria did not really involve them, as they could only be spectators, not actors in the drama.

They were too young to have seen much of World War II and one way or another had escaped Korea and were free of the permanent dark spots within the soul that marked writers like James Jones and myself, who were also in Paris at the time and who thus had a different view of the world from them.

Unlike other little magazines, such as the *Kenyon Review, Poetry, Story* and *Partisan Review*, to name several that have come and gone or have changed unrecognizably, the magazine they debonairly were conspiring to produce had no thesis to promote except, as it turned out, that of eclectic excellence. I must confess at this late date that I was somewhat surprised when a group that I considered rather light-minded and dilettantish turned out a quarterly of such bold and professional quality.

I should have been warned that something serious was in the air when the *Paris Review*'s first award for a short story was given to a very young man named Philip Roth, presented by Aly Khan in the rather incongruous luxury of his mansion facing the Bois de Boulogne. Even so, given the wandering habits of the editors and contributors and the exigencies of the careers ahead of them—novels to write (Styron, Mattheisen, Marquand Jr., Harold L. Humes, Blair Fuller) and explorations of the Amazon, Africa and the Arctic (Matthiesen again), activities such as boxing professional heavyweights, living through a training camp of the National Football League as a rookie, photographing the biggest elephant in the world on its native grounds, playing the triangle with a symphony orchestra, swinging from a circus trapeze and memorializing these excursions, among many others, in hilarious books and television shows (Plimpton), I privately predicted a short life for the infant publication. And now, lo and behold! it is twenty-five years later (where has all the time gone?) and the magazine is still with us, elegant and vital and from its pages has come a series of searching interviews with writers of all sorts that has made an important contribution to the understanding of modern American literature. The people who were responsible for it then and whose names still are associated with it, though graying or balding here and there and not as quick on the tennis court as once they were, are just as pleasant to be with as they were then, and, if they were inclined to boast, as they are not, could look back with satisfaction and say, "Look what we have accomplished."

At any rate, my house is still open to all of them, even if it isn't in Paris or on the Basque Coast, and the booze is still free.

In the United States, the magazine had a number of offices—the first set up by Thomas H. Guinzburg at 2 Columbus Circle where the Huntington Hartford Museum afterwards stood, and then a railroad loft at 401 East 82nd Street with a burlap-sack curtain which separated the front office from the "back room." A number of transients took up a temporary residence behind the burlap sack. . . .

The present office is in a ground floor room on East 72nd Street in New York City. The Editor and his family live upstairs. A lion-trainer's chair, laced and ripped by claws, hangs from the ceiling, its seat inscribed with a salutation by Dave Hoover, the star of the Clyde Beatty-Cole Bros. circus to commemorate an occasion when he took the Editor into the lion's cage with him. There are also hooks in the ceiling from which to hang the staff's bicycles to give everyone more room below. . . .

[A view of the activities at East 72nd] has been supplied by Elaine Dundy, the former wife of Kenneth Tynan, the critic, and herself a novelist (*The Dud Avocado*) and essayist:

Norman Mailer tells me that what he most recalls about the *Paris Review* parties in the fifties and sixties was their charged atmosphere. "All those writers," he says, "myself included—walking rigidly through that packed room towards the drinks, our heads erect, only our eyes swiveling sideways to identify the enemy."

Twenty years ago Stephen Spender, comparing the English Literary Scene with the American one, wrote that the former resembled a cozy conspiracy while the latter a battleground or brothel. Clearly he had done his research at the fortnightly literary salon held in the *Paris Review*'s offices on 72nd Street which was also the apartment of host George A. Plimpton. For over a decade it was the only Quality Lit game in town.

I, too, remember those parties filled with their dangerous, challenging, sometimes near-fatal mixture of novelists, critics, editors, and publishers stewing together in the pressure-cooker of that long narrow room. And I remember the thrill of fear with which one realized that once across the threshold the only exit offered seemed to be the icy East River darkly flowing outside the windows.

However frightened, no one seriously engaged in the literary scene dreamt of missing these regular confrontations and no one dared come unarmed. Norman Mailer brought his seconds, his boxing chums. Terry Southern brought his fellow hipsters, Boris, Kooky, and Shadow. Bill Styron brought his charming wife, Rose. And Jimmy Baldwin brought the fire next time. I, myself, wore several suits of armor. Sometimes I came as a wife, sometimes as an adventuress. I never came as a novelist, except as an amateur one, deflecting the foe with assurances that my first novel was a fluke; for what was immediately apparent in those days was the lack of serious literary ladies. The women there, highly decorative for the most part, were strictly utilitarian: wives, mistresses, girlfriends past and girlfriends possible. In all the years I attended these soirées I never once came across Mary McCarthy, Carson McCullers, Eudora Welty, Flannery O'Connor, Katherine Anne Porter or even Lillian Hellman.

Only now recollecting in tranquility these discordant gatherings do I realize what was taking place was not merely a series of black comedies or shell games. What emerges for me now is something ineffably poignant. Beneath the surface squabbling, sniping, and stalking, the antagonism went deep and it was real. It was an antagonism based on warring philosophies. Each of the young men there—the writers, poets, editors, and publishers—genuinely stood *for* something . . . which meant each was against something else.

Hip, Beat and Square were philosophical concepts that translated themselves into literary styles. The poets Ginsberg, Orlovsky and Ferlinghetti were, of course, Beat. Mailer at that time was so obsessed with Hip that in *Advertisements for Myself* he ran a list, pages long, of things he considered hip with their dreaded square equivalents: "nuance," for instance, was hip and "fact" square. Styron's novel *Set This House on Fire* hadn't gone past the fifth page before the "I" of the story was stalwartly declaring himself a Square. Southern's philosophy was that of the arch-prankster-intriguer: the gadfly in the Venetian manner of Mosca or Iago.

By word and deed guests expressed themselves with unrestrained freedom. Often the words were very funny. I remember Mailer attacking a rival as "White, Protestant and wrong," and Southern informing a startled middle-aged wife in a hat that "There are more things in heaven and earth, Mrs. Sprague, than are *dreamt* of in your philosophy." Mike Nichols reported the following exchange upon being introduced to a Hipsteress:

Nichols: "How do you do?"

Hipsteress: "I thought you'd be cleverer than that."

Clashes were not only verbal but, at a fair rate, physical. Sometimes they involved animate objects, sometimes inanimate. It was in dealing with these skirmishes that George Plimpton excelled. Benevolently watching over us all with a sort of awed enthusiasm, our host, with his infinite tolerance of his guests' vagaries and umbrages which could end in fisticuffs, collapsed coffee tables, broken glass, or tears, really made the whole thing go with a stylish swing. One guest, momentarily out of control, who saved up her money and apologies for a month before confessing to bashing an enormous wall mirror in the room, was quickly absolved by him with a generous "It's all right. It was bound to happen one day." That grateful guest was I.

One of the curious aspects about the magazine, especially as time goes on, has been the feeling of support given it by those no longer actively involved. When he came through Paris in the early seventies William Styron would drop in the little office on the Rue Vernet. Maxine Groffsky remembered that he would always ask with great concern, "Maxine, how are we doing on subscriptions?"

"I'd look at him in surprise," she recalled. "We had all of 213 subscriptions in Europe. I'd say, 'You must be kidding, Bill.' But he *did* care. People who had been associated with the *Review* came to the office as if they were on a pilgrimage. They sat around. They wanted to know if everything was O.K. They cared. They had a wistful and nice nostalgic feeling about it."

Apparently, friends, as well as the writers and editors had a proprietary feeling about the magazine and the people who worked on it. Jacqueline Onassis wrote a note about the 25th Anniversary:

A 25th Anniversary issue of the *Paris Review*? That cannot be. It and you belong to the time when everything was beginning.

The *Paris Review* weaves in and out of my Paris memories. All the most brilliant and romantic young men were involved with the magazine and all the girls were vivid. We were discovering a city, discovering Europe, literature and art *sur place*—slight expatriates all, determined that our lives would not be mundane.

There was a certain amount of running off to Pamplona and talk of the Black Sun Press!

I remember sitting with you in an airless hole of a night club on the Boulevard Raspail when I was a Junior Year Abroad student. You, rather pale in a black turtleneck sweater, told me how the blue notes of saxophones through smoke-filled haze ushered in the dawns for you, and how you would walk the gray Paris streets in the first light back to a strange bed. Your evenings sounded exotic to one who was spending hers swaddled in sweaters and woolen stockings, doing homework in graph-paper cahiers. . . .

Every time I open a *Paris Review*, I pause at William Pène du Bois' drawing of the Place de la Concorde. You can feel his delight in every element translated into every line. That drawing represents the way I felt about Paris.

Now there are students running off to Paris to be like you. Congratulations, dear George.

E.V. Griffith

Poetry Now

E.V. Griffith

E.V. Griffith was born in Swatara, Minnesota, in 1927, and has lived on the north coast of California, in the heart of the redwoods country, since the age of nine. He graduated from the University of Minnesota, where he studied under Saul Bellow and Robert Penn Warren; after college, he returned to California, where he has edited, in succession, two important literary magazines: *Hearse* (1957-61; second series 1969-72) and *Poetry Now*, which first appeared in 1973. Chairman of the panel on Literary Magazines at the 1975 Library of Congress Conference on the Publication of Poetry and Fiction, Griffith made his living as a career civil servant and official in his home county in California until 1980, when he took an early retirement to devote full time to editing and publishing.

Poetry Now—And Then

Poetry has been a part of my life for as long as I can remember. When I was five, an older sister who liked to play "school" taught me to read, using Longfellow's *Hiawatha* as one of our textbooks. We played the game almost daily, and by the time I started first grade, I could read at third- or fourth-grade level. And I mean really *read*—not just sight-read, from memory—for those were the great days of phonetic learning, and I can well recall my sister's adjuration, "Sound it out! Sound it out!" when I would stumble over the names of Hiawatha's human and animal brethren.

When I was in the fourth grade, I went to a one-room school—eight grades in one room. The teacher made us all memorize a poem a week, and on Fridays we had school recitation—each student repeating, in turn, the poem he or she had learned. Memorizing came very easy for me, so the teacher would assign me harder—and *longer*—poems each week, and while my schoolmates struggled haltingly through quatrains, I would spiel off poems like Alfred Noyes' "The Highwayman" or Stephen Vincent Benet's "The Mountain Whippoorwill."

In high school, I had two superb teachers, Violet and Gladys Shulsen, sisters who both taught English. They loved poetry, and loaned me poetry books from their personal library, urging me to start a library of my own. The summer I was 16 (1943), I pitched hay for a local farmer for 25c an hour to earn money for the first three poetry books I ever bought: Robert Frost's *North of Boston* (then priced at $2.00), Sara Teasdale's *Flame and Shadow* ($1.75) and Edna St. Vincent Millay's *Second April* ($2.00). I chose those particular titles because some poems which I liked in my sophomore English text were reprinted from those volumes.

The buying of those books is one of the keenest memories of my teen-years. At that time, I lived in a rural area, two miles from the nearest town (of 350 souls), in a county without a single bookstore. I ordered the books from the publishers in New York (a different publisher for each book), writing my order letters in longhand on lined binder paper, and paying for them with Post Office money orders. I had never bought a money order and didn't know the procedure (in those days, you filled out an *application* for a money order, and the Post Office then sold you one). The postmistress helped me with the application, first making certain I had the *money* for the enterprise (we were known to be poor). I had a very unreal idea of how long it would take the books to reach me. More than a month went by, and I walked to the Post Office two or three times a week, expectant, then disappointed. The Frost book came first; I opened it immediately, and walked home up the highway, book in hand, reading.

Those three books started a poetry collection which I've added to from that time to this; it now contains well over 2,000 poetry volumes, which are the ones I've winnowed out to *keep*.

When I graduated from high school, I served in the Army a couple years, during the last part of World War II. By this time I had started writing poetry— bucolic sonnets that appeared in the *Saturday Evening Post, Saturday Review of Literature*, and *Ladies' Home Journal* when I was 19. At war's end, I was able to go to college, thanks to the GI Bill. I chose the University of Minnesota, where I had the good fortune to study under both Saul Bellow and Robert Penn Warren.

At Minnesota, I joined the staff of the campus literary magazine, *The Minnesota Quarterly*; I became its poetry editor, then, in my senior year, its editor-in-chief. The publication was intended for campus writers only, but I persuaded a reluctant Board of Publications to let me also solicit manuscripts from outside writers. Soon the *Quarterly* was publishing the likes of James T. Farrell, Jesse Stuart, and Langston Hughes. My assistant editor was Lloyd Zimpel—later a short-story writer and novelist—and it was he, more than anyone else, who first *truly* introduced me to the Wild, Wonderful World of Little Magazines. Zimpel knew a Minneapolis store that stocked a few dozen titles—virtually all there *were* in those days: *Accent, Origin, Goad, Golden Goose, Inferno, The Bridge* and others long passed into history, but of blessed memory. We bought them all and, between classes, pored over them hungrily, sitting on the bank of the Mississippi near the bridge from which John Berryman would later jump.

My experiences editing *The Minnesota Quarterly* and my excitement over the format and content of the other Little Magazines of the early Fifties made me want to start a Little Magazine of my own. I picked a name for it: *Hearse*. I don't recall the exact genesis of the name. After college, I came home to California, and began to assemble the material that went into the first issue of *Hearse*; it appeared in 1957. It contained only 24 pages, plus covers, with work by 30 poets (among them Joel Oppenheimer, Robert Creeley, Larry Eigner, Jonathan Williams, Langston Hughes), and a reproduction of a painting by Lawrence Ferlinghetti. I printed only 100 copies, and mailed most of them, free, to poets and English Department chairmen. It drew some nice responses; William Carlos Williams sent a note praising it, and there were some other good reactions as well. That first issue has become a collector's item; one rare book dealer is now cataloging a copy of it at $400 ("*Rare! One of only 100 copies!*"). (I only paid *$30* for the whole issue.) As a footnote I should mention that the first issue was printed by a mail-order printer—Ottumwa Duplicating Service, of Ottumwa, Iowa. The local hometown printer to whom I'd taken it refused to print it because of alleged "obscenity"—a line in one of Joel Oppenheimer's poems read: "His balls are a restricted area," and the Ferlinghetti painting, "Open City," a powerful depiction of a weary, hollow-eyed prostitute staring out over the city, while two sailors wait in the background, showed what the printer called "visible breasts."

In format, *Hearse* was a center-stapled booklet 5½ x 8½" page size, printed on an offset press on a medium-grade white book stock. The wire staples which held the pages together had a propensity for rusting. The cover stock was Rhino bristol, a different color each issue, with the name *Hearse* printed in black ink. (A few issues varied this by using *white* cover stock, and a *colored* ink.) The "type" for Issues 1 through 6 was IBM-electric-typewriter type, which my Iowa printer (his name deserves recording: Earl Rollison) retyped from my own manual-typewriter copy. The format owed much to—in fact, almost *copied*—the format of another Little Magazine of that period, Carl Larsen's *Existaria*, which was also printed by Ottumwa Duplicating Service.

The Ottumwa company printed the first six issues of *Hearse*. Rollison and I never met; all of our transactions were by mail. I would send him my copy, and the finished issues would come back to me by parcel post. (And in fairly small parcels, I should add, since I only printed 100 to 300 copies of the early issues.) Issue 7—and all of the issues thereafter—was printed in my (by-then) home town, Eureka, California, by letterpress, from linotype-set metal type, at the same printshop which had refused the first issue. (There was by then a new owner.)

In launching *Hearse*, I had given little thought to how I was going to distribute it. A few bookstores handled copies (Gotham Book Mart in New York City, City Lights in San Francisco), but mostly distribution was by mail—with about one-half of those early-issue copies going for free. I sent copies to contributors, to hoped-for contributors, and to other editors, in exchange for their publications. (I have always maintained an active—and substantial—exchange list.) That there were relatively few subscribers never bothered me; in fact, I preferred it, since I disliked the record-keeping chores that went with maintaining subscriptions. There was no other staff, and I handled all correspondence. A

139

subscriber to the early *Hearse* had a rather rough time of it, and, in retrospect, I admire the hardy ones who endured. *Hearse* had no fixed publication date; I simply brought out an issue whenever I felt like it, and had enough material. So there was no way of knowing if an issue was just late, or if, indeed, there would *be* any others. I recall reams of correspondence from the patient, persistent Serials Librarians at certain universities who wheedled, cajoled and badgered to obtain "all issues to date" for their archives. All *Hearse* issues were priced at $1.00 per copy, irrespective of the number of pages per issue (as few as 16, as many as 88).

I let *Hearse* lapse in 1961, because of other obligations. In 1969, two things happened which brought me back to publishing again. In culling some old files, I found a hefty envelope of unpublished Charles Bukowski poems, which Bukowski had apparently sent me some time previously (the postmark-date was not readable), but which I had filed away and forgotten. Among these manuscripts was the long poem "The Days Run Away Like Wild Horses Over the Hills." I wrote Bukowski, asking if this poem was still available, and saying that reading the poem made me itch to start publishing *Hearse* again. He replied that the poem was still unpublished, and that if I wanted it for *Hearse*, I could have it. (It later became the title poem of one of Bukowski's best collections.)

In this same period, I had a note from Mrs. Winfield Townley Scott, whose husband had died the previous year, inquiring whether *Hearse* was still "active," and generously offering me four of the last poems Scott wrote before his death.

With the Bukowski and Scott poems for openers, I put together the first number of the so-called "second series" of *Hearse*—Issues 10 through 17, which appeared from 1969-1972. When I launched this renewal, I toyed very seriously with the idea of converting *Hearse* to a tabloid newspaper format, but in the end kept it in the same "booklet" format as the earlier series. Printing was by letterpress, the printings first at 1,500 copies, then later at 2,500 copies, per issue.

The reborn *Hearse* was extremely well received. *Library Journal* reviewed it, calling it "one of the better edited, more important little poetry magazines in America," and library subscription agencies began placing orders for their clients. This time the subscriptions were properly attended to, and subscription income *almost* made the magazine break even.

The initial series of *Hearse* had drawn some good poets (Kenneth Rexroth, Allen Ginsberg, Paul Blackburn, LeRoi Jones, Richard Brautigan, to name a few not already cited), but the new series brought an increasing flow of the "arrived" and "arriving": Marge Piercy, Philip Booth, James Tate, David Ignatow, John Haines, Robert Mezey, Diane Wakoski, Michael Benedikt, X.J. Kennedy, Marvin Bell, Harold Norse, David Wagoner, Daniel Hoffman, and etc., etc.

It was a good time, one might suppose, to simply rest on one's laurels. But the idea of a poetry magazine in newspaper format kept nagging away, and by the time *American Poetry Review* was launched as a tabloid early in 1973, I'd already started to put together the first issue of *Poetry Now*, which appeared later in that same year. I wanted to be able to run "poet profiles," and photos of the poets, and these things did not seem adaptable to the format of *Hearse*.

William Childress, a fine writer and longtime friend, had recently inter-

140

viewed Josephine Miles, and offered me his profile of her for *PN*'s first issue. And I had a lot of poems on hand, accepted for *Hearse*, which I simply shifted into the new publication. Thus the first issue of *PN* went together fast and easily. I then decided that a good way to launch *PN* was to give away free copies of the pilot issue to the 1,300 poets then listed in the CODA publication, *A Directory of American Poets*, as well as to some 700 Little Magazine editors, book publishers, media people and libraries. That way everybody who ought to know about it would learn of it all at once. And that's what I did. A lot of subscriptions soon came back, and a flood of manuscripts.

At first, I thought of keeping *Hearse* and *PN* going simultaneously, but that idea seemed so impractical that it was quickly abandoned. *Hearse* died again, for a final time, its unfulfilled subscriptions honored by *PN*.

Working with *PN*, in the tabloid newspaper format, has been as satisfying as I had always thought it would be. The format is one that I think readers are instinctively comfortable with; after all, they're used to reading newspapers. So *PN* has had that going for it from the start; it holds well in the hand. *PN* runs 48 pages per issue, and with its tabloid dimensions (11½ x 15"), has a feeling of substance and heft to it that most smaller poetry magazines lack. Each issue has a dozen or so photos of poets. I'm always curious as to what poets I've read, but never met, *look* like. (It is rarely like I think they will.)

My wide reading and appreciation of *all* kinds of poetry throughout literally my entire life has made me, I think, more eclectic than most editors, which is important, since, by owing no allegiance to any particular school or coterie, I can publish the best work available to me in all moulds. Each *PN* includes approximately 100 poets—around 150 poems—in a mixture of both "arrived" and "arriving" poets, plus talented newcomers. A newcomer, in this definition, is someone who has not yet appeared widely in magazines, and who has not yet published a book through a major publisher. I include a newcomer's page in every issue, and also devote one issue each year, *in its entirety*, to newcomers—so *PN* is more receptive to new talent than most magazines. Also into the editorial mix go a number of prose poems; I have a great fondness of the prose poem as a genre, and respect for those who can write them successfully. (Too many poets who attempt prose poems simply end up with a kind of stylized prose.) I also include some 20th-century poetry in translation in each issue of *PN*.

One "constant" in each issue of *PN* is a profile/interview with a leading contemporary poet. The profiles are wide-ranging: William Stafford, Mona Van Duyn, Donald Justice, Edwin Honig, Dave Etter, Thomas McGrath, Peter Viereck, Richard Eberhart, Vassar Miller and Robert Peters, for example. Unlike the traditional "Question"/"Answer" interviews which other magazines publish, *PN*'s profiles are a combination mini-biography/bibliography/craft interview, with accompanying photos. The profiles will eventually be published as a book.

PN's method of "reviewing" current books of poetry is to simply present two or three poems clipped from the book being "reviewed," reproduced without comment except for the name and address of the publisher, and the price of the book. Books chosen for review come from both Commercial and Small presses—about half and half. The annual Newcomer's issue reviews only *first* books.

The reception of *PN* has been extremely gratifying. The initial notices were good—and they have gotten even better. Bowker's *Magazines for Libraries* (4th ed.) calls *PN* "Far and away the most interesting and readable poetry magazine in America." (Heady praise indeed.)

During the years I edited *Hearse*, I wanted to bring out some books and chapbooks of poets I liked, and Hearse Press was born, as an "adjunct" of the magazine. Seventeen titles were published under the Hearse Press imprint, the most significant of which was Charles Bukowski's *Flower, Fist and Bestial Wail*—Bukowski's first book. In a similar manner, Poetry Now Press is being established as a book-publishing "adjunct" of *PN*, with a number of anthologies and individual titles in early prospect.

After nearly 30 (!) years in small press editing-and-publishing, I cannot now conceive of a time when I will *not* be involved in such endeavors in one way or another. Poetry still pleasures me, as it did when my older sister taught me to read, at age five, from Longfellow's *Hiawatha*, and when, at age 16, hands blistered by a pitchfork wrote out an order for Frost's *North of Boston*. ("You *do* have the money, don't you?" the postmistress inquires across the decades.) And today's Little Magazines—at least the *best* of them, now when there are hundreds to choose from—still excite as did those copies of *Accent* and *Inferno*, read so long ago between college classes in Minneapolis.

The lifespan of the "typical" Little Magazine is, as experience teaches, abysmally brief. In the first issue of *Hearse*, in 1959, I urged readers to purchase single copies of—or, better yet, subscribe to—ten current Little Magazines which I myself had just subscribed to: *Existaria, Emergent, The Miscellaneous Man, Trace, Experiment, The Colorado Review, The Chicago Review, The New Orleans Poetry Journal, Sparrow*, and *Poetry Broadside*. A year or so later, seven of those ten were no longer publishing.

They come and they go. At the present time, *PN* exchanges with around 200 Little Magazines, and other editors send me copies as well, so some new issue arrives every few days. Some I especially admire are George Hitchcock's *Kayak*, David Wagoner's *Poetry Northwest*, Daniel Halpern's *Antaeus*, DeWitt Henry's *Ploughshares*, David Ray's *New Letters*, Joseph Bruchac's *The Greenfield Review*, and Marvin Malone's *The Wormwood Review*. There are many others that are also indispensable. Those I've just named have all been around for a number of years, and I admire not only their consistently high quality, but also the fact that their editors have found the time and heart to keep them going. *Kayak* has survived for more than 60 issues as a quarterly, and *The Wormwood Review*, an "irregular" quarterly which mails out a full year's issues all at one time to save on postage costs, is just shy of printing a *90th* issue.

As this is being written, *PN* has just published Issue 35—and looks ahead to years of others. Having started two magazines—*Hearse* and *PN*—it is unlikely that I would ever want to start another, especially when *PN* is being well received, and I am content with what I am doing. The "formula" for future *PN*'s will not change: a poet profile; a healthy mix of "established" and "new" poets; "book reviews" via clip-out samplings; 20th-century poetry in translation. These ingredients, properly assembled, should produce a series of issues as strong—and spirited—as those in the past. And as the feller sez (I *think* it was the feller): "Why tamper with success?"

We grow older and mellow—and, if it all turns out right, we come into our own. *Hearse*—once called "controversial"—has now assumed the status of a "classic" ("in the tradition of the *great* Little Magazines, like *Blues, Blast, Broom*," one critic exuded). *PN*—*never* controversial—has established a solid reputation as one of the biggest—and best—of the current Littles ("far and away the best and most readable"), and increasingly shows up among dust-jacket listings of "prestige" credits of prior publication ("His poems appear in *Harper's, The New Yorker* and *Poetry Now*").

PN, especially, has also brought *personal* honors, some of which I have declined, but a few of which I have accepted. In the latter category was serving (twice) as a member of the CCLM Grants Committee dispensing National Endowment for the Arts largesse to Little Magazines; serving as a judge for the Fels Awards; and chairing the panel on Literary Magazines at the 1975 Library of Congress Conference on the Publication of Poetry and Fiction. (It was at that conference that Daniel Halpern made the comments which later caught the attention of James Michener and led to the financial underwriting—by Michener and others—of the National Poetry Series . . . be that for good or ill.)

Six general comments, after three decades as an editor/publisher:

1. Publishing a Little Magazine or operating a Small Press can be very self-satisfying—even exhilarating—but, except in the *rarest* instances, cannot earn one a living. Almost every editor I've known, whose publications have survived for more than a few issues, has had to dip into his or her own pocket—frequently (and sometimes *heavily*, in these days of steadily-increasing printing and postage costs) to sustain the publication.

2. While most assuredly not "everyone can do it," there is no "ideal background" for an editor/publisher of a Little Magazine. Many editors are academics—especially those who edit publications which emanate from universities. But one editor I admire (Warren Woessner of *Abraxas* and Abraxas Press) works as a chemist; another (Marvin Malone of *The Wormwood Review*) is a practicing pharmacist; and a third (Terrence McMahon of *The Fault*) is a hardhat—a bona fide member of the Operating Engineers Union. And I've earned my *own* livingg as a career civil servant and official in County Government in my home county in California.

3. The *best* Little Magazines are those edited by single individuals, who have total control over contents. A good magazine needs a tone, an integrity, a signature—and one person can shape these things for it better than an "editorial committee" can. Magazines that are edited by committee often end up dull.

4. Flashy type and deckle-edged paper do not in themselves a good product make. It is *content*, not appearance, that is important. I remember with pleasure John Bennett's *Vagabond*, which he ground out on a second-hand (1928 model) duplicator; and Douglas Blazek's *Olé* and Judson Crews' *The Deer and Dachshund*—both produced by mimeograph.

5. "Editing a Little Magazine and not promoting it is like winking in the

dark. *You* know what you're doing—but nobody else does." (This is someone else's quotation—I'm not sure whose—but I certainly concur with it.)

6. Little Magazines are Important—but only a few of them ever *change* anything (and usually not until *Later*).

Hearse

Poetry NOW

VOL. VI, No. 5 [Issue 35] $2.00

Tom Jones

RICHARD EBERHART

RICHARD EBERHART was born in Austin, Minnesota, on April 5, 1904. His father, A. L. Eberhart, was an industrious, self-made man, who worked for the Hormel Meat Packing Company in Austin, with which he held several positions, eventually becoming its vice president. By carefully investing in the growing Hormel organization, the senior Eberhart accumulated a small fortune, and by 1916, was able to build for his family a handsome home in Austin, on a forty acre estate, at a cost of $50,000. This home, called Burr Oaks, was a huge wood-and-stucco construction, with 18 rooms and a gymnasium in the basement sufficiently large that it could be used to play basketball or as a ballroom, as the circumstances warranted.

Duane Locke

Poetry Review

Duane Locke

Duane Locke, editor, *Poetry Review* (alias *University of Tampa Poetry Review* alias *UT Review*-1962-and still continuing, although less passionately and regular), was born December 29, 1921, Vienna, Georgia; present residence: 2716 Jefferson Street, Tampa, Florida 33602; married: Frances, an elementary school teacher; occupation: Professor of English and Poet in Residence at University of Tampa; although in 1981-82, "the happiest time in my time," was on sabbatical; publications: over 600 poems in over 400 different little magazines, a number of anthologies, and 12 small press books of poetry.

A Brief Autobiography

Once an interviewer asked, "It says in *Contemporary Southern Poetry* that you are a prolific poet. What causes you to write so many poems?" My answer: "I have suffered. I was an introvert in the Tampa public school system."

My torment as an alien in an extroverted school system began my urge to edit a little magazine. I wanted a tangible revenge on a society whose values I despised. I acquired a toy printing press and satirized big bands, small bands, hayrides, dances, sports, parties, and most all of the activities that people cherish. My magazine had a circulation of two, myself and a six-year-old boy who lived next door. The boy constantly complained that the magazine was hermetic and obscure and he disdained its predilection for the rarefied and recherché.

At college, the University of Tampa, a professor, Douglas Angus, inspired me with a love for contemporary poetry and introduced me to little poetry magazines. He was a rare English professor, for he had a genuine and deep sensitivity to poetic art, and did not get by as the common variety with mechanistic methods and the dispersing of copies information. But his being a man of erudition, sensibility, and strong emotions made him unpopular with the less learned men of feeble emotions who composed the administration. He soon left the university, and his departure delayed my development. After him, all my undergraduate English professors were less-than-mediocre and excessively ignorant in matters of modernistic poetry—although they were vivacious, colorful, and bon vivants.

Being at a backward university caused me to seek civilized values elsewhere. I started going to New York every summer and discovered the little magazines at the Gotham Book Mart: *VVV, View, transitions, Tiger's Eye*. I remember my excitement when I saw Maxwell Bodenheim and his poems tacked on a Greenwich Village wall. I became attracted to the poetry of Charles Henri Ford and Jose Garcia Villa. I discovered Gerardo Diego and Vicente Huidobo, and was so excited I tried my first attempt at writing poetry. My initial creative efforts in the Spanish avant-garde manner were only short lived, for I met with a crushing and violent opposition from my ignorant professors and miscellaneous poetasters around Tampa.

Finally, I went to graduate school at the University of Florida. Now my professors were learned, but they were passionately concerned with literary scholarship and not the creation of poetry. I do not think that any of my professors had ever read the work of a living poet. I became a literary scholar, specializing in the poetry from Donne from Marvell, and was sidetracked from the more worthwhile activities of writing poetry and editing a little magazine.

When I got my Ph.D. I made the first major mistake of my life by accepting a job at my hometown university, The University of Tampa. I should have been more adventurous and gone to one of the other universities of a much higher quality that had offered me a better position—one in which I would never have had to teach Freshman English, but I was a coward. At the University of Florida, the leading literary scholars came to see me and begged me not to go to the University of Tampa, saying that I would waste my life at such a place. At the time, I did not understand what the phrase *waste your life* meant, but now that I have wasted my life by teaching at the University of Tampa, I understand the phrase fully.

When I commenced my academic career at the University of Tampa, the pace was leisurely, my colleagues, although oblivious of modern poetry and little magazines, were colorful, vivacious, and bon vivants, and also very tolerant of idiosyncracies and thus congenial to the development of individuality. I started four scholarly works on (1) the influence of medieval symbolism on the poetry of Donne through Marvell, (2) the metaphysical suggestion of John Keats' imagery, (3) a literary criticism based on classification and evaluation of sentences, and (4) English prosody, with special attention on the placement of related consonants in making poetic music. I never finished one. After squandering some time on the trivialities, escapisms, and parasitism of scholarship, I met David Wade, a poet, who always carried a copy of *Howl* and used words such as *Auerhahn, Hawk's Well Press*, and *Totem Press*. His enthusiasm for innovation revived my interest in modern poetry, and finally I started serious writing. Unfortunately, when I finished my first real poem, I was already too old for "The Yale Younger Poets Series." After publishing my first 200 poems, I started editing a little magazine.

148

As time went on the unviersity began to change, a new breed came into power; drab, methodical, mechanistic, intolerant, opportunistic, and antagonistic to individuality—a breed I would call "the real enemies of civilized values and imaginative literature." But this new breed were experts in standardization, syllabi, spy systems, close order drill, and reducing a member of the faculty to a cog in a wheel. I saw myself growing old among my enemies, but the editorship of the little magazine had a strong therapeutic value, serving as an antidote to my insular, provincial, and antipoetic academic surroundings.

Our magazine survived financially through university support, although spiritually and humanly only a few at the university were concerned with our existence. Students of mine in a prosody class suggested that we start a little magazine. R. Morris Newton begged a mimeograph machine from a priest, but it would not work. Finally, the university consented to let us use their mimeograph, and the president, David M. Delo, supplied money from his personal fund for other expenses. Later on, a group of poets, Alan Britt, G.F. Robinson, Silvia Schiebli, Richard Collier, and Steve Barfield, made enough money through poetry readings to buy an offset, and gave it to me.

On the day the university president promised to pay our expenses, we added "University of Tampa" to our modest and humdrum title "Poetry Review." I insisted that the university would have no supervision over the magazine, and thus we became an independent magazine patronized by a university. Now, I regret the addition, for I am nearing retirement age (about five years), and when I am finally freed from economic imprisonment at the university, I do not want anything around to remind of my servitude and sentence. I have already started inking out all except "Poetry Review."

When I started the magazine, the person who helped me most with advice was Kirby Congdon, and later on, Gerard Malanga helped us gather some excellent poets. Rich Mangelsdorff and Hugh Fox supplied inspiration.

One of our most exciting days was when we received a bunch of poems from LeRoi Jones. That was before he became Amiri Baraka. A disappointment was that I never received a poem from my favorite poet, Richard Howard.

I suppose what I regret most about editing a little magazine was the time and energy it took from my own writing. I feel that editing a little magazine, as well as teaching at the wrong university, was harmful to my development as a poet. If I could sell my soul to Mephistopheles and relive my life, I would never, in spite of the excitement, edit a little magazine. Instead I would devote all my energy to my own poetry, and I would not have waited until the age of 40 to start writing.

I never thought of a little magazine as a way to make a living, for I feel that anything that aspires towards the highest excellence automatically precludes profit.

I never had an editorial policy, for I distrust any type of formulated belief. There is something repellent about a mind that makes all decisions before the problems arise.

In the '60s, the little magazines, mainly, the unpopular and impoverished, had an élan, were valorous and adventurous; but soon became extinct. Now, the little magazines seem tepid and standardized.

The little magazines that I liked most were Fred Wolven's *Ann Arbor Review* and Harvey Tucker's *Black Sun*, the small press, Harry Smith's *The Smith*. I also remember with affection, *Ghost Dance, Mimeo, Input, Gunrunner, Beanbag, Intermission*, and *Poets at Le Metro*.

I disliked all insular and insensitive magazines such as *Caterpillar* that are frantic about one limited mode of expression and blind to all others. But I did not hate them too intensely, for due to their overwhelming numbers and prevalence, I would have been consumed by hatred and had little time to do anything else.

The main qualification that a little magazine editor must have is the capacity to endure the following types without developing a disdain for the entire human race and becoming addicted to the daydream that evolution had stopped with the phylum *aves*: (1) those 10,000 or so untalented and empty people who are ardently convinced without the least doubt that they are the unrecognized poetic geniuses of this century, (2) those many inerudite and unlearned editors who foolishly believe that in their genes was the ability to be the final and ultimate judge on what constitutes a worthwhile poem, and (3) those stupid people, usually high school teachers and college professors, who dismiss without reading, or making an effort to understand, all modernistic poetry as not being up to the quality of the past.

I feel that since government grants were based on supposed merit and not on chance, they were harmful to little magazines and poets. In August 1953 the Federal Arts Project did not demand evidence of artistic qualifications and thus made it possible for the lesser known, more independent, and more adventurous to be eligible for financial aid. Out of this group came Arshile Gorky, Jackson Pollock, Willem de Kooning, William Baziotes, Mark Rothko, Adolph Gottlieb, Philip Guston, and James Brooks. Before, when artists were screened by committees for their merit, very little art of any worth was produced. A study of the history of human opinion concerning the arts convincingly demonstrates that most people who believed themselves capable of judging merit were wrong. Grants should be based on a lottery, names drawn at random, and not on the delusion that a committee will be found that is capable of making a selection based on achievement. I know my plan will be a great disappointment to many egotists and megalomaniacs for it will deprive them of a source for self-esteem, but the furtherance of the intense, complex, and deep little magazines and poets seems more important.

I have not found either COSMEP or CCLM to be helpful, but I did enjoy the social life at their meetings.

I suppose I will survive the '80s by enduring a teaching situation that is somewhat uncongenial to my basic values, but in hopes of not having to teach, I have been applying for every form of grant. I would like to dedicate these last years of my life to writing poetry and not editing a little magazine, but I do not expect I will get a grant—unless my method of chance and a lottery is instituted.

Before I close my comments, I want to thank the many students of mine who physically and spiritually aided me with the magazine. I have already mentioned the poets who read, and they also served as a collating machine. We organized a system of about 20 students walking around a table. Some of the others who devoted considerable time to our enterprise were Joseph Rodiero, Nico Suarez, Lizabeth Fairclough and Jane Leonard, who is still here and still helping.

Morrison 1985

Morris Edelson

Quixote

Morris Edelson

Quixote magazine, Quixote Press, publisher, Morris Edelson, began 1965, Madison, Wisconsin.

Subsidiary enterprises: Nude Playwrights' Theater; Madison Film Club; Marxist Drinker's Society; Angry Arts Festivals; Valhalla Coffee House—all in Madison, Wisconsin 1966-69. *The Rag* newspaper, Austin; Fly By Night Printing, Austin; the anti-Glen Scott, anti-Social Dem Deb Group, Austin, Texas, 1974-76. Takeover newspaper, *The Journal of Psychedelic Drugs, The Venereal Wart Newsletter*, RPM Printshop, Madison, Wisconsin, 1976-79. *US China Peoples Friendship Newsletter, Career Digest*, The Reaganomics Guns Not Butter Vaudeville Company, Houston, Texas, 1979-82.

Major Publications:

The Great Bourgeois Bus Company, Ed Ochester, 1968

Four Polish Poets, Victor Contoski, 1967

Going to Bed, Margaret Savides Benbow, 1974

A Charles Bukowski Sampler, Charles Bukowski, 1966

Modern African Revolutionary Poems and Songs, Emile Snyder, 1965

The Madison Poems and Collages, d.a. levy, 1968, reprinted in color 1980

The Opium Must Go Thru, Charles Potts, 1968

Singin' in the Drain, Tuli Kupferberg, 1968

The First American Book of Anti-War Poems and Songs, ed. Robert Bly, 1966

The Communist Manifesto in Cartoon Book Form, by George Rius—10 editions, first 1969

Incitement to Nixoncide and Praise for the Chilean Revolution, Pablo Neruda, 1968 (note: this issue is the "authorized" one issued from Chile, threatened with lawsuit by John Crawford who brought out the capitalist edition some nine years later)

The Madison, Wisconsin, Telephone Book, 1978 (issued jointly with Bell Telephone Inc.)

Madison Undercovers, Morris Edelson, 1979

A Roll in the Hay Gets You An A; Graduate School Revisited, Morris Edelson, 1979

Heroin Smuggling from the Golden Triangle, Robert Solomon (with STASH Press), 1979

The Yankees and the Cowboys, Carl Davidson, 1978

Places *Quixote* was produced, partial list:
  Cellar, dirt floor prone to flooding, on Brooks Street next to YMCA, Madison
  Lutheran Church, University Avenue, Madison
  Wisconsin Alliance Office and editors' living quarters, Williamson Street
    next to Smith Cycle Shop, Madison
  RPM, Madison
  Fly by Night and Red River Womens Press, Austin
  Takeover newspaper office basement, Madison
  Draft Resistance office, Madison
  Texas Research Institute for Mental Science, Houston
  Boiler room, Spaight Street, Madison
  Naurotowica Street, Lodz, Poland (rubber stamp edition)
  rjs's farm, outside Cleveland, Ohio
  Sy Gresser's game room, Washington DC (book of Gresser's poems mailed to
    him unassembled—staff and family met and worked in 1969 before we
    left for Poland)

Staff Members: many, many

Publisher's data: DOB, April 25, 1936, Los Angeles, CA; PhD, U of W, Madison,
  1973

Arrests:
  Criminal trespass, Beaumont, TX, 1964; criminal trespass, Selma, AL, 1964;
  blocking traffic, Madison, 1968; disrupting public assembly (speech of
  George Wallace), Madison, 1969; assault with deadly weapon (on the occasion of the visit by the American Nazi Party to radio station WORT, Madison, WI); shoplifting, Austin, 1978

Disposition of cases: Charges dropped. Poll tax repealed. Defeat of invaders in
  Viet Nam. Segregation declared illegal.

Work experiences of publisher: numerous; presently working in fetal alcohol
  syndrome studies at Texas Medical Center, authoring book on the Vickie
  Daniel case (ex-waitress kills most prominent young politician in state), res-
  taurant reviewing for *Texas Monthly* magazine, copy editing for three truck
  magazines, teaching English at the U of Houston downtown college, writing
  weekly news story for *Career Digest* news, and serving on board of US China
  Peoples Friendship Association, paid grant writer.

Size of FBI file: 4 pages, dealing largely with work in Poland, cultural production in Madison, Wisconsin

Size of penis: $2^{1}/_{8}$ " flaccid; usual condition; $5^{1}/_{8}$ " tumescent

Hobbies: Bicycling, wandering around universities looking for an honest intellectual, traveling through Cajun areas and marshes

Reading: bulletin boards, crime reports, scientific and trucking journals, history
  and politics. Murder trials recently because book on same is coming up and
  out: "Half Price and the Dairy Queen" tentative title.

Gulf Oil Corporation

Dear Sirs and Mesdames
December Press

Since I have become a successful executive, I seldom look back on the follies of a misspent youth, except with bitter tears and self-remorse. Therefore, a questionnaire, an unlovely exercise in semi-commo at best, on my little magazine empire building and final ascent into a more responsible area of endeavor, can only be painful to contemplate and arduous to confront. I pause only from intercontinental concerns crowding my mahogany desk next to my exclusive, and should I say to forestall any visits from one of the perpetrators of this minor headache, locked liquor cabinet, and I write this counsel only to assist those whose minds may yet be clouded by some foggy notions that publishing their own drivel somehow will make it less drivelous, and that putting dark impressions on lighter colored materials will add up to fame and fortune.

I must choke back a sigh when I remember first discussing literature with those giants of the scribbling art, James Dickey, Felix Pollak, and Victor "Cleanhead" Contoski. Alas, how they all thought that literature would justify their personal nastinesses, failed marriages and shady backgrounds: Contoski's connection to a Polish grandmother, Pollak's use of state time and funds in his position as Rare Books Librarian in Madison to write what he called poetry, and James Dickey, poet and womanizer in residence at the University, hoping to achieve even greater fame than his Coca Cola commercials had brought him. Yes, those were the days when his novel *Deliverance* was impregnated in his soul. I recall his arrows of love and passion flying about the hilly woods of the Army Math Research Center, shortly before that building was blown to smithereens by the New Year's Gang. This was early in the '60s, and it is difficult to recall those long and learned discussions we three had, in our canoe, running the rapids through the locks in the Yahara River, paddling furiously towards the 602 Club and Bar.

Of underground publishing I had heard some hints, in 1955, before I was forcibly ejected from my comfortable existence in a dormitory at Southern Methodist University. There, before being expelled from school after a literary argument became a legal one, I would glue my aural orifice to a shortwave transmitter, hearing of Fidel and his monthly sheet called *Gramma*. It was a combative little paper, one which I emulated later, when I too was a soldier, facing the Russian Army in East Berlin. Brick by brick, as they built a monument to free expression, I began to create my far-reaching plan for my present eminence. My practice runs took the form of maneuvers in the *Stars and Stripes* newspaper, my editorship of the battalion newsletter, and my staging of the annual Tittichop

Follies, bacchanals lauding the achievements of our forces, which composed the first combat helicopter units of the US Seventh Army. We sold helicopters to the world and to the Pentagon, preparing them for grand adventures in rice paddy lands with the eversoportable instrument whose capabilities we were demonstrating.

It was from this experience I arrived in the '60s where, with the application of chemicals to cellular material in the collective cortex, all hell began to break loose. The old ways were dying, it seemed, the new ones seeking an expression. Editing resembled breaking a mustang; writing was an effort to explain one's life, shape the world, grab a life raft in the swirling change. No one slept, we considered daily publication, we kicked in doors to university printing machines and grabbed off mimeo paper from scared registrars.

We thought publishing, and we formed a gang, renegade to all except that which outshouted us, a way to *take* a living; and those who objected were pushed to the wall or into their own publication, still not secure from our depredations. Let us recall, after taking an Alka-Seltzer, Warren Woessner and James Bertolino, poets who insisted on having our seal of approval, now both respected academics of $40,000 annual net worth to society, they claim (and have convinced at least a few people). Let us recall that they came into our offices and typed up their own poems, did all the physical work, paid for publication, and sniveled along until they got their own little volumes, their fingernailhold on the ladder of some literary reputation, published with our imprint—they suffered woe enough almost to forgive their lack of talent: our typist, Margaret Savides Benbow, would improve their poems when they weren't around, by adding or subtracting words; I, grown impatient one night, scissored several of Woessner's lyrics in half, and ran them improved, and thus we ran. Felix Pollak, on state time, devised our logo, "If you want to see your poems published the way you wrote them, send them somewhere else."

This was not simple perversity, but an editorial decision, reaction to "concrete poetry" impossible to reproduce given our simple resources of one of those long-armed IBMs, with a carriage return like a kick of a mule, and the Multi 85, the night-table sized printer. All we could do is what we could type, and we thought photo-offset a Ford Foundation plot to engorge and then enfeeble the humanities—and we were right. Few could appreciate or even value our foresight in those days: Richard Kostelanetz ignored our counsels and editorial pleas and went straight to the purgatory of those waiting for a grant, clutching his concretetions around him . . . d.a. levy ended his sprung loose composition with a rifle slug to his own head, after losing many verse debates in our cellar. . . . William Wantling wore his own life down to the last Camel and broke its back after visiting our assemblage in Madison (the annual COSMEP meeting) . . . and concrete poetry, poem as object, poem as playtoy poets put on their tweeds and their glossy covers, roared their gibberish from every podium, and rammed the abstract expressionism of literature up the eager chambers of the trying-to-be-arty, the Trick Quarterlies and the Hype Period reviews, the regionals and the fugitives, the beats and the Eliotic, and there was a great darkness on most of the land, except in San Francisco, except near Chicago, except in Cleveland.

156

So we published the exceptional, and still do, yes, lord, yes, and distribution and publication remains more or less the same. Since we still have our trusty old double-barreled multilith hanging over the mantelpiece, it still comes down and spits now and then, and we as then xerox, handwrite, rubber stamp, water color, and offset print what we think ought to get out. There was never a conflict about giving or selling our magazine, since we did both, and meant to do. We always enjoyed those who gave their magazines away since we could then staple them inside our own publication, encompass them, as it were, as examples of bad art.

Good art, to us, said something about the unequal power and wealth of the country, and the self-defeating nature of the aim to accumulate. Satire and humor, indirection rather than pedagogy, the techniques of good art as taught by craftsmen, were the chosen forms. In addition to this desire for good art, we also had the purpose of illustrating the decadence and emptiness of poetry such as that by Woessner, Dickey and the genteel ladies of Beloit College—so we ran their work as well as others, without comment. Today, since so many of those wallpaper literati have achieved some nook or hole or other from which they vent their noxious gases in comfort, we feel less obliged to mess with them.

And the readers wrote and tried to knock us down, and yes they did, and had us arrested one night. Let those of you who hate my achievements thank Jerry "Pocky" Pochkar, a simpering English major, whose right to the jaw downed me on the ice; and thank Dean Crocodile Ginsberg (not Allen), who called the police on our performance of a poetic play. Well, yes, it was good publicity, but it had its cost, d.a. levy being hounded out of Cleveland ran right into the same problems, masked even more nauseatingly by fatuous allusions to good taste in the little academic villages.

And the money poured in, and we got the keys to the joint, so who needed foundations, the snooty banalities of the Coordinating Council of Literary Magazines, a Titanic-styled do nothing conglom; who needed the even more offputting simpers of a Judy Hogan, or nacreous decay of a Richard Morris of COSMEP, amateur hustlers looking for a money fix, and hearing success stories from tough-minded dilettanti like Harry Smith and his pal HL Van Grunt? Thank god for the death of the NEA! And three cheers for the senility of the Foundation Ford. And may writers be fined like overtime parkers, idiot inheritances ripped from their grips!

And thus we said, and say it again: You want a medal already? So the readers paid for a while, it was fashionable in those days to accept guilt and pay Eldridge Cleaver or some other paper panther to tell you how you were all crummy because you didn't have cancer, a work-related injury, or a proper rapport with the beatified lumpen. We hired a protection racket expert who made sure that once a library or reader subscribed, they continued. This was Doug Blazek, Chuck Buks' Boswell, whose belches were more fearful than napalm, the terror of the smaller academic Wisconsin library, for a decade or two. His tricks were to send the librarian at home some several hundred mutilated cards from the card file, or the first two pages of the rarest book on the shelves. Old librarians had their earpieces coated with Elmer's glue, while the younger shelvers in

157

the stacks had to replace whole rows of bottom books dislodged by our man's steel toes. They paid up and paid again.

Yes, it is a tough world out there, and we survived and came back from the jungle to fame and fortune. It was writing that made us and writing we lived by. And alive we could share, and share we did.

So, we were, Cleanhead, Pollak, Dizzy Contoski, Ed "Fingers" Ochester, Darius Andrew Levy, Margaret Benbow Savides, Mary Duncan, Jack Gilbert, David Hilton, John Crewdson, and I, played collective (1) Robin Hood, (2) Fidel, (3) Heraclitus; set out to make trouble, record history and make a little of it ourselves, challenging the boojays whenever we could. Art was action, anger, but recorded, pictured, so we tried writing it down.

Our first issue, now selling for a cool $1,000 in the Amsterdam markets, saluted the fallen warriors of the literary landscape, those with wounds in their face and front, not the leprous lizards of language graft. At Wisconsin there was a proud record, *The New Student, The Rocking Horse, penny sheet* and *Carrots and Peas.* Saul Bellow grew out of and away from that proud past at Wisconsin, Sinclair Lewis had written there, by our time there was only a Socialist Club and a Literary Committee, both registered with campus gestapo and certified safe. The tide of history washed all this away and floated us up into the rolling tides. With the beats, and the drugs and the Viet Nam War, the secrets of America were exposed, and everyone wanted to talk about it, rage at the atrocities of the system, of the war on the poor.

There were days, in 1969, when we published an issue a day of our "megazine." I remember it well, a group of four tending the little press, six or eight people stacking and stapling, applying duct tape (as was levy's wont), and Margaret Benbow making the typer smoke. Anna Taylor, Diane Wakoski, Shirley Perry and Liz Uhr, all published writers now, took their turns at the typer; rjs (Robert Sigmund Sherman, a Cleveland associate of levy's) helped me run the multi; while Bertolino and Woessner ran coffee, and we produced issues, and anthologies of the work of Roger Mitchell (now chairman of the English Dept at Indiana U), James Hogan (editor of *Harper's* magazine), levy, and Cleanhead. Margaret would take her breaks with a card table full of magazines outside the (WAR) Memorial Building on campus . . . Contoski would repair to the English Department supply room, or wait until night and go over the transom, and return with reams of paper . . . and some sympathetic or amused colleague of mine would go teach my classes. I was a Teaching Assistant at the time, and getting my GI Bill for education, and blowing them both on our books, mags, plays and films. The libraries' subscription money, special contributions extorted from people who were afraid of us, and blackmail kept the whole empire afloat.

And that's what I learned in our days of youth, when we ran 500 copies of dreams and shouts and stapled them together with our socks and mailed them to Harvard, and other subscribers who wanted it personal and sweaty, right off the press. The bribe and the boot get things done; it's even more true now than it was in the '50s and '60s. I nailed the words of Lee Wallek, the eminent literary critic, who had a great influence on our social concerns, nailed them right over

158

the press, in gilt and plastic: "Money is good, more money is better." Money represented frozen force, the persuader and terrifier, and it alone got things done. Oh the quacking poets who never knew that! What skid row, what straightjacket are they in now? I thought Woessner and Bertolino, and all those *Beloit Poesy Journal* bards, all those regional poets and corny voodoo dancers (Robert Blah from Minnesota for one) would just go croaking and croak. I thought they didn't know. Too many survived, times are not tough enough; I regret even publishing their modified lines. And the stock market is too strong, the dollar too sound yet, since I believe *The Smith* still pollutes the mail—may they raise the rates, double, triple them! And oh lord Hyperion and Paul Foreskin still darken the land; and every English department itches to have the forests decimated for pentameters yet unaborted.

Well, moving along the cafeteria of memory, not every tray is full of barf: Steve Kowit is a Pacific lighthouse, with his Gorilla Press, and Brent Northup peers through the fogs of Seattle, he and Susan in Bellevue, Wash. San Francisco? I don't know about it, haven't stopped in since Janis Joplin wrote me her lyrics at the Blue Onion and tried to tickle my nethers with her horny hand— they were always either sucking their thumbs there or sitting on them, or both alternately, until the Beats arrived, and maybe it's gone back that way. Who hasn't City Lights bookstore ripped off? Shortest list in the world. In the '60s, despite loping Len Fulton and his aptly named dust books and his inaccurate lists of publications which had a little life of its own, despite the Beats, and despite New York, the Midwest was the hotspot and goodspot of literature. And I appreciated it, though lord where did it go: Nobel Prize deserver Curt Johnson, the Cleveland gang, and Madison-Minneapolis forming a little geographical peanut that I am not claiming superior to any other, just a very active, alive, inquiring, self-aware, and fun place to be, which some people were trying to make into a revolutionary enclave, some into a Parnassus or Passaic of Poetry, and some, most, just jiving and thriving in, sleeping and partying around and typing it up.

It was young and it was fun, we were heady with tear gas, and we had clear consciences and the power of battalions, and a cause and some loves. The enemy reeled before it counterattacked. And I hope I made this clear, the earth shifted slightly to accommodate us, and that wasn't enough, we were going to dig clear to China, and grow rice on the mountains.

Remember those crazy days, those poems ending: ". . . the next sound you hear will be gunfire . . ."; ". . . eat this poem, and you will never die . . .";". . . the rotten teacher with his pus-filled mind must go, go burn Viet Nam . . ."; ". . . stuff my nose with onions, close my eyes with silver, stop my mouth with garlic, and tell me lies about Viet Nam . . ."; ". . . you can have your fuckin' city back . . ."; ". . . here in the vortex of Wichita . . .".

Well, they finished the Berlin Wall while I watched; and our unit transferred to Viet Nam—maybe you read of the 54th Transportation Battalion—and I went back to civilian life in Boston when Kennedy, the first one, was shot, then to Wisconsin when the anti-war protests started. On the vast tableaus of the steady erosion of the System, the little magazines, even our own efforts, were more

159

effects than causes, but enough of the latter to make it fun. We all profited from our efforts, if we stayed alive, or came back from the grave. Ed Sanders got a best-selling novel out of it (*Tales of Beatnik Glory*), and Ginsberg his professorship in Boulder, CO. My old buddy Tuli Kupferberg, who lent a hand on many an issue of our mag and did the songs for The Fugs, moved right up the ladder of success to a prestigious apartment address on Prince Street in Manhattan. Paul Foreskin in Austin parlayed his nodding acquaintance with literacy and littles into some kind of position with an arts council there. Pat McGilligan, whose little book, *I Aim for the Stars*, formed one of our 1970 issues, became editor of *Playgirl* on the strength of his publication in the littles—who says the money is not there? It all depends on what one knows one is worth.

For myself, publishing corporate brochures, I think, still allows me to fulfill my literary and social interests, as well as earn a five-figure salary. The annual report for example, this year, clearly and damningly shows oil pollution just beneath the rig in the middle of the Gulf. You don't have to point things out— people are smart enough; an oil slick is worth a thousand slogans. Our company newsletter routinely rattles our top corporate brass; our device of misspelling their names is as keen a piece of sabotage as I ever devised when I was trying to bring the war home and dump a mortar shell on the Badger Ammunition factory. And what about the stock option the company allows us? Rotten capitalism? Not a bit: with a ten-share sale, you can make a run on the Board and get a little panic reduction of Gulf net worth: that's where they live, those greedy top brass, that hurts the enemy, don't you know?

Let's get this clear: little magazine publishing should have taught anyone in it who the friend (one who gives you money) and who the enemy (one who demands money, energy, health etc. from you) may be. That's what the clarity demands of the '60s were about and that we won: a little less muddle, if you please, know yourself and know your pocketbook from a hole in the ground. And then a way out of the conflict between "wait your turn" and "we want it now"—"you've got it now, and it's going to get more." Pair of dice now, that's where we're at, and the little mags that were good showed us that; my time with the Multi explored that truth. Thank god I learned that quick enough to leave it all behind: we shot at noon, stripped in the evening and burned at night, to print all that anger and prophetic demands: now my tender corporation, stretching its quivering neck over the blade of collapse, meekly waits my foot to render it dead. Midwife at its failing, I am well-fed and kept; it's almost as much fun as being a young editor again. Excuse me, I have to get these magazine packages franked in the company mailroom before the security guard comes to fetch them in the company truck. This is a generous corporation—it supports public television, both sides of the revolution in Nicaragua, and quite a few ecology and health activist nuts: I am sure it would be glad to support my literary magazine, if it knew, but I think it even more virtuous of it to support those good activities which it does not even suspect the existence of. Lord I love an unknowing giver! Those picky endowments can go get ants in their grants.

(1.00)

ex-MAYOR

(cover art: SOGLIN AT FIFTY by George)

Merritt Clifton

Samisdat

Merritt Clifton

Merritt Clifton was born 9/18/1953, Oakland, California.

Education: I was about two-and-a-half, in my highchair, when I happened to notice that the "Wh" on my old man's box of Wheaties and the "Wh" on my mother's Whirlpool washing machine were symbols for the same sound. This is my earliest clear memory. Within a few weeks, pestering my folks for help, I'd taught myself to read. Proceeded to get expelled from the Sonoma County Public School District at age eight, for being two grades ahead of age-level *after* repeating the 4th due to "immaturity." Completed the 5th in three months at a Seventh Day Adventist academy. Missed a full year. Returned to school in Berkeley, CA, 1963. Participated in first wave of Berkeley school desegregation, 1964. Flunked out of all heavy academic subjects but English & history; spent high school playing baseball, painting watercolors, hanging around street-corners, breaking into the newspaper racket as cub muckraker, & beating shit out of whoever crossed me. Entered San Jose State University (SJSU) in fall '70; got kicked out of journalism & English departments before writing my own special major in creative writing. Then got kicked out of 41 units of individual classes before graduating with distinction in '74. Got kicked out of theatre arts M.A. program later that fall. For source of real education, see Work Experience.

Family Obligations: hitched to the brilliant, beautiful, but reclusive P.J. Kemp—hitching ceremony, however, was strictly Big Brother's idea. No kids, 10 cats. Dwell on the Kemp family subsistence-level dairy farm, helping sling hay & so forth in trade for living & workspace. Extended family includes most living things (am uncertain whether bureaucrats are really "living"), & obligations toward them include vegetarianism, raising hell against war, pollution, & government, & otherwise practicing the gospel preached.

What I Do For A Living: haven't rightly figured that out yet. Edit & publish *Samisdat*. Write for innumerable litmags, alternative newspapers, etcetera. Survive, somehow, on the uncertain proceeds. Barter a lot. (& if I ain't got cash, the bastards can't tax it.)

Publications: somewhere over a thousand, but quit counting years ago. Founded *Samisdat* in '73. Contributing editor to *Small Press Review* since '75;

2 percent owner of *The Townships Sun*, local monthly alternative newspaper, since '78. Acting managing editor, Tau Delta Phi Press, 1972-77. Environmental/investigative correspondent to *The Sherbrooke Daily Record* since '78. Columnist, *The Book-Mart*, since '79. Columnist for other litmags including *The Pub, The Northwoods Journal, Stony Hills, Azimuth, & The Smudge Review*. Contributing editor, *Quester*, 1976-78. Editor in various capacities, *The Reed*, 1971-73, while at SJSU. Spent two years on editorial staff of *The Daily Jacket*, 1968-70, a small semi-pro newspaper published from Berkeley High School 1957-71; was briefly editor-in-chief, 1970, but fired three times in two months, the last time for a violent run-in with black militants who offered to dictate editorial policy. Books: novels *24×12 & A Baseball Classic*, novella *Betrayal*, non-fiction titles *On Small Press As Class Struggle, The SAMISDAT Method, The Pillory Poetics* (3 editions), *Relative Baseball, Le Ballast D'Amiante/The Asbestos Line*, fiction chapbook *Two From Armageddon*, sampler *Three Of A Kind*, poetry chapbooks *From The Golan Heights, Vindictment, & From An Age of Cars*.

Work Experience: my old man had this bright idea about getting rich in real estate, so hocked himself up to the eyeballs to buy a succession of rundown semi-slum to out-&-out ghetto apartment houses, in & around Oakland, CA. From age 11 on, my younger brother & I were his chief maintenance men, housepainting, laying carpet, collecting rent, & generally trying to keep the buildings intact while the tenants attempted urban renewal from the inside out. Earnings from this—20-60 hours a week, average wage 40¢-$1.00/hour—went toward college. For pocket change, hustled shopping carts, speculated in baseball cards, did odd jobs, sold newspapers; eventually became copyboy with *Oakland Tribune*, 1970. Subsequently worked as woodcutter, Alaskan pulpmill hand, firefighter, & stevedore for smugglers; I.D. card photographer; newsletter editor; stage carpenter; & by 1975 just woke up one day to realize I'd survived six months on nothing but writing/editing/publishing income.

Samisdat

"Head Fucking Bastard In Charge" proclaims my letterhead. Merritt Clifton is synonymous with *Samisdat*, & vice-versa; my magazine & chapbook series are the most cohesive outward expressions of whatever I am. Editing as I practice it is an art form in itself, using other artistic elements—essays, fiction, poetry, graphics—to produce a multi-dimensional whole greater than the sum of parts that usually can stand alone, but stand together to mutual advantage. I accept or reject material according to whether or not it fits into my own self-conception—if it's something I'd like to have written myself, it's in, & if not, it's out, regardless of any other standards. According to my current promotional flyer:

"*Samisdat* writing distinguishes itself through passion, purpose, and commitment. We live to encourage life, & to oppose whatever destroys life, on whatever pretext. We respect the laws of nature, not of government; the morals of practical consideration, not those of superstitious dictate."

This isn't just hype. It's my personal creed, a statement of ideals I strive to meet, & of beliefs reached through considerable hard knocks & soul-searching. Here is where I stand; *Samisdat* is my banner, manifesto, 40 acres and a mule.

I wasn't always this openly egotistical, though despite outward gestures to the contrary, *Samisdat* did spring like Athena, grown and armed, from my own head and no one else's. Originally, in 1973, I proclaimed myself only "editor-in-chief," delegating much more responsibility than I should have to various associates who I hoped would do much more work than they ever did. I didn't yet realize the essential individuality of a good little magazine, having always before worked on cooperatively run student publications that, like slow-pitch softball teams, gave everyone a chance & so thoroughly leveled out competition that talent—especially mine—got continually frustrated.

"Editor-in-chief" evolved into "Bastard" first. I had to be a bastard to get anything done. Letters from would-be contributors and comments from my "staff" soon changed a personality trait into a title, Resident Bastard, while my chief & only serious assistant in the early days, Tom Suddick, became Bastard Of Ceremonies. I became the official Head Bastard after contemplating words of advice Len Fulton sent in early '75: "I'm the final stop-and-go man here at *SPR*," he wrote, "and that's going to be the case until and unless some mighty big bastard comes along and shows me a better way." Resident Bastards tend to be viewed as temporary obstructions between a would-be contributor's ego and an unearned splash in my pages. As Resident Bastard, I received letters addressed to Publisher, demanding that I fire myself for conduct unbecoming an editor—like bouncing drivel, labeled "drivel." As Head Bastard, that stopped. The word "head" also reflected my own increasing intellectual awareness about what I was doing. The monster, already walking and talking, had begun to think as well. "In Charge" and "Fucking" have been added as promotions for work well done. However, I don't anticipate any further self-promotions, lest I become as encumbered with titles as a banana republic dictator, & as infatuated with my own past distinctions as opposed to present consciousness.

I began *Samisdat* because I'd become mightily pissed off. I'd had a lifelong dream of founding my own publishing empire, gradually tapered down by age 19 into a more precise & immediate intention of obtaining a press somehow, learning to use it, & developing my own readership, since nobody else cared to publish what I considered my most important work. I'd kicked the concept around over beer with various cohorts at SJSU. But, having no money and no actual knowledge of printing, I'd deferred ambition for several years—I'd otherwise been ready to start at age 16—while internal fires smoldered.

Since my violently hostile junior high school days, recounted in *24x12*, I'd suspected something powerfully wrong with the Almighty Way Things Are. Growing up in Berkeley, & having in fact been present when John Thompson & Doug Palmer commenced the poetry reading in 1964 that became the Free Speech Movement, I'd had a first-hand view of the leading "alternatives" offered during the late '60s, but the self-censorship, hypocrisy, sexism, & general tyranny-of-the-majority I saw among the radical left only mirrored the aspects of the Establishment I fought against.

165

And I fought, always, with every weapon at my disposal, leading a small vigilante band against rapists and muggers by night, writing advocate journalism on behalf of the environment, feminism, & press freedom by day, painting water-colors visually expressing my protest by dawn and twilight. Though a member of the Ecology Action wing of the SDS in 1969-70, and a highly active & visible Nixon re-election campaign volunteer for six months in 1972, I never actually *belonged* to any political faction. I helped block National Guard trucks and ex-pose police brutality at People's Park, 1969, while wearing such a close crewcut that some of the Guardsmen thought I was one of them, out of uniform. As a Nixonite, I had the longest hair and wildest beard I ever saw in any Republican headquarters, & spent many of my evenings writing anti-Vietnam War stories and poems.

Nothing fit. Feminist mags rejected me for being a man. Black militants hated my guts for being a guilt-free honky, son of a slumlord, though my father & I both grew up as dirt-poor and oppressed as any of them, & though I'd shared the ghetto dream of a jailbreak through professional baseball, only to be rail-roaded off one otherwise all-black team when seven of the eight other players refused to take the field with me. A powerful public speaker, with or without a microphone, I couldn't even manage a conversation with a girl. I knew I wrote fiction as well or better than any of the people published in the slicks, yet re-ceived only form rejections from slicks and litmags alike. I immersed myself in the Bible, searching for clues to why illogic and nonsense reigned, conceiving great admiration for Jesus H.—as opposed to Jesus "Christ"—without ever be-coming at all religious; the dude simply joined a pantheon of heroes already in-cluding Ted Williams, Muahmmad Ali, Henry David Thoreau, Ralph Waldo Emerson, Mark Twain, Jesse James, Thomas Paine, Abe Lincoln, & various others whose only common denominator was enough balls to keep right on roll-ing after their legs were chopped off.

The Nixon campaign experience, recounted in *Betrayal*, fired me most. I'd done everything the Horatio Alger way, I thought, & been burned. I'd honestly tried to work from within, by the book, plotting, conniving, & hustling with the best or worst of 'em, only to wind up with blood on my hands, the blood of dis-tant Vietnamese and of baseball teammates, who got drafted while I didn't. But jealousy burned as well: seeing Joyce Maynard, for instance, my own age but an Ivy Leaguer, almost effortlessly making the bigtime writing ideas not all that dif-ferent from my own—with the difference that I lived mine. The final incentive to founding my own mag came when, for the third year in a row, my fellow staffers on the SJSU litmag, *The Reed*, bounced what would have been my first published story, at the last possible minute, after it had already been scheduled for inclusion. That final spark ignited a whole keg of pent-up gunpowder. With-in 24 hours I'd hit the streets of Berkeley with a typewritten prospectus, selling $75 worth of advertising. Tom Suddick matched that $75 with his income tax refund. I kicked in another $75 I'd earned at odd jobs to complete our first *Samisdat* budget.

From the start, *Samisdat* operated according to several premises I've upheld ever since, unconventional but effective. First, we've never spent money on production for the sole sake of appearance. We've always used the cheapest production methods available to us; when we went to typesetting from typewritten format, it was because typesetting became available to us at a price enabling us to profit by resultant savings on paper and postage. When we began using photographs, it was because we obtained access to economical halftoning. The popular notion that appearance sells litmags is absolute bunk, as my three years of *Reed* experience made manifestly clear to me: the last issue published before I founded *Samisdat* received national honors for production quality, but lost over a thousand dollars, while an issue I produced in the *Samisdat* format, with the same contributors as the fancy issue, sold 487 copies in 10 days & cleared the profit that kept the mag alive. I knew I couldn't sustain *Samisdat* if it lost money. I knew my audience wouldn't be large, at least at first, & that it would consist mostly of starving writers & artists much like myself. Therefore, to achieve maximum sales, it would have to be priced at minimum cost, & cheap production became absolute necessity. I don't think any litmag has ever charged readers less per page of literature in the decade we've been operating.

Second, Suddick cintributed the principle of "ad-hocracy," or doing jobs as they required attention, publishing & mailing as material dictates rather than according to a set schedule. I didn't fully understand "ad-hocracy" at first, but essentially it's Zen, drawing form from events instead of attempting to impose preconceived form upon them. Each *Samisdat* has a central theme, for instance, yet I've never announced a thematic issue or specifically solicited contributions to fit with others already accepted. What I need, I know by now, will come in the mail when I need it. Editing well is just a matter of recognizing it when I see it. As a semi-pro ballplayer, I first acknowledged this principle in the relatively narrow art of hitting:

> Like films on stance & swing
> without the cage,
> like headfirst slides on paper,
> we are taught through theory.
>
> But fifteen hundred minor league at-bats,
> Williams says, are minimal.
> That's three years, at least.
> Theory?
> As Berra says, & even Williams admits,
> "You can't think & hit."
> Just know what you've done
> when you've done it.
> & if you don't, Williams adds,
> *you don't belong up here.*

I still send that poem with letters of advice to other aspiring editors. Those who understand it, invariably make good.

Principle Three was that we'd earn our own way. No handouts. I figured I could lose $1,000 on the first four issues. After that, each succeeding *Samisdat* would be published exclusively on proceeds of the last. To continue publishing on a losing basis would also mean publishing for inextant readership. I did take some very bad conventional advice at first, giving away about 1,500 copies of my first four issues to well-known writers, libraries, et cetera, in hopes of building reputation & circulation, but I gradually learned that my own initial stingy impulse was right: a litmag is valued only if sold, with the price in cash or equivalent value demanded for every copy. Since getting that through my skull, complimentary copies have gone only to contributing authors.

Principle Four is the personal touch. No forms. No delays in responding to submissions. No polite nothings. I've wiped my ass with photocopies manuscripts, sent razorblades with rejections in a couple of cases where authors played headgames with me after I'd published *Erratica* editor Don Dorrance's last work before he killed himself, & nobody's more ferocious in response to formula hackwork. But by the same token, no author submitting here has ever received less than a prompt, honest verdict if SASE accompanied the manuscript, & whenever I can lend a hand in any way, whether with criticism or a steer to another mag or personal advice, I've done it. I view my mailbox as my bedroom/office, submissions as visits. One doesn't respond to human beings with forms. It's simple as that—& while I probably get more hate mail than anyone else in the racket, I get more sample orders & subscriptions from appreciative authors as well.

I did not, however, have the least idea what I was doing in founding *Samisdat*. I made some intelligent guesses, based on past experience with *The Reed* & several newspapers, but my ignorance was nonetheless so profound that I actually pasted my headlines together from letters clipped out of slick magazines before learning, four issues later, that rub-off decal lettering existed. Though in the midst of the so-called small press movement, & already aware of many of the most significant litmags in it, I didn't recognize their kinship to my own activity. To a kid growing up in Berkeley during the '60s, the Beatniks looked a lot like the Establishment. Underground newspapers such as *The Berkeley Barb* & litmags I'd read including James Cooney's *Phoenix* & Curt Johnson's *December* all impressed me as institutions. Discovering Len Fulton's 1973 *International Directory Of Little Magazines & Small Presses* while placing a consignment at Moe's Books on Telegraph Avenue opened up a whole new worldview to me. Heated correspondence with Norm Moser also helped: I rarely understood a word that he said, & much of it was gibberish, but he also became the first editor other than myself to publish my fiction, the first editor of any experience to pass along advice & encouragement.

While slowly, painfully losing my thousand dollars that summer, publishing an 80-plus page monthly, I gradually realized that to continue successfully I'd have to study a segment of literary history not taught in SJSU classes—publishing history, without which, I found, the rest is incomplete. I reluctantly suspended my own publishing activities in September, 1973, with a premature announcement of bankrupt termination. Meanwhile I read every litmag I could find in the SJSU & Berkeley Public libraries, cover to cover, making notes on contributors, formats, duration of existence—anything that seemed significant. I learned that most litmags were always in financial trouble. I learned that for the most part I'd been doing all right, even if I had sold only six full subscriptions & received only two renewals (Gabriele Rico & Stella Zamvil, two beautiful women). When poet Jayne Beilke sent me $37 she'd saved toward helping us out, & when it arrived along with a job as an I.D. card photographer on the same day, my 20th birthday, I felt impelled to begin again. Same format. Same contributor base, primarily SJSU students, creative writing classmates, whose best efforts Suddick & I shanghaied. But new self-confidence, new perspective, and new immediate objectives.

Originally, Suddick & I expected to make ourselves famous, influential; to gain clout in the New York literary establishment without having to go east & kiss asses. Now I realized it wouldn't happen. What's more, I didn't care any longer—not a lot, anyhow. Joyce Maynard could have her wealth & fame. I'd devoted myself to working toward changing the Almighty Way Things Are from the bottom up, the only way that can ever be lastingly successful, showing others what's wrong with it & then, as important, setting a personal example of what to do about it. How to "Live Free Or Die" instead of suffering zombie-hood working for the man.

As usual, my attitudes seemed wildly self-contradictory to those around me, including fellow small press people. *The Barb* gave us two big write-ups within two months; the first, high praise, interpreted me as I viewed myself, as a non-libertine libertarian, yet somehow missed the underlying point of *Samisdat* completely. The second thoroughly slammed & damned us, for adopting outer camouflage hiding our point. Reviewer J. Edgar Poet—actually John Thompson, I believe—thereby helped much more than he realized or probably intended. I understood at last that my contradictions reflected not confusion over ideals but rather over labels; that in order to publish a magazine fairly representing myself, I'd have to separate it from any identification with existing political/social/academic terminology. In short, I'd have to evolve my own philosophy, and express it clearly; I couldn't borrow anyone else's.

Certainly not COSMEP's. My first contact with COSMEP came after Tom Suddick & I rejected Norm Moser's infamous novella—the same one almost everyone's rejected—& he responded by threatening to have COSMEP blacklist us. In addition, he claimed COSMEP director Paul Foreman would soon visit to kick my ass. Foreman arrived about half an hour after Moser's letter. He didn't offer to kick my ass (& besides, I'm bigger, though he's no midget). But he did talk to me like a union shop steward, issuing a join-or-else ultimatum. I bucked Teamsters & Operating Engineers under similar circumstances—I'll join a union if someone sells me on the concept, but not because some goon says "Or else." I was damned if I'd take that crap off fellow writer/editor/publishers. As a newcomer, I was naturally paranoid about COSMEP's power to blacklist, & as already mentioned, much of the small press looked like the establishment from my Berkeley perspective. When Richard Morris repeated Foreman's line to me, without denying Moser's, I counterattacked, accusing COSMEP in my next issue of attempting to form an alternative New York Litmob, of mirroring the system it purportedly opposes. That criticism still goes, though I realize by now that even if they wanted to, neither COSMEP nor the alleged Litmob could effectively blacklist anybody.

First contacts with individual small press people were equally disappointing. For about two years, until I firmly established my Head Bastard identity, I found my exchange/review copies were almost always greeted with gushing praise, accompanied by ill-written, inappropriate manuscript submissions. After I bounced the manuscripts, the praise curdled into condemnation. Most small press people, I realized, are in it from desperation. Like many writers, little magazine editors view alternative publishing as a means to an end, not an end in itself. Becoming an editor is a means of gaining political leverage, toward advancing up some ladder. The ladder is really more like a squirrel-cage, however, since the harder they climb, the farther away success seems to be, until they finally collapse of exhaustion. Then, like any tired rodents, they're apt to bite the hands that feed them. Observing this helped overcome my own ambitions toward status-seeking—helped me bend the wires and escape a prison of unrealistic expectations. When I asked myself *why* I might want wealth and power, it was always because I wanted to change the Almighty Way Things Are. But following Establishment rules for doing it could only strengthen the Establishment's hold on others' imagination. Better to start changing what I could, where I was.

Meanwhile, I've never quite forgotten the alternately hostile and exploitative attitude I encountered as a newcomer. In my first two years, only the late Dale Donaldson of *Moonbroth* offered practical business advice, suggesting the per-page pricing system we've used ever since. Only fellow newcomer Kurt Nimmo, later of *The Smudge*, and Fred Merkel of Garage #3 Press, extended technical help. Only Len Fulton and Ellen Ferber of Dustbooks, among the known and established, welcomed us as peers, however inexperienced. (And Curt Johnson sent exchange/review copies in response to ours, without comment, but taken as friendly acknowledgment because many others took our copies, sent their manuscripts our way, & never did send us their magazines.) Remembering how much a friendly hand could have meant to me then, I've always gone out of my way to help & encourage other newcomers. This was the initial idea behind *The Samisdat Method: A Do-It-Yourself Guide To Offset Printing*, priced close to cost ($2), but a money-maker now simply because it's in constant demand. All told, we've probably helped 25-30 other litmags and presses get started, of which about two-thirds are still operating. *The Samisdat Method* has helped another few hundred strangers into the business.

I graduated from SJSU in June, 1974, and like most college graduates, anticipated that I'd soon find a regular 9-5 career. *Samisdat* I'd continue in my free time. Fortunately, none of the newspapers to whom I sent my resume needed help right about then. Equally fortunately, a Class A minor league baseball team called the Portland Mavericks needed pitching, and had heard I could throw blue smoke. If I didn't succeed there, my younger brother claimed he could get me well-paid muscle work at a pulp mill in Ketchikan, Alaska. This led to the series of misadventures recounted in *A Baseball Classic*.

170

I packed *Samisdat* into a typewriter case and a knapsack, heading north. Washed out of baseball after throwing three innings of no-hit relief but walking and letting score the winning run in my only exhibition game. Nearly starved in Alaska, got sick from the muskeg water, caught on at the mill but hated it, & returned to California at the end of the summer determined to make it somehow as independent, self-employed writer/editor/publisher, damned if I'd ever work for the man again. I'd gone through SJSU on a total monthly budget of just under $100, including books, tuition, food, clothing, shelter, and entertainment (the odd six-pack). Between *Samisdat* and freelancing, I now earned enough to spend $125 a month. I also managed to save enough to acquire my first printing press, an ancient Davidson 241 Dual, designed to print one side of each sheet by offset and the other side, simultaneously, by letterpress. The letterpress unit was missing, also one of the two ink-form rollers, but I didn't let that daunt me. My father & I reassembled the press from buckets of parts in his basement, strictly by the seats of our pants. Within a month we had it working.

By this time we'd already gone heavily into book-publishing, the natural and inevitable complement to putting out a litmag. Maine poet H.R. Coursen, our first non-San Jose or Berkeley contributor, suggested this first in late '73. He offered to buy half the press run, enough to insure our breaking even, if we published his chapbook *Lookout Point*. The manuscript impressed me, we couldn't lose, & so we did it, coordinating publication with a two-day writing festival we organized at SJSU in early '74. *Lookout Point* somehow or other became runner-up for the '74 National Book Award. We began producing other poetry chapbooks on the same basis. Suddick meanwhile was expanding the Vietnam war story that had led off the first *Samisdat* issue into a short novel, *A Few Good Men*, actually a group of eight interrelated stories based upon his own wartime experience. He put up a third of the cost of publishing it—the cost of binding—& I kicked in the rest. Little noticed then, it's sold some 30,000 copies as an Avon mass-market paperback since '78, and is still in print.

The press permitted even more book-and-chapbook publishing; we've issued a book, chapbook or regular magazine issue every three weeks, on the average, ever since. I soon discovered a good reason to be prolific—the backlist. It's easier to promote books one title at a time. Because we're so prolific, almost every book we've ever done has been badly underpromoted, including my own most especially. On the other hand, book orders don't start trickling in until after the book has a reputation. This means a gap of from six to nine months, in most cases, between sending out advance copies and making a buck. With a short list, that's a good way to starve. Publishing a lot of books, on the other hand, means that somebody's always ordering something. I've also learned that requiring authors to put up the cost of paper and printing supplies, modest though the investment is, usually insures their best promotional efforts. They have to make their money back. They also get to keep 100 percent of whatever they get for their half of each press run. This kind of incentive encourages them to do the hustling most authors consider beneath their status.

Learning something about the business end of publishing gives the authors a more realistic set of expectations, while having a lot of them out promoting themselves is a bit like having a sales staff for *Samisdat* as a whole. Many of our authors today are repeat customers. Of course some newcomers, full of Hollywood mythology, will exclaim that if our authors are furnishing cash for materials, and if we ourselves aren't doing much vigorous promotion (though we do set up many reprint opportunities), we're running a vanity press. This overlooks three significant points. First, we do always distribute half the initial press run. In order to eat, we have to sell enough subscriptions to unload most of those books. We can't just stuff them in a closet and say we've distributed them, as I've seen some other publishers do. (I suspect that among poets there are more undistributed chapbooks in closets than either queens or skeletons, by a 1,000-to-1 ratio.) Third, any author who's ever dealt with me knows that I am, indeed, the Head Fucking Bastard In Charge, the last editor who'd ever compromise personal standards.

Then there's the most underappreciated point, among those who have never run a printing press: it's hard, dirty work, especially when using junkshop equipment & do-it-yourself methods. Anyone who does his or her own printing—assuming it does get done—isn't pulling a hustle. Simple counterfeiting would be little more difficult. Which brings up another of my many realizations, shattering previous illusion. In June, 1975, I published my own first novel. I'd always imagined that first novels debuted, if not to major reviews, then at least to celebration and acknowledgment; that the event brought a thrill. My first novel brought instead just a 60-hour sleepless marathon, including 18 hours at the often malfunctioning Davidson Dual. I didn't get any special charge out of it until Mudborn Press brought out the deluxe second printing over five years later. By then I'd learned that alternative publishing is *always* tough, grubby, pissing in the wind. One can't ever do it for any reward beyond simply getting the message out to the few people one can get to listen. Anything else that happens is luck, a special treat, a happy accident.

1973-74 were *Samisdat*'s start-up years; 1975-77 a period of transition leading up to our present activities in Richford, Vermont, and Brigham, Quebec. Our initial attitude of skeptical dissent evolved into a coherent philosophy during this time, & the philosophy became a lifestyle. Tom Suddick & the other San Jose writers who dominated the early issues drifted out of contact, though Tom returned as an active contributing editor 1979-80 and still assists with special projects. We acquired equipment, learned to use it, & traded up toward our present array—a Multilith 85 offset press, Gestetner 300 hand-cranked mimeo for backup, an IBM Executive "C" typesetting typewriter, and a contact-frame used for plate-burning and exposing negatives. W.D. Ehrhart, Mark Phillips, Tobias Grether, Jesus Bill Robinson, Lorna Dee Cervantes, Jo Schaper, & most especially P.J. Kemp all arrived within a six-month period, contributing manuscripts, muscle, inspiration, & philosophical influences. rjs, Scott Mace, & Stella Popowski formed a second wave about 12-18 months later.

Ehrhart was the second Vietnam veteran to become a *Samisdat* regular, Suddick having been the first. We'd published other Namvets in between, without ever making much of it, unaware that they'd been defacto blacklisted virtually everywhere else. Perhaps it was because most of the COSMEP litmaggers had

172

been anti-war activists, who regarded the vets as monsters. Perhaps editors, like the rest of America, just didn't want to be reminded. Whatever the reason, Ehrhart was first to tell us about the difficulty he & other literate vets faced in finding publication—even though (or maybe because?) they were mostly working like hell to keep us out of similar disasters already developing in Latin America. With Ehrhart's help, we went on to publish more Namvets during the next few years than any other magazine large or small, until the blacklist was broken and the war once again discussed in public. Some of them, Ehrhart included, have risen to national prominence. They've helped our own recognition rise with theirs.

Phillips, through his short stories, correspondence, and bullshit over beer, helped clarify the essential link we felt between what factory-work does to people and what supposedly enlightened, civilized people do to the environment. He participated in Woodstock while I was at People's Park. He shoveled slag for Niagara Mohawk while I did the same for the Ketchikan Pulp Company's wood-burning powerhouse. He got kicked out of classes in Buffalo while I got kicked out in San Jose. He also watched his father die of a job-related cancer while I founded *Samisdat*, turning his thoughts inward while mine moved outward. He hasn't yet become a fluent essayist in his own right, but I've borrowed and enlarged upon many of his ideas. He also personally helped move us across the continent in April, 1977, by appearing twice in times of crisis with the hand we needed. His odyssey from muscle-work through academia to homesteading in the Adirondacks more or less typifies that of many *Samisdat* people, perhaps including ourselves.

Tobias Grether, a Swiss-American inventor and philosopher, taught me to think clearly, consistently. More than any other individual, he helped me structure the *Samisdat* philosophy into something more than just a collection of beliefs—into something one can live by, conscientiously, without either oppressing others or compromising oneself. After 20 years of struggle, on his own, Grether hired me to ghostwrite *Homochronos*, a privately published opus describing evolution as a process of expanding time-consciousness. The higher the life-form, he argues, the greater the awareness of past and future. The more intense this awareness becomes, the more intensely we use our intelligence. Human progress comes about through imagining and acting toward an ever more distant, yet also more concretely visualized future. We developed technology to bring tomorrow closer; now we study ecology toward accomplishing what lies beyond technological grasp. Increasing time-consciousness is also the central activity involved in individual growth, from infancy to mature adulthood, a stage relatively few ever reach. As infants, we employ only the "force-cycle" of thinking and acting, responding physically to immediate stimuli. Very soon we come to use the "faith-cycle" as well, connecting actions into sequences that may or may not be cause-and-effect. Because we do such-and-such, we expect so-and-so to happen; if it doesn't, we repeat such-and-such, perhaps with added rituals, rather than admit error and change expectation. Finally we discover the "reason cycle," where, desiring a certain result, we work backward to find out what, if anything, might accomplish it. The reason cycle can only be used in relation to material

173

objects, where all the variables can be discovered. The trick to maturity is knowing when and how to use each particular mode of thinking to best effect. Perspective in time provides the key.

I had already been at work on the essays that became *The Pillory Poetics* for over a year when I met Grether. I had already noticed that both "modern," image-centered poetry and traditional, verse-form poetry tend to focus on *how* something is said rather than upon the message itself: why and what. I had also realized that so-called internal criticism—the "New Criticism" of the 1930s—tends to encourage devoted study of nonsense, the interminable series of scholarly papers on James Juice being Exhibit A. But until Grether presented me with both the notion of time-consciousness and his means of distinguishing products of acting in one thought cycle from those of another, I hadn't been able to find a definition of poetry, or the short story, or the novel, that could accurately explain what each genre is without falling back on often contradictory elements of form. Suddenly I understood that literary genre are different means of capturing time, and that the distinctions between them are the distinctions between time-units. A poem is an instantaneous realization. It may *remember* events taking any amount of time, but the memory bursts forth all at once into the new context. A story, on the other hand, traces the evolution of a significant realization through a period ranging from about an hour to under five minutes. A novel searches for the realization, and may move through years or even decades. The easy way to figure out what any given piece of writing is, or should be, is to consider how much stage-time it would occupy if performed as a play. Try putting any poem through a performance, without acting out past events and without expanding the script. It can't be done. The essence of each poem is internal. But any good short story will make an excellent, if brief one-act play (speaking internal monologues aloud), and good novels can always make good full-length plays or motion-pictures, budget allowing. (Unfortunately, producers rarely do have the budget to accurately reproduce everything a novelist imagines, which is why screenplays so often fall short.)

But *The Pillory Poetics*, a literary philosophy, was just the beginning of Grether's influence here. The ideas in *Homochronos* are also a powerful argument for personal liberty, for live-and-let-live, for self-governing free enterprise, for honest and responsible individual conduct, for unenforced social cooperation. Every individual, Grether deduced, always acts as best he or she can in the present to achieve a more desirable future than might otherwise be expected. Each of course has a different vision of "desirable," the motivating factor behind trade. Evil is simply what happens when some compel others to seek a future they don't personally choose. The compelled people either fight back, producing war, or submit, limiting their imagination, obeying stupid orders because they won't have to answer for the consequences. At present, and throughout history, most people have spent most of their lives obeying the stupid orders of priests, politicians, soldiers, and bosses. The argument that we need priests, politicians, soldiers, and bosses to keep us from all raping, robbing, and killing one another fails because most of us do these things only under orders, direct or implied, suggesting that the victims deserve it for being female, the enemy,

174

or both; and because if we really were all booodthirsty rapacious Yahoos, the great majority of us could never be controlled by the relative few who make the rules. Always non-violent anarchists by personal inclination (though able and unafraid to use violence, as in apprehending those doing others harm), we now could explain exactly what we aim to replace the System with, when once we persuade others to abandon it: nothing. We don't need no steenking badges to be decent, productive citizens. *Freedom Comes From Human Beings* supplies examples, and every *Samisdat* story, poem, or work of art suggests the possibilities.

Jesus Bill Robinson, like Grether, is an entrepreneur who lives by this creed. He told me once that my version of his biography was "like a Commie rewriting history," but since I took every word of it from his own letters, I'll recite it again anyway. His old man was a tent-circuit evangelist. At age 18, when Jesus Bill got polio, his old man threw him out into a snowbank & conducted a three-day revival meeting to expel the devil from him. Jesus Bill finally hitchhiked to a hospital on his own. When he returned home, with a permanent limp, his old man knocked him off his crutches for reading sinful literature. Bill hit the road again. During the 1950s he learned to fly planes with the U.S. Air Force, then flew for Hughes Air West. In the '60s he ran a Cadillac agency, before bullshitting his way into an engineering job with Honda-America. By the early '70s he'd organized a militant consumer group, the Honda 4-Cylinder Owners' Association, bitterly attacking his former bosses over built-in, calculated-risk safety defects. For kicks and extra cash he made biker movies with Jane Fonda. Somehow he acquired a weekly newspaper with offices on either side of the U.S./Mexican border, near Jacumba, California. He took his usual bull-in-a-china-shop approach to journalism, the Mexican government tried to close him down, & he took his revenge by springing various Americans from Mexican jails.

At some point amid all this, he pursued an investigative scoop by riding in a B-25 full of dope. U.S. Border Patrol planes began a hot pursuit. The pilot panicked and tried to knife Bill to get rid of witnesses. Bill shot him dead, crash-landed the B-25 in the desert, and somehow got clean away. Resettled in Ocotillo, TX, he got into book-publishing, took over a Texas-born atheist newsletter called *Quester*, & hired me on as contributing editor. During 1976-78, we exposed & ridiculed the rising fundamentalist tide together, figured out how to build our own exposure and plate-making units, & lent each other lots of moral support through all manner of personal, financial, and legal crisis. The John Birch Society finally chased Bill from Ocotillo to Arizona—& a few days after he moved, a hurricane completely flattened the town. Wrath of God!

Jesus Bill's most visible contribution to *Samisdat* was typesetting the first three issues we ever had typeset, but his most significant contribution is intangible—a strengthened spirit of maverick resistance to the Almighty Way Things Are. Jesus Bill is now roaming the Pacific Northwest. I consider him a traveling nose-thumbing ambassador.

Lorna Dee Cervantes, now editing *Mango*, was the first of several apprentices we've had, volunteering her help by way of learning how to assemble and print books & litmags. We'd known each other on sight for several years before she finally worked up the nerve to introduce herself. Unable to afford a subscription, she'd shoplifted *Samisdat* in stores at first, then read it in libraries, & although she didn't actually get involved directly until mid-'76, I count her among the few who have been part of our whole evolution. With Fred Merkel and Jesus Bill, she helped us dope out do-it-yourself printing. She introduced us to Indian & Chicano culture. We in turn printed her first *Mango* on the *Samisdat* press, trading her the paper in exchange for her help in moving the press from Berkeley to San Jose. Later we loaned her the money to buy her own first press. She meanwhile brought us into the Willard Street Cooperative—a courtyard full of shacks originally built to house farmworkers, back when San Jose consisted of orchards. P.J., then an illegal alien, was safe there, among others. The Hell's Angels served the district in lieu of police, & weren't bad neighbors. Fellow Cooperative members included novelist James Brown & artist/poet Adrian Rocha, both of whom became *Samisdat* regulars. Our seven months together became a successful experiment in semi-communal anarchism. We remember Lorna's personal struggle to overcome racism, poverty, and political oppression every time we raise hell on behalf of the Akwesasne Mohawks, or Central & South American peons.

Jesus Bill always had one annual deadline, he used to claim: he got all his work done by May, his wife since 1952. Since late March, 1976, I've been able to respond that I get much of mine done by June, short for Pamela June (P.J.) Kemp. P.J. wasn't the first bright young woman lured to my doorstep by scintillating correspondence, but she was the first to stick around long enough to become inkstained inside & out, to be blamed for corrupting *Samisdat* by disgruntled would-be contributors, and to have a significant, lasting influence on our operations. During the final year of my ghostwriting contract with Grether, and especially through the frantic push to meet deadline, P.J. did virtually all the *Samisdat* production work, much of the editorial screening, and about half the reviewing of publications received. She intuitively deduced, from knowledge of photography, the do-it-yourself exposure-and-plateburning system Merkel and Jesus Bill later perfected for us. Coming from a subsistence dairy farm in green, wet Quebec, where the seasons are as pronounced as the year-round desert shadows in San Jose, P.J. hated California. She also recognized that economic survival would become increasingly difficult amid a booming city, while her mother and brother would face equally mounting difficulty maintaining the farm without extra muscle for haymaking. She therefore worked out the tradeoff forming our present economic basis. *Samisdat* shares the family homestead, contributing to the grocery kitty. We help with haymaking and miscellaneous other chores instead of paying rent. Between her brother's milk herd and the garden P.J. helps her mother maintain, we're actually 90 percent food self-sufficient.

Since we moved to Quebec in April, 1977, P.J.'s direct contributions to *Samisdat* have been somewhat less prominent than during her defacto editorship—numerous stories and poems, some published under pseudonyms, some reviewing 1977-78, and some service as first reader of fiction submissions. But I count our evolution in perspective during the past five years as an indirect contribution whose weight cannot be measured. Living on the land, we have become concerned with it, emotionally as well as intellectually. Living in a "foreign" country, though just half an hour's drive from our Richford, Vermont, post office box, we have come to appreciate the difference between how Americans view themselves and how others view America. More precisely, we now appreciate the ever more obvious contradiction between the "American" ideals as expressed in the Declaration of Independence and Bill of Rights, and official U.S. government policy. Like Thomas Paine, who saw it happening 200 years earlier, we consider ourselves patriots in exile, while politicians and bureaucrats profane the words expressing our most sacred beliefs. We are also more acutely aware of what Paine and others achieved, since Quebec as yet has no effective Bill of Rights: freedom of speech, press, religion, and movement are all customs here, unprotected by law should Big Brother wish to end them.

In 1978 P.J. launched her own publishing series, perpetual motion machine. Her alternative science magazine, *Fourth Dimension*, published four critically successful issues 1979-80, and now appears as an irregular inclusion in the *Samisdat* series, though still under the perpetual motion machine imprint. *Fourth Dimension* might most accurately be described as the non-fiction discussion of ideas *Samisdat* itself advances in fiction, poetry, and the "Pillory" essays.

As retiring as P.J. generally is, rjs makes her look like a raving extrovert. Steve Sneyd introduced us shortly after *Samisdat* arrived in Quebec, but we'd been receiving his Ground Zero publications and cryptic notes for over a year before we learned what the "rjs" initials stand for, by which time what rj himself stands for seemed vastly more important. He began his alternative publishing career as the columnist Captain Zero in the late d.a. levy's *3rd Class Buddhist Junkmail Oracle*, an uncommonly perceptive underground newspaper issued from downtown Cleveland 1966-68.

levy himself was a slightly-built ex-sailor, who circa 1960 noticed Lake Erie pollution while sitting on the docks between unsuccessful attempts to find work. He began writing poems about it, influenced by the Beats. From desperation, he hawked the poems to strangers on the street. After he obtained and repaired a junked mimeograph machine, he began publishing poems of others as well, becoming an increasingly effective voice against not only the impending death of the lake, but also against the Vietnam War and the cultural attitudes producing both. In short, levy became politically dangerous. One evening in 1966, he mimeographed several poems by teenagers in a church basement, by permission of the minister, and read them aloud. They contained four-letter words. One of the teenagers tipped off the police, who arrested levy for pandering pornography and contributing to the delinquency of minors. After levy explained to the court that he supported himself and his 17-year-old wife on the 87¢ a day his poetry earned him, judge Frank Celebrezze remarked, "Bail of $2,000 isn't too much for a great poet," sending him to jail. This is the same judge Celebrezze who later dealt institutional authority a landmark blow by striking down Ohio's mandatory public schooling law; one wonders if the levy case haunts him. At any rate, the injustice done levy was so apparent that a prominent New York physicist posted the bail, from sheer disgust, while even Cleveland's establishment newspapers howled protest. For the next two years, levy's most productive, he was repeatedly arrested and detained, often without charges, but was never convicted of any offense. His publishing assistants were rjs, Tom Kryss, and Al Horvath, among others. Just before Thanksgiving, 1968, he gave them his books, burned many of his manuscripts, ordered his wife to leave him, and finally, on Thanksgiving Day, shot himself with a .22 rifle.

rj, then 19, found the body. He carried on, with the others, for another decade before proclaiming his semi-retirement from publishing. Meanwhile he too had moved from the city into the country and begun growing most of his own food. He became the world's leading expert on restoring and repairing Multi-50-80-85 series presses. And he became an effective, if gloomy environmental crusader. For us, he established a direct link to levy, a spiritual ancestor (though still just 26 at his death); supplied technical advice and scarce replacement parts; and provided the final kick in the butt we needed to get off the grant dole.

We'd never philosophically believed in grants, but took $1,000 in 1974 and another $500 in 1975 because the Coordinating Council of Literary Magazines made it available, & like other young piglets we felt entitled to whatever stimulated our nostrils. Then we squealed long and loud when the grants quit coming, coinciding with our attacks on corruption within CCLM and the sponsoring National Endowment for the Arts. Our philosophical objections surfaced here. We never expected to get another grant, & continued filing applications pro-forma into 1977, just to stay on the CCLM mailing list. But when Diane Kruchkow & others decided to divvy the slop-bucket equally among all applicants late that year, we accepted another $931.36, spent mainly on contributor payments and editorial attacks on the grant system. "Hypocrisy!" shrilled many, whom we ignored, since they had their hooves in the trough themselves. But rj didn't, hadn't, & wouldn't. Moreover, he suggested that the best way to demonstrate our opposition would be to demonstrate conclusively to other alternative publishers that, available or not, they don't *need* grants. When the NEA offered us $1,000 in August, 1978, we remembered rj & felt nauseous until we'd returned it with a letter suggesting they shove it, sideways. Whereupon rj organized a promotional campaign that boosted our circulation 25 percent. Most of the subscribers, including Kryss, who pays for his with art & baseball cards, are still with us.

Of the others who joined us during our transitional years, Stella Popowski has contributed most obviously. A Polish-born artist, educated in France, she fled to Mexico with her mother after World War II, married a rich man to get into the U.S., 1968, divorced him, refused to take his money, and at age 62, knowing little English, set out to make her living as a Haight-Ashbury street-painter during the "Summer of Love." We've published her work during this period as a chapbook, *Purely Popowski*. Today she enjoys modest success in Newport Beach, mailing us thick portfolios of pen-and-inks clipped from her sketchbook once or twice a year. We probably have 500-600 unpublished Popowski drawings on hand, have already used perhaps 200, and expect she'll remain a regular well into the next century.

178

Scott Mace, now editing *Bug Tar*, and Jo Schaper, of Blue Pentacle Press, are more former apprentices who lent much time and muscle, & progress toward deserved distinction in their own right.

Samisdat began to feel rooted in Quebec and New England during 1979. During 1977-78, we were strangers here, but in late '78 I "inherited" 2 percent of a struggling alternative newspaper, *The Townships Sun*, when publisher Bob Dawson decided to give it away to people in Quebec's rural Anglophobe community who might be able to keep it going. *The Townships Sun*, circulation about 3,000, appears monthly, & is actually Quebec's third-largest English-language paper, based in Lennoxville. I'd written for it before, but now I began contributing investigative features every issue, focusing on the environment—acid rain, nukes, long-range high-voltage electrical transmission, river pollution, big businesses with bad attitudes, et cetera. Meanwhile, the Canadian Pacific Railroad laid asbestos waste as track-ballast on a route bisecting the Kemp back pasture. When P.J. brought me samples, I began investigating that as well, for Quebec's second-largest English-language paper, *The Sherbrooke Record*. In exposing the safety hazards of asbestos, I took on, simultaneously, Canada's single largest corporation, the Quebec government's plan to nationalize the asbestos industry as basis for an independent economy, General Dynamics, whose King Beaver Mine sold the asbestos to CPR, and the various branches of the Canadian government who stood idly by while all this was happening. Five government investigations and much national radio and television exposure later, the fight's still going on. Then-*Record* editor James Duff was sufficiently impressed to hire me on as a more-or-less fulltime environmental/investigative correspondent. I take my payment primarily in typesetting and offset camera services, time-consuming work I used to do myself. This frees my time for muckraking while enabling us to publish more material at less cost of subscribers.

The newspaper work entrenched us in Quebec—though on at least one occasion I've been face-to-face with a gun-toting clown who thought I belonged elsewhere. Meeting James Cooney of *The Phoenix*, Jack Powers of the now vanished Stone Soup Gallery in inner Boston, & Don Roger Martin's Randolph Gang established our New England connection. New Englanders have always been prominent in *Samisdat*: first Coursen, then Miriam Sagan, who sent her first-ever poetry submission here, made her print debut in our fifth issue, and had her first two chapbooks published here, 1975 & 1978. And the Payack brothers, and many more. But Cooney, Humphrey Olsen of *Snowy Egret*, and Henry Geiger of *Manas* are the old bucks who've been publishing to promote similar ideals since Hector was a pup (1938, 1922, & 1947, respectively), & visiting Cooney for the first time, in his 250-year-old farmhouse/printshop overlooking the old haunts of Ralph Waldo Emerson, Margaret Fuller, Henry David Thoreau, & Emily Dickinson, finally gave us some sense of belonging to a geographically local as well as philosophical tradition.

Swilling beer, swapping memories of resistance and Ted Williams, & listening to Hank Williams records with Powers about a year later added a connection to more recent New England intellectual history. Powers comes from Roxbury, son of an Irish prizefighter & a devout Roman Catholic mother, youngest of four sons who served, respectively, in the Army, Navy, and Air Force. He himself was to become either a Jesuit, a Marine, or both. Instead, when drafted in 1959, as a 19-year-old Jesuit seminarian, he declared himself homosexual when he couldn't qualify for conscientious objector status under the stringent religious grounds then required. After drifting to San Francisco, where he mingled among the Beats and wrote his own first poems, and after a stint as a newspaper reporter in New Hampshire, Powers returned to Boston and opened Stone Soup in 1963. For the next 17 years, the Stone Soup storefront was hub for activities including peace and anti-nuclear marches, alternative energy exhibits, urban farming projects, art shows, concerts, poetry readings, and all sorts of publishing. Urban redevelopment finally claimed the storefront, but Powers continues many of the Stone Soup activities from a nearby apartment, just two blocks from the Common, close to where Isaiah Thomas built the first American alternative publishing empire circa 1776. Stone Soup and *Samisdat* have combined energies for a small but invigorating group reading every year since 1979.

Martin made his reading debut at the last one. He's another longtime outlaw & local organizer, town sot & unofficial poet-laureate of Randolph, Vermont, whose residents and happenings he records as faithfully as the newspaper, with greater insight of course, and no fear of wrathful advertisers. Making contact in '79, he's been sending his own poems & actively scouting other local talent for us, helping some with printing and promotion, talking increasingly seriously of founding a litmag of his own. His most noteworthy discoveries so far are gentle environmentalist poet Cathy Young Czapla, & her husband John, whose homicidal illustrations are inspired in part by throwing scrap for Vermont Castings.

Evaluating everything we've done over the past decade, I have to believe our chief contribution to life, love, & literature is essentially the same as the contribution of the others acknowledged here: inspiring further intelligent & unflagging resistance to the no longer so Almighty Way Things Are. We have never reached a "mass" audience, & never will, because we don't address masses. Rather, we address conscientious, dissident individuals, who often feel alone until they somehow learn we're here, take courage, & carry on. If our example teaches anything, it is how to amplify one's voice not through volume of sound but instead through intensity of message. As Walter Cummins, a favorite *Samisdat* fictionist, wrote once, "One of the most important characteristics of your operation is the fact that somebody cares a great deal about the work published or rejected, & that other people share the concerns." And if there be one central theme to *Samisdat*, it is that we face no Apocalypse, nor any Second Coming or Judgment Day, only tests of individual strength of character we can meet: each of us is his or her own messiah.

The small press has changed considerably since we started, yet much of the change has come full-circle: from typewriter/offset & mimeographed litmags to slick book-mags produced on grant money back to typewriter/offset & mimeo. The significant change is internal. Today's small press people are no longer spoiled baby-boomers, for the most part. At least not those we're most in touch with. Rather, we're survivors & new-wave punks equally determined to make it

180

on their own, their own way. As inspiring as the old-timers are the Daniel Betz/ Peckerwood Bruner/Bruce Combs generation of upstarts, learning from our mistakes. While grant cutbacks suffocate the alternative publishers active just for ego-boost at others' expense, many more upstarts shall emerge. Like sagebrush, we bloom, wild & spiky, whenever a dry spiritual ecology needs regeneration. Big Brother tried to irrigate us out of existence, to turn us into tame lawn-grass, but we're back, the Indians, antelope, & buffalo soon to follow.

And then there's Robin Michelle Clifton, the *Samisdat* spiritual mentor who signs each "Pillory" essay, whose fearless reviews have been our most popular (and most hated) feature since our fifth issue, back in '74. Of her, I can only state, Our name is Legion, for we are many, adversary to every bastard who thinks he's God because he can command pigs to rush over a cliff without asking questions. We figure Jesus went on to much better things.

Sayeth the Lord, thy Head Fucking Bastard In Charge, amen.

A.D. Winans

Second Coming

A.D. Winans

A.D. Winans is a San Francisco-born (1936) poet and writer whose work has appeared in more than 300 literary and commercial magazines and anthologies. He is the author of seven books of poetry, most recently *The Reagan Psalms*. A former agent of the Office of Naval Intelligence and the Defense Investigative Service, he resigned to become a full-time small press publisher after he refused orders to destroy information which might be revealed re the Committee to Re-elect President Nixon during a background investigation of the President's brother, Donald.

A Literary Journal and Press

I first learned about the "small press" literary scene in the late 1950s when I read my first issue of *Beatitude* magazine, edited by the poet Bob Kaufman and William Margolis. It was a simple "mimeo" publication featuring some of the best "beat" writing of those days. My knowledge would be expanded in the 1960s when the movement seemed to flourish with both intensity and high-grade quality, not so much in general appearance, but in what was happening with the written word. I grew to identify with what was then called "meat" poetry and the magazines I enjoyed most were *Olé* by Doug Blazek and John Bennett's *Vagabond*. I was also impressed with *ARX*, a publication put out by a group of young kids in Austin, Texas; and then, of course, there was a magazine called *Hearse, Zahir, December, The Smith*, and a host of others which made those days exciting and alive.

Later, in the late '60s, I was hanging out at local bars with Poet/Publishers Kell Robertson (*Desperado*) and Ben Hiatt (*Grande Ronde Review*). It only seemed natural that my own magazine and press, Second Coming, would itself develop and get off the ground in December 1969. The first issue appeared in print, on the newsstands, in 1970.

183

It is not easy writing and publishing your own magazine, though I found it a lot easier at that age than I do at 45. Since I have had to also work for a living, at a variety of jobs, it meant that my own writing was always being short-changed at one level or another. I don't regret the sacrifice nor the efforts put into editing and publishing at all, although I do plan on publishing only the magazine in 1982 (no books scheduled for publication) and perhaps well into 1983.

At no time did I ever think of "little mag" publishing as a way of making a living. I knew that Len Fulton had virtually cornered the one market for small press publishing and that was indexing and maintaining records of books in print. This is a much-needed service in small press publishing, but far too boring a piece of work for me. Later the "how to" book publishers would come into the forefront of small press publishing and like Fulton would find a way of making a living from small press activity. This too was and is alien to me, but then poets are indeed "alien" creatures.

As I said, I have been publishing since 1969/1970. Second Coming recently published its 10th Volume (vol. 10, nos. 1 and 2) and its 11th volume is in the working stage. I occasionally fall behind on schedule, but a rush of energy here and there usually brings me up-to-date before too long. One of the problems is that I will not publish an issue until I have the work on hand that fits that particular issue. I do not run on quantity but quality and some of my "enemies" (young turks for the most part) can't seem to understand this.

The format of *Second Coming* has changed from an un-copyrighted print run of 300 copies to a copyrighted issue of 1,000 to 2,000 copies. I have published local, national, and internationally known and unknown poets and writers. We have presented quality art work, photography, fiction, plays, reviews and translations in both regular, special, and anthology type issues. The two best sellers were the special Charles Bukowski issue (1972) and the *California Poets Anthology* (1976). Bookstore sales have been marginal and personal subscriptions disappointing and sporadic at best. The main support has come from library sales and "word-of-mouth" followers who buy not only the magazine but the book line as well. The book line (26 to date) has carried the magazine along with grant support, but out-of-pocket expenses have always been a sizable contribution and hence the need for me to work at outside jobs.

In 1975 *Second Coming* became a non-profit, tax-exempt literary corporation. It made grant-seeking easier and assisted in making up a large portion of the deficit. I still give away over half the print-run to prisons, old-age homes, individuals, and other outlets interested in literature. I see no conflict in giving away copies of the magazine as "reading" distribution has always been a primary focus of *Second Coming* as opposed to "dollar" diplomacy.

My only editorial objective was and remains to this day to publish the best work available to *Second Coming*, within a framework of presenting a balanced (as much as possible) presentation of women, men, third world, prison, and even academic work.

My early publishing philosophy was perhaps tempered with awe and excitement; much of this excitement has left me; but enough still remains to make me keep going. An editor/publisher must change with the times and move in the direction of the new flow of energy around him/her. Volume 10 of *Second Coming* was entirely fiction and prose; Volume 11 is a special prison issue; Volume 12 will feature a huge anthology presenting the *Best of Second Coming*. When *Second Coming* begins to be predictable, then it will be time to cease publication or tuck itself away into a coma to rise again when and if the need is there.

The response to the magazine has been 90 percent favorable. Reviews have always run 9-1 in favor of what was being done and published. There was the usual "sour apples" complaints from poets who I have not published; lost friends angry that I did not understand and publish their work; but any literary magazine worth its weight must undergo this kind of criticism.

I really don't know what the most single significant aspect or editorial accomplishment is. I suspect the special Charles Bukowski issue is among the top three issues. The author himself claims it is the most definitive issue done on him. The worst seller, a special *New Zealand Anthology*, is a significant issue (in my opinion) as far as comparative literature is concerned. And, finally, Volume 10, nos. 1 and 2, should go down as a rather remarkable bringing together of some of the most outstanding and diverse writers alive today: Herb Gold, Ishmael Reed, Charles Bukowski, James Purdy, James Drought, Jack Micheline and others stirred into one melting pot.

I don't have any regrets for any issue I have put together, nor would I attempt to try and outline the least significant achievement. That would be much like rating one of your children against another and looking for flaws.

The "little" magazine scene when I started was filled with excitement and an "aliveness" hard to describe. The editors were mostly poets themselves and the magazines' styles often reflected the viewpoints, hopes, and despairs of the poet/editor/publisher. It was a work of labor and love. Most of the work from typing of the finished manuscript to collating and folding was done by the poet and his friends, often followed by a satisfying drunk at a local bar or some friend's home. You knew that when the ultimate product was finished you had been there from the time the seed was planted to the final birth. And even then it was not over. Like early Brautigan, the editor/poet walked the streets, more often than not, hawking or giving or even bartering away the vision for anything from a dollar to an exchange of poems on the street. There was a sense of feeling and belonging shared from long night conversations of anti-government nature to shared correspondence with poets never met some 3,000 miles away. You might say it was *Family*.

By contrast—the present scene is more sophisticated—sometimes too incestual—sort of like the glitter of stars on a clear night—the product is indeed beautiful to view from the eye but, alas, too soon forgotten. Grants have made publishing easier, for sure, but they have also taken away some of the close-knit ties that made early publishing camaraderie a thing to respect and hold in wonder. How-to books and money-making visions have pushed the small press publishing scene into an area I am not at all comfortable with. Thus (at this writing in 1982) I seriously weigh whether I will renew my membership in COSMEP (Committee of Small Magazine Editors and Publishers). As Dylan said, "The-Times-They-Are-a-Changing."

It is difficult to determine where small press publishing is headed. I say this only because of the unsure state of grants and funding available to small presses and magazines. The true littles such as *The Smith, Poetry Now, December, Vagabond*, etc., etc., etc., will survive as long as the energy allows. I think in the long run that the cutting of grant funds will only make for a healthier small press and literary magazine scene. One can always go back to "mimeo" publishing if he has to, or must, and with the cut-back in grant funds the only real ones to be hurt will be those marginal writers and publishers who in truth contributed little or nothing to the scene to begin with.

I probably put the same thing into my magazine and press as did any dedicated editor/publisher. In the beginning (first few years), I did everything from the typing, paste-up, to the final product (with exception of actual printing); that final product included licking stamps, running to the post office, being a secretary, promotion manager and distribution manager. The money was never a prime concern. I worked for it, supplemented it by grant money, and had a few donations from friends here and there. The time and psychic energy was, however, brutally draining on both me and my life as a poet and writer. It is the latter that has caused me to make a decision to "slow" down out of necessity and commitment to my life in that area.

I think small press editing and publishing altered my life in that it made me more aware of the sweat and labor such a life involves and it brought me into contact with new writers and poets and even non-writers of great literary knowledge and intelligence. I think it was far more rewarding than bad on me and I would do the same thing over again if given the same set of circumstances. I believe that small press publishing, like writing, is something you're more or less born into rather than consciously making a choice of doing it, at least if you go on into ten or more years of publishing. Was it worth it? God Yes it was.

Magazines I still like today include anything John Bennett puts out, Harry Smith too. I still enjoy *Zahir, Beatitude* (sometimes), *Gargoyle, Bogg, Gravida* (when it was publishing), and a few others of greater or lesser merit.

It would be hard to give a list of magazines I dislike, simply because I don't read them more than once or twice before putting them out of my mind. There is a long list of such as *Partisan Review* and *Hudson Review*. Why would I dislike them? I think the question is why would I like them? They are boring, dry academic work. Add the language magazines to that list, too. Add anything that takes life rather than gives.

I haven't the slightest idea of what the background of an editor/publisher of a little magazine should be. I would be prone to suspect the backgrounds would be as diverse as those of any other profession. Barring the academic journals, where surely we know the backgrounds of the editor and publisher . . . who knows what makes a good editor or publisher? You sure as hell won't learn in the classroom.

I have already touched on grants and COSMEP. Suffice it to say that I think grants did more harm than good: they pitted poet against poet, writer against writer, editor against writer, and rewarded more second-rate people than Mayor Daley of Chicago did with his old-time ward bosses. David Wilk and Mary

MacArthur [former NEA Literature Program Directors] to me, are simply little better than war criminals. Sound harsh? Perhaps, but it's true. They did, in their own way, more to harm small press publishing while rewarding friends of freinds than any previous NEA administration with perhaps the exception of the Jack Shoemaker carpetbaggers. But in the year 2000 no one will even remember them. COSMEP is little more than a paper dragon flying this way and that way in the wind, paying the salary of Richard Morris (whom I like) and wining and dining board members at meaningless board meetings held throughout the U.S. They may as well be given a seat at the U.N. for all the good they do.

The "little" magazine and "small press" does not fit into today's society, and why should it? It is a minority in a majority of rather blase, non-thinking people—the kind that would elect a richard nixon or ronnie reagan to rule the land. The small press scene remains small simply because the country as a whole has a paucity of wit, energy and charm. As James Drought said to me in a letter: "I meet individual after individual searching for some character, some class, some cultural roots. There is nothing; it's such a waste of food and resources— the lives lived by our individuals all over this country."

And so the vision and search goes on and it's presented in the *better* of our so-called *small* literary magazines and presses. For better or worse, we are here to stay.

I guess that answers the 21 questions presented to me by Diane Kruchkow and Curt Johnson. I don't know how many words it came out to be and neither do I care.

I didn't give my opinion on God (the jury is still out). I still remain anti-government (politics), all governments, and yes I still enjoy sex now as much as I did when I was eighteen. I still maintain a bit of innocence, or so I am told, though I suspect it is becoming somewhat tarnished.

You have my permission to "sigh," cry, or even laugh. But a subscription to *Second Coming* would be even more welcome.

187

Alta

Shameless Hussy

Alta

Alta was born in Reno, Nev., 1942; educated at UCBerkeley; married and divorced, 2 children; 11 books; founder & publisher of Shameless Hussy Press. We can also tell you that at one time *Seventeen* magazine refused to print the title of her press. Alta's answers were brief, and thus we are enabled to print the questions sent the contributors to this volume, together with her responses. The editors' letter to potential contributors began:

We are compiling a book on the little ("literary") magazine of the '60s and '70s to be published by December Press. For obvious reasons we'd like you to be a contributor to this volume.

Will you take time and about 2,500 words (more are welcome if you feel inspired) to tell about the little mag editor's/publisher's life as you knew it back then?

It would be nice if in the course of your response, you'd answer all or most of the 21 questions appended, but don't feel you have to. If you feel like it, give your opinions on God, politics, sex, and/or whether or not you think you've lost your innocence. (And when that happened and what precipitated the event.) Other anecdotes are also welcome.

A photo of yourself (or two—then and now) and a cover of your magazine would be appreciated and printed, along with your date and place of birth, education, present residence, family obligations, and what you do for a living. Publications, work experience, prejudices, and so forth would also fit here, as well as a biblio of your magazine (press), with subjectively emphasized highlights. All of this paragraph's requested info in headnote form, if you will.

In the piece itself, mostly on your experiences as part of the little magazine subdivision of this continent's culture. And how you and your magazine survived the '60s and/or '70s—humanly, financially, and spiritually—and how you plan to survive the rest of the '80s. The more personal and opinionated, the better, your response.

189

And here are the 21 Questions, with Alta's responses following in italics:

1. When did you first learn of the little magazine—or underground publishing?
1967.

2. What prompted you to edit/publish your own little mag? If you also wrote, how did you manage to wear both hats?
Berkeley women's conference, 1967. A friend suggested, "Why don't you do an anthology?"

3. Did you think of little mag publishing as a way to make a living or part of a living? If so, was it?
Never. No way.

4. How long did you publish? How many issues? Why did you stop (if indeed you have)? And what are you doing now and how did little mag experience relate to it?
Five years. Five. Fatigue & lack of $. Good experience.

5. What format and how many copies of an issue did you sell or put into good hands at the most? At the least? (Out of what size printings?) Was selling vs. giving away any kind of philosophical conflict for you?
1000-3000. Nah.

6. Did you have an editorial philosophy (objective)? If you did, how successful were you at putting this into practice?
Feminist. Totally successful.

7. If you're still publishing, how did your early publishing philosophy (or practice) differ from your present one?
I'm more lenient in politics, more stringent in literary quality.

8. What, in general over the years, was the response to your magazine?
Shock.

9. What do you regard as the most significant aspects or accomplishments of your editorship?
Opening the world of publication by & for women.

10. What do you now regard as the least significant (or most regretted)?
Huh?

11. What was the little magazine scene like when you started?
Fun-o!

12. What is it like now, by way of contrast—if any?
I don't kno.

190

13. What do you think of contemporary small press publishing, as distinct from little magazines? Where do you think small press publishing is headed? How does today's little magazine relate to today's small press? To the commercial press?

In all directions.

14. What did you put into your little magazine in terms of time, psychic energy, and money—and where did you get the money?

Lots. Lots. Lots. Welfare & lovers.

15. How did publishing a little magazine fit into your life? Did it alter your life? If it did, in what good ways? In what bad?

Kept me from drinking. (Not really.)

16. What did you get out of publishing a little magazine? Would you do it again, everything else being equal? Was it worth it, in retrospect?

Kicks. Sure.

17. What other little magazines did you (do you) like?

Hundreds, esp. Aldebaran Review, The Ladder, Aphra & New (all defunct).

18. Dislike? Why?

Male porno rags.

19. What do you think the background of an editor/publisher of a little magazine—ideally—should be?

Whatever they want.

20. What do you think the net effect of government aid to little magazines (and small presses) has been? Were organizations (e.g., COSMEP) helpful?

Helped financially, but fostered competition. Sure.

21. How do little magazines fit into U.S. society today—on levels not just limited to literary? And how do today's small presses? Or should they fit in at all?

Fit schmit. Do pansies fit? Violets?

LEAP LEAP

John Milton

South Dakota Review

John Milton

John Milton was born in Anoka, Minnesota, May 24, 1924. B.A. and M.A. in British literature, University of Minnesota; Ph.D. in American literature and creative writing, University of Denver. Married in 1946 (after three years of Army service) to Leonharda Hinderlie, in St. Paul, Minnesota. Daughter Nanci born in 1957 in Minneapolis. Wife is artist and teacher. Daughter is actress, dancer, and teacher, living in California. J.M. spent almost 30 years in St. Paul, tried North Dakota for a few years, has been in South Dakota at the University since 1963.

Bibliography is approaching 300 items, including 10 books as well as a number of edited books. Teaching and editing have taken too much time.

In the class predictions for graduating seniors at Murray High School in St. Paul, Minnesota, 1942, the name John Milton was followed by a terse notation, "newspaper editor." That high school no longer exists, having merged with another, and so there is no one for me to tell that the prophecy was fairly accurate. However, what I really wanted to be was a writer. When I look at the hundreds of little mags and literary journals of the 1980s, I find very few whose editors are not also writers of some kind. This condition could be viewed sardonically because sometimes it appears that if a person fails as a poet he tries a novel, and when he fails at that also he becomes an editor. At worst we are reminded of "those who can't write teach writing," and we might try an extension, "those who can't teach writing edit writing."

All of this can be discouraging when I realize that I have done it all—written in several genres, taught both expository and creative writing, and for the past two decades edited a literary quarterly. If all of it has failed, where do I go next? Trying to rationalize may just cloud the issues, but I tell myself that I quit writing poetry only because the world was getting too cluttered with poems, that I have not succeeded as a novelist only because of the provincial and blind New York editors, and that I have kept the *South Dakota Review* going this long only out of sheer stubbornness. In any case, there can be no question about the total frustration arising from multiple interests.

So, why not be content with writing some poems and stories? Why start a magazine, as I did in 1963 at the University of South Dakota? It certainly was not the high school prediction. It wasn't for money. In truth, the magazine sprang from my personal and academic interest in Western American literature. As a graduate student at the University of Minnesota I was forced to major in British literature even though I argued at length in favor of American. When I went a step further and asked that I be allowed to write my dissertation on the Western American novel, I was laughed right out of the school. Some years later I went to the University of Denver, a Western university, and received better treatment. Meanwhile, I had been writing articles on Western fiction, and I thought there should be a journal that would give long overdue attention to major—but ignored—novelists like Walter Van Tilburg Clark, Frank Waters, Harvey Fergusson, Vardis Fisher, Frederick Manfred, Wallace Stegner, and also provide an outlet for emerging Western writers of all kinds. And that is, essentially, how *SDR* got started.

When I moved to the University of South Dakota in 1963 as chairman of the English department, the first or second thing I did was ask my dean for money to publish a magazine. He came up with $400 (the current budget is between $10,000 and $12,000—more about that later), and I hastily scraped together a few articles and poems, some Western and some not, and had 500 copies printed at the local newspaper plant. Design, format, and type styles were less than ordinary, but the copies sold and we soon had a subscription list of several hundred names. The dean was appalled. Subscription list? he asked in wonder. He thought the one-time publication would satisfy me and I could get back to being his English chairman. Over a six-month period I gradually convinced him that *SDR* must go on—forever, if possible. He was skeptical, but he funded a second issue and I found a better printer in nearby Sioux Falls and set up the format in 1964 that we still use, except for the cover.

In 1964 I had help from several people and we published two issues and expanded the subscription list. The materials became more Western-weighted, but we also decided to accept manuscripts from all parts of the country. Perhaps we were afraid of becoming provincial, but I wrote in an editorial that we wished to send Western literature to the rest of the country and to bring in to South Dakota or the Upper Midwest the best writing we could find elsewhere. Sort of a cultural exchange program. It has worked well. A few local cranks have complained when we went outside the state for material, and more than a few New York City writers have complained that they cannot get published there and won't we please take care of them.

Over the years we have published two issues devoted entirely to South Dakota, three or four devoted in the same way to the Upper Midwest, two given over to American Indian writing and art, a dozen or more special issues of the West, and a host of what I call general issues. The latter kind became more feasible after the birth of another journal, *Western American Literature*, which I also had a small hand in starting. It caters more to the academics, leaving *SDR*

194

considerably more flexible. I like this arrangement.

When I say "we" published, or "we" decided to do this or that, I am only being editorial or royal in usage. In actuality, for the past 15 years, there have been two people keeping *SDR* in business. Five or six young ladies have, one at a time, done the subscription paper work and the billing and the mailing. All have been indispensable to me because I soon discovered that the editing itself took more time than I could really spare. To make it somewhat easier, I resigned the chairmanship of the English department. Currently I teach half time and edit the *Review* half time. The magazine went quarterly in its third year, and a budget was set up in the College of Arts and Sciences. The dean insisted that I appoint a committee to oversee the editorial work, and for two or three issues I listed some names on page 2; then, when he had forgotten about it, I dropped the names. And so, for better or for worse, *SDR* has been a one-man journal. The workload is a real burden for one person, but a great deal of time is saved in making decisions. The autocracy has at least been efficient.

Funding has been a perpetual problem. For 2 years out of the last 18, the College budget was sufficient. Just as I relaxed a little, then, the budget was cut in half. In spite of recent inflation, the contribution from the College has never again reached the figure of those two good years. In other years—which means most of them—the necessary funding has come from a variety of sources. The two largest and therefore most significant contributions came from a private foundation in Minnesota. During the '60s there were several small grants from CCLM, but I no longer apply there because the small amount of money each time was hardly worth the effort of making out the application. The big money always seemed to go to those journals that already had much more money than anyone else. Politics, I suppose. A few years ago I was personally invited to apply for a large development grant from NEA—in fact, urged to do so—but then my application was quickly turned down. More politics?

For those special issues which dealt largely with South Dakota material, *SDR* got several small grants from the South Dakota Arts Council. Because it was the Council's policy not to support literature, it stipulated in each case that it was paying for copies of the magazine, or for color separations. Twice *SDR* reveived substantial contributions from subscribers—these got us over at least one serious crisis. And once, way back, when there seemed to be no hope of printing another issue, the president of the University gave me the money left over from the snow removal fund—it had been a dry winter. Twice, when nothing else seemed ready to solve the money problem, we combined two issues in one, cutting the annual cost by one fourth.

The money problems exist largely because I insist on a quality journal, not just the contents but also the physical object—paper, type styles, format, and printing method (letter press for years, now offset). Paper is no longer as good as it was 10 or 12 years ago, yet it costs more; otherwise we have held quite closely to the original specifications.

Important as it is, I do not like to talk about money. It takes some of the joy out of editing, of planning special topics, of looking for new writers. The biggest pleasure for me is finding a good story or poem by an "unknown" and later watching the continued success in other journals, or in books, by that writer. Culturally isolated in South Dakota, I also use *SDR* as my connection with the world beyond my adopted state. The friends I have made, even though I have met or seen very few of them, are of the utmost importance. Those would-be contributors whom I have angered are soon forgotten. These are the people who are more worried about publication than about writing, who are terribly ego-centered, who do not accept criticism, and who seem to feel that it is an editor's obligation to publish them. They are easily identified because their manuscripts are almost always accompanied by letters explaining how talented they are and how many journals have already published their work. Perverse as it may be, I am reluctant to publish someone who sends along a list of 200 previous publications and obviously wants to add one more journal title to the list. I won't play numbers games. Curiously, most of these people are mediocre writers, and I wonder about the sanity of those editors who have already published them. I fear that many editors have games of their own to play.

Given my own editorial prejudices, it may seem strange that stories from *SDR* have been prominent in Foley's *Best American Short Stories*. Two stories have been included in those volumes and dozens have been listed in the "Roll of Honor" or in the "Distinctive Stories" lists. One year (here goes the numbers game) *SDR* ranked second behind *The New Yorker* or third behind *The New Yorker* and *Esquire*—I don't remember which. I've been impressed by the number of younger writers who, after appearing in *SDR*, went on to publish books, either poetry or fiction. (On such occasions, because of my dual role as editor and writer, I feel both pride and jealousy.)

It must be said, I think, that in the priorities of the journal, our first concern is still for articles on literature, especially Western American literature. Fiction comes second because of the limited number of outlets, and poetry is last for two reasons: (1) there are hundreds of all sizes and shapes of poetry magazines, and (2) good poetry is getting scarcer every year, although the number of poems increases. It seems fairly important, though, that all three kinds of writing be given attention. Again, money has something to say about how much can be included each year. In good years we have seen issues of around 175 pages; in bad years we have dropped as low as 60 pages for an issue. One thing about publishing a literary journal, each year is a surprise, whether good or bad. But one thing seems certain, that *SDR* will remain a kind of middle-class journal, envying the relative wealth of *Texas Quarterly*, *TriQuarterly*, *Chicago Review*, and even *Kansas Quarterly*, while at the same time being considered rich by many of the smaller struggling journals.

The format of *SDR* has not changed since the second issue. Trim size is 6x9" and the printing has been done both by letterpress and offset, with the basic type style Times Roman 11 point. The normal print run is 900 copies, of which 500 go to subscribers and, for quite a few years, 100 went to our New York distributor. Quite regularly we got 80-90 returns from New York, prompting the distributor to insist that we change the cover and make it more attractive. We did so. Nothing happened. Eventually we agreed to terminate our arrangement, and there were some hard feelings on both sides, each blaming the other for the lack of sales. As fate would have it, our Twin Cities distributor in Minnesota dropped us at about the same time, and then the Plains Distribution Service went out of business. It seems as though we are conspired against. At present we have no distributor of any kind, relying entirely on mail subscriptions.

For a "normal" issue I now keep the print run at 600-700. For special issues I gamble on extra copies. Once, back in 1967, I ordered 1,200 copies of an issue devoted to the Southwest. They sold so quickly that I immediately had 1,000 more run off. Sales lagged almost instantly; it has taken 15 years to get rid of most of the second printing. In 1969 I again tried a larger printing, this time for an issue on American Indian writing and art. After it sold out I turned the issue over to *SDR*'s sister organization, Dakota Press, as a book, and *The American Indian Speaks* went through four printings with sales of almost 4,000 copies, the only item in nearly 20 years that actually made money for either *SDR* or Dakota Press.

It has been the special issues that have given me the most pleasure, have provided the most fun, and have been the most rewarding experiences. But, I soon discovered that the more fun I had, the harder I worked. This seems to be an inevitable condition for an editor. I'd like to run through some of those special issues and may as well do it in chronological order.

For the Autumn 1964 number I conducted a symposium by mail among novelists who were concerned with the American West. The eight participants were Forrester Blake, Walter Van Tilburg Clark, Harvey Fergusson, Vardis Fisher, Paul Horgan, Frederick Manfred, Michael Straight, and Frank Waters. A.B. Guthrie, Jr., refused to take part on the grounds that he had nothing to say. The questions were aimed at the place and role of the Western novelist and the effect of his environment upon him: "What are the characteristics of the American West, especially the chief motivating force on fiction?" And, "Does the western novelist have any special problems because of his regional background?" There were ten such questions. The symposium has been reprinted in anthologies and stands as the first "collective" statement by a group of Western novelists.

The Southwest issue that I mentioned—Summer 1967—featured a 60-page autobiography by Dorothy Brett, the titled English woman who came to this country with D.H. Lawrence and remained in the Taos, New Mexico, area until her death a few years ago. Although Brett continued to work on her autobiography, turning the material over to a neighbor, no other portion has been published. I would like to get my hands on the rest of the material. (As of this writing, I have not seen the new movie based on D.H. Lawrence's stay in Taos, and so I cannot evaluate the treatment of Brett, but I remember her fondly as I look again at the photographs I took of her in the El Prado house.) Another Southwest issue, Spring 1969, was given over to a single manuscript of 13 pieces, written in the 1930s by Taos chiropractor I.L. Udell. "Doc" Udell, who also painted, was almost a legend in the Taos valley, but his manuscipt lay unnoticed until a friend of mine helped unearth it. The information on Taos of the 1930s, and Spanish witches, and the Penitente religious cult is invaluable. I don't remember how many copies were printed of that issue—perhaps 1,000—but it sold out quickly and has never been reprinted because I turned the rights over to a lawyer who said that he represented Udell and wanted any further proceeds from the material to help support the ailing good doctor. As far as I know, nothing has been done, and I feel deluded and gullible. I will not give up material that easily again. (I had better say here, however, that *SDR* does not assume ownership of most of the material it publishes, having it copyrighted only for the protection of the writers.)

For the 194-page Indian issue (Summer 1969) I traveled 4,000 miles and spent a full year on the gathering, selecting, and editing of the materials. Many of the stories and poems came from students at the Institute of American Indian Arts in Santa Fe. Among the painters whose work was reproduced—much of it in expensive color—Oscar Howe had also attended the IAIA when he was young. Of the others, R.C. Gorman, Navajo, has since become one of the wealthiest and best-known painters in the country. (I'm guessing, R.C., but it sure looks that way.) The issue was highly successful in every way, financially and influentially. It was the first of its kind and it spawned more imitations than I could keep track of. Some of the pieces turned up in four or five other collections, usually by permission, but not always. As for me, I suffered a peculiar fate, being proclaimed an expert in Indian literature and approached by far too many people for expert advice. I hereby disclaim any such expertise and do not wish to be disturbed any further. Just because I have a lot of Indian friends, some of whom are writers or painters, well . . . .

At the end of 1969 I put together an issue on Sinclair Lewis and Frederick Manfred, two writers from my home state of Minnesota. Two years later *American Indian II* (what a clever title!) appeared—Summer 1971—with fewer writers and more depth than in *American Indian Speaks*. It sold out rapidly but, with what turned out to be excellent foresight, I rejected the idea of a second printing. Over the years I have been told that the first Indian issue was much better than the second, although I disagree.

The number of which I am most proud bore a book title, *The Writer's Sense of Place* (Autumn 1975), and it was adopted as a text at several schools. Of 87 writers in all parts of the United States to whom I sent a list of questions, 54 responded, either answering the questions or addressing the general topic in essays of various lengths. I insist that I am not a name dropper, but it gives me pleasure to find in the pages of *SDR* such people as Andrew Lytle, James T. Farrell, Gary Snyder, Grace Paley, Erskine Caldwell, Tom McGrath, Josephine Miles, Richard Eberhart, W.D. Snodgrass, Max Evans, Frank Waters, Frederick Manfred, Richard Hugo, William Stafford, Wallace Stegner, Madison Jones, Rudolfo Anaya, William Eastlake, Ross Macdonald, Richard Wilbur, and many more. A good representation of all parts of the nation, of men and women, and of nationalities and minority groups. And all of these writers dealing with—and not agreeing much of the time—one of my favorite concerns, "place." Preparing that volume exhausted me. Fortunately, I was then in the third year of my weekly allergy shots and was otherwise beginning to feel better than I had in almost ten years. The emotion that remains with me from *Sense of Place* is gratitude for busy writers who would take time to participate in a project originating in that presumed cultural wasteland, South Dakota.

I would like very much to think that *SDR* has watered that wasteland more than a little. From the mail I get from all over the world, it would seem that South Dakota is finally on the map. Yet, within the state, from my own adopted people, there is little recognition and little thanks. (Some notable exceptions to that condition, of course, but by and large South Dakota remains an agricultural state with little concern for the arts, for writing, or for a literary journal.) Perhaps it is this lack of recognition at home that turns me away, to other places, for the special issues that not only please me but also delight readers in those faraway regions. An issue on New Mexico novelist and American Indian scholar Frank Waters proved popular in the Southwest. (That was Autumn 1977.) More recently I decided that I had maligned Los Angeles long enough, refusing to admit it into the definition or discussion of the American West on the grounds that it was at best an end-around run from the East and at worst something very peculiar that could not be named. I asked ten writers with considerable Los Angeles experience to do essays on the subject "Los Angeles as West." Not quite by coincidence, this Spring-Summer 1981 issue came out during L.A.'s Bicentennial and was made a kind of official publication for that event. It changed many people's ways of thinking about Los Angeles, including my own. After an absence of almost 25 years, I now feel a renewed fondness for Los Angeles and for Southern California, arising from a new understanding of the mystique of the place. It is experiences like this that keep me interested in editing *SDR*. The fringe benefits are worth more than the basic wage.

All of this is probably pretty dull stuff. The individual adventures, the spats, the relationships with contributors who do not know me except as an editor, the problems of editing without rewriting, the feelings I have for hundreds of writers and would-be writers, the frustrations of trying to convince people that a literary magazine is a worthwhile endeavor—all of the daily contacts over an 18-year period—these would make a book, perhaps even an interesting one if my memory proved adequate.

When I started—and *SDR* was my second magazine—the little magazine-small press scene was relatively subdued. In the Great Plains region there were the *Southwest Review*, the *Arizona Quarterly*, the *Colorado Quarterly*, and *Prairie Schooner*, and that was about it. One of those four is no longer with us. By the mid-'60s, however, little magazines were springing up all over the place, and a few of them have survived. The most noticeable growth has been in the number of small presses, some of them so small as to hardly warrant the name "press." I am sure that this phenomenon has been the result of increasing commercialism among the major publishers in the East. I am convinced that most of the best fiction and poetry lies unpublished or eventually acquires a few readers through small press publication. We cannot predict the future. It is at least conceivable that one day there will be no printed books and all communication will come off electronic machines, but I continue to believe that enough of us deplore that possibility, condemn the kind of thinking behind it, that we will eventually succeed in preserving the written word as perhaps the most valuable and vital single thing in human history. I have been beaten down too often to retain my youthful idealism, but I would not continue to edit a literary journal, or to write stories and poems, if I did not think there was a chance to continue and revitalize the literary arts.

The big hurdle, it seems to me, is not enthusiasm (or the lack of it), not money (entirely), not the absence of readers, not a dwindling of dedication, but the simple facts of distribution. Our Dakota Press, which operated in conjunction with *SDR*, has died for lack of distribution facilities. *SDR* hangs on to its 500 loyal subscribers and gets into the world's best libraries, but it will never have enough buyers to make it a self-supporting endeavor. At times this makes me almost as angry as my inability to crack the eastern publishers as a writer. But the anger is brief. I happen to believe in what I am doing. And so do all the other editors and writers working on the periphery of the BIG SUCCESS. Blessings on us all.

SOUTH DAKOTA REVIEW

autumn 1968 / volume 6, numb / $1.00

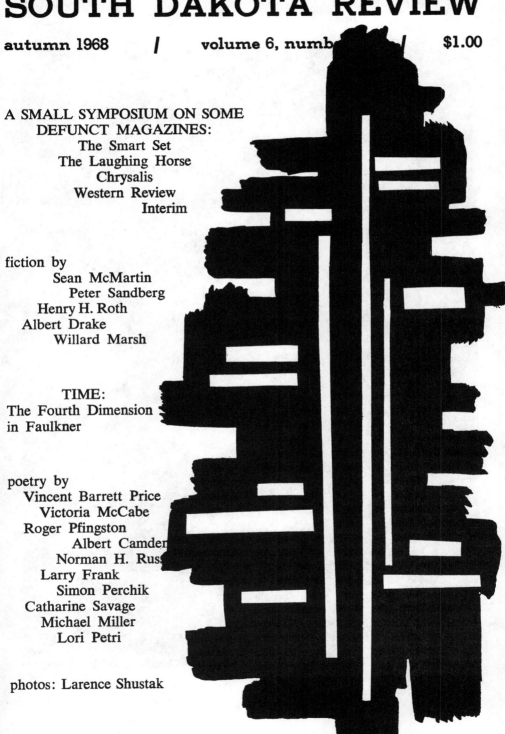

A SMALL SYMPOSIUM ON SOME
DEFUNCT MAGAZINES:
The Smart Set
The Laughing Horse
Chrysalis
Western Review
Interim

fiction by
Sean McMartin
Peter Sandberg
Henry H. Roth
Albert Drake
Willard Marsh

TIME:
The Fourth Dimension
in Faulkner

poetry by
Vincent Barrett Price
Victoria McCabe
Roger Pfingston
Albert Camden
Norman H. Russ
Larry Frank
Simon Perchik
Catharine Savage
Michael Miller
Lori Petri

photos: Larence Shustak

Morty Sklar

The Spirit That Moves Us

Morty Sklar

Morty Sklar was born in 1935 in New York City.

Education: Newtown High School; the U.S. Army, 82nd Airborne Division, 1954-56; Queens College; heroin addiction, 1960-66, N.Y.C.; Phoenix House, 1966-69, N.Y.C.; University of Iowa, B.A. 1973; the Actualist poets and Little Mag editors of Iowa City, from 1971 . . .

Present residence: Iowa City (P.O. Box 1585, IA 52244)

Luckily, for the past year I have not had to do as much outside typesetting and other work as much as usual, due to the mild success of our anthology, *Editor's Choice: Literature & Graphics from the U.S. Small Press,* 1965-77 (publication date, December 1980). As important as earning money for physical sustenance, is living as cheaply as I can.

A book of my poems, *The Night We Stood Up for Our Rights,* was published by Toothpaste Press in 1977. Other poetry, and fiction, have appeared in Little Mags, and a letterpress chapbook was self-published in 1974. Because of preoccupation with my magazine/press, I've written little the past few years, and sent little out for publication. A first novel, 300 pages written, waits to be completed.

Jobs I've had include (chronologically): *Long Island Star* delivery boy, at which time, age 12, I first read Henry Miller's *Tropic of Cancer,* or *Tropic of Capricorn,* I don't remember which, which I'd stolen from a doorstep (I hadn't known, when I took the package it was in, postmarked from a foreign country, what was in it); shipping and receiving in my father's hardware store; bus boy and waiter; soldier; panhandler, thief, speed and heroin pusher; office clerk; bus driver; drug counselor; typesetter . . .

Prejudices I have include: not liking the profit-oriented way of operating which underlies most endeavors in the U.S.A.; not liking writing and other artwork which doesn't express some kind of human concern and energy; not liking negative contracts between people, made to protect some narrow and stingy way of living.

Volume 1, #1 of *The Spirit That Moves Us* appeared 1975. Volume 6, #1 was published 1981. A special issue, *The Actualist Anthology* (Vol. 2, #2 & 3: 1977) has a generous sampling of the work of 14 poets who lived and interacted in Iowa City from the early to mid-'70s. This was part of a group which had its life outside the university community and the Writers Workshop, altho a few had at one time been in the Workshop, and one even taught there. Among them are Anselm Hollo, Sheila Heldenbrand, Allan Kornblum, George Mattingly, David Hilton, Cinda Kornblum, Darrell Gray, Dave Morice, Jim Mulac, and Morty Sklar.

At the other end of the spectrum, in terms of focus, is *Editor's Choice*, 501 pages of work selected from nominations by editors, of work from their presses/ magazines. Other special issues include *Cross-Fertilization: The Human Spirit as Place* (Vol. 5, #3: 1980); *The Farm in Calabria*, by David Ray (Vol. 5, #1 & 2: 1980; published back-to-back with a regular magazine section; *Nuke-Rebuke: Writers & Artists Against Nuclear Energy & Weapons* (1984), and Jaroslav Seifert's *The Casting of Bells* (1983). Seifert is the Czech poet awarded the 1984 Nobel Prize in Literature, and *The Casting of Bells* was his only work available in English at the time he received the Nobel.

The Spirit Moves On

I had seen Little Magazines before arriving in Iowa City from New York City in 1971, but I had no context to put them in. I hadn't realized they are a large part of our literary culture and heritage. In Iowa City in 1971 there were Littles such as *Toothpaste* edited by Allan Kornblum (8½x14" stapled mimeo which has since evolved into the letterpress magazine *Dental Floss* and Tooth-paste Press); *Gum* (4¼x5½" stapled mimeo), edited by Dave Morice who does *Poetry Comics*; *Search for Tomorrow* (5½x8½" perfectbound offset), edited by George Mattingly who's been publishing Blue Wind Press books; *Suction* (8½x11" stapled mimeo), edited by Darrell Gray, who was a focuser of the community energy come to be known as Actualism; *Me Too* (8½x11", then 5½x8½" saddlestitched offset), edited by Barbara Sablove, Mary Stroh, and Patty Markert; and others.

Several things prompted me to edit/publish my own literary magazine. First was the desire to pack a magazine full of gutsy and effectively rendered poetry (and later, fiction and artwork). I also embraced the idea of editing as a way to define my aesthetics. As an editor I function, in a way, like a photographer, recording what signs of life I see. As I began to edit I realized the personal pressures editors are under—from writer-friends, writer-editors and well-known writers, all of whom one feels uneasy about rejecting.

Along with some local writers, we publish writers from all around the country and from other countries. Our recent issue, Volume 6, #1, contains work by nine foreign authors (out of 37 contributors to the issue). All but three of the authors are living. In this same issue, along with works by Charles Bukowski, Gloria Dyc, Leonard Nathan, James Bertolino, and Lyn Lifshin, are works by Ai Qing of Peking, China; Jarkko Laine of Turku, Finland; Alberto Vanasco of Buenos Aires, Argentina; Eric Akerlund of Falun, Sweden; Gunter Bruno Fuchs

204

of West Berlin; Jose F. Lacaba of MetroManilla, Philippines; Frans Nadjira of Sanur Bali, Indonesia; Fernando Pessoa of Portugal; Francis Jammes of Bearn, France.

Practically all the work published in *The Spirit That Moves Us* is unsolicited, but I always jump on writers whose work I hear and like at readings, or which I have read.

As far as writing and editing/publishing, I find it difficult to do both. I tend to get involved in one or two things at a time and take them as far as they'll go. There was a time I snatched poetry from the air, and a time I sat down at least five of seven mornings for three pages of my novel, whether it took four hours or an hour-and-a-half. If an hour-and-a-half, I'd often keep on writing, maybe as many as ten pages, and maybe even write again that evening. If that sounds nostalgic, it isn't . . . I intend to again become very involved in my own writing. The hang-up is promotion of the mag and press. When a promotional or fund-raising effort doesn't pan out, I'm soon thinking of what else to try (after first considering quitting the whole thing).

When I started the magazine in 1975 I didn't think of it as a way to make money. In fact, a few years later, when I began thinking perhaps it might be able to pull in $500-$1,000 per year, and I began to do big promotional mailings and other things to drum up business, it still barely paid for itself, and that's all it does now, with occasional grants and all. By now, with many fine reviews in such publications as *Serials Review, Library Journal* and *Choice*, as well as *Small Press Review, Gargoyle, New Pages, Northeast Rising Sun, Margins* and others, and with all the mailings and paid and exchange ads, I think I should be able to at least pay myself for the typesetting.

To November of '81 we had published 12 issues, four of them double issues, with three of those special issues.

Format is 5½x8½", perfectbound (saddle-stitched in earliest issues, and an extra clothbound edition of *The Actualist Anthology*), typeset on a table-top IBM Composer and printed offset by the lowest-bid/fine-quality printer (first issue was mimeographed, with an offset cover). Length varies from 48 to 144 pages. Over the years, each issue sells about 600 copies, subscriptions included. An exception is *The Actualist Anthology*, which has sold over 800 copies since 1977. I like to exchange with other magazines, send out a lot of review copies, and samples to libraries, bookstores, distributors, and people whose work I'd want to consider for publication. I like to have enough copies of an issue to assure having complete sets. All that, plus the everlasting hope of the mag really taking off at some point, has prompted me to do print runs of at least 1,000 from the beginning, and as high as 1,800 (1,500 paper and 300 cloth of *The Actualist Anthology*).

My editorial philosophy follows my feelings about writing and other arts: they are best when expressing human feelings and concerns. Style-oriented work doesn't make it on its own; content-oriented work doesn't either. I go for work which says something to me, either with its voice or its eyes.

Response to the mag has been pretty positive, both in direct comments from people and in reviews.

The most significant aspects of my editorship are my ability to choose work, not people, and having been at it so long!

When I started in 1975 there seemed to be more originality in the looks and content of little mags. Now, too much work, by both writers and editors, is either too tossed-off or too much in the middle range, dynamics-wise.

I think small press book publishing is headed the same way as, for instance, stone-ground whole wheat flour and other whole and unadulterated food: as people learn more to know the difference between good and poor, and rely less on image, they look to the small press more in the same was as they look into natural food stores and home gardens. The small press has published some lousy, as well as great work, but so has the big commercial press.

I put at least 30 hours per week into the mag and press. Less than 2 percent of the poetry, fiction, essays, and artwork submitted ends up in the mag, so that entails a lot of reading. During the past three years a lot of time has been spent setting up systems to operate in, which meant taking all our fairly organized data —such as subscription lists—and inter-relating them. For instance, when a manuscript arrives, a submission card is typed out, if there isn't one yet for that person, and purchaser and subscription files are checked to see if that person has bought anything from us. The reason for that is not to judge the manuscript by what the person has or has not bought, naturally, but to determine whether or not to insert a mailing piece in the return envelope. If the person has either submitted work before, subscribed or purchased a copy of the mag or a book, we enter the date of their submission in those files. This system also allows us to maintain a more personal relationship with people. I use the file cards to jot notes pertaining to a book they may have published, a job they may have or something personal they said. Also, thru my ex-wife's student status at the university, we have entered all our reusable data in a computer, which prints out mailing labels in zip-code order. We keep track of all contributors, subscribers and purchasers by the use of "Address Correction Requested" and "Forwarding & Return Postage Guaranteed" on mailing pieces.

Concerning psychic energies invested: Until a short while ago I had a strong conflict stemming from thinking of publishing as being secondary to my own writing and the need to make a living. I still want to get where I can dedicate a lot of time to writing, but I have come to feel that publishing is something I have to do also, and not time stolen from my life. I have been most discouraged by, for example, having had a rave review in *Serials Review* and a good short review in *Choice*, both in December 1980, followed by only three new library subscriptions in the 12 months following. I'm also most discouraged by having attractive, informative ads in *American Book Review, Small Press Review, San Francisco Review of Books, New Pages, Gargoyle, fiction international* and other places, and receiving very very few orders as a result. What do you do after responses like that? Quit? No. Can a parent quit a child when it doesn't behave or if people don't "buy" the child? Direct-mail advertising has proven to be the best bet for the mag and books. And reviews of books, if not mags, in library journals do bring library orders. And distributors do sell books, and collect money from bookstores, even if they don't sell mags.

The first issue of *The Spirit That Moves Us* was paid for with money I received by having been "relocated" from a $50/month apartment where the new post office was built. The next two issues were partly paid for by a State Vocational Rehabilitation program grant. The fourth was the first partly funded by the Coordinating Council of Literary Magazines. Since then about half the publishing expenses have been paid for by occasional grants from either CCLM, Iowa Arts Council or National Endowment for the Arts. I've hustled around $2,000 for *Editor's Choice*, ¾ of it from local businesses and people and the rest from Gannett Newspaper Foundation. That is something I now have to do with the magazine, since it is now (February 1982) five months past the usual CCLM grant application deadline and we've received no application.

My office is part of our small apartment, and back issues and books are stored in friends' houses and in the basement in our apartment building. Until a year ago I paid only $30/month for three years for an office in a local church.

Publishing altered my life by putting me in touch with the world of independent non-commercial literary publishing and offering me the opportunity to both be influenced by, and influence, writing and others' publishing. Sometimes editing simply reinforces my lifelong beliefs, and other times it stretches my mind. The whole process is more satisfying all the time, even with the disappointments, and frustrations such as not having a distributor for the mag, and having a relatively small active subscription list (presently 155 individuals and 63 libraries). It's a relationship based on love and purpose, and as such grows deeper with time. In a relationship, when something is wrong one thinks in terms of challenge and making things right—or at least working toward making things right. As Jose Villa said, "In getting there is perfect arrival."

The background of a little mag editor should be, ideally, his/her background —life, influences, experiences. It's not the background which counts most, but what the editor is trying to do and how well he/she does it.

The net effect of government aid to little mags and small presses has been twofold: financial encouragement of both worthwhile and not-so-worthwhile publications. I see it as a basically important thing, with whatever faults it may have. The most important question which arises in terms of government grants is that of their potential to "alter" the editors' visions, to put it mildly. I think that their potential to do that means simply that the world (we, as humans) is not perfect, but anything may be mishandled—or handled well—by people. The individual responds to his/her environment. It's not, except in extreme, inhuman situations, the "thing" which makes our lives, but us. To say otherwise is to say the material world completely controls the human/spiritual world. What grant applicants have to face, then, if they choose to stick to their ideals, is the possibility they won't get the money they want. But so what? The money is not as important as the quality of life and living, and so nothing is really lost except a chance to make things financially easier.

Government grants have also helped the small press thru aiding distribution organizations such as Bookslinger, and service organizations such as Committee of Small Magazine Editors & Publishers and Poets & Writers Inc.

Along with their contribution to our culture, small independent mags and presses fit into our society as an expression of freedom of choice and, if you must, as part of the free enterprise system. They fit in the way grass and wild-flowers fit in when they creep up thru cracks in the sidewalks of our civilization.

The Spirit That Moves Us

Poetry, Fiction, Essays, Artwork
Volume 6, Number 1

ISSN 0364-4014

$1.50

John Bennett

Vagabond

John Bennett

John Bennett is editor of *Vagabond* magazine and press. His own works, as author, include the novel *The Adventures of Achilles Jones,* and the short story collections *The Night of the Great Butcher, The Party to End All Parties, Whiplash on the Couch,* and most recently the books *Tripping in America* and *Survival Song* (parts I and II), and a series of White Papers.

Rundown on *all* of it? That's a tall order. Just say that John Bennett began publishing *Vagabond* back in 1966 out of a grave disenchantment with 20th-century living. It was something to do besides giving up totally, becoming a total cynic. About the same time I made a breakthru and my writing came alive for the first time. That was the story *The Night of the Great Butcher.* I've gotten a lot of mileage off that story. It's like burning your bridges behind you, in a peculiar sort of way. It's like leaping from the ledge of one burning building to another. One step ahead of total disaster all the time. Spiritual disaster. Just a cunt hair away from throwing in the towel. Forging alternatives to what your society tells you are ultimates. Gradually evolving a little character. The dividends begin coming in. I've used writing as a weapon. I do war with it. No wonder New York won't touch me. I don't understand what's the big deal about New York. That's just more hype. A person's life shouldn't be so dependent on a far-away city. I don't need New York and I don't need a string of letters after my name and I don't need a new Datsun. I am not driven. These things mean nothing to me; I know, because once they did. I woke up one night in a strange bed dreaming the American Dream. I found the bathroom and took a long piss. I stared out the window over the bowl at the night sky. No moon, just stars. That's where it's at, I said to myself. Then realized I'd stopped pissing a long time ago. Flushed the toilet and left the bathroom. Didn't go back to bed.

Is any of this making sense to you? It's coming straight off the top. Or

211

maybe it's coming from down deep up thru a brass pipe under about 800 lbs. of pressure. I like to think that's where the good writing comes from, that's how it gets out. The *Butcher* stories were alive and cooking and the novel *The Adventures of Achilles Jones* was alive and cooking and for a long time I diddled around writing poems that just didn't have the same pa-zam, for my money. Looking back on this period, I'd say it was a time of crisis. Life is a time of crisis, tho, so what of it. But you can't just sit around being the last angry young man year after year. You can't just go around *reacting*. You've got to start building. Am I getting in over my head here? Maybe. I'd been living off the fat of my anger and by the time I'd finished the *Achilles* novel I'd begun gnawing the bones and it was obvious something else was called for. It was time to start climbing out of the hole. Well, I left the poems and over the years did two more novels and half of a third. It felt better but it was still a transitional period. Since I wrote the *Achilles* novel back in '71-'72 I've been up in the air. In the process of leaping from one ledge to another that is far, far away. I think I landed in the past year or so. I think, that is, that I'm hanging from the ledge by my finger tips. All I gotta do now is pull myself up. And, while I'm waiting for the strength to do that, hope and pray that some crazy sonofabitch doesn't step on my fingers.

That's the whole thing in a nut shell. In my writing and in the *Vagabond* books I've published I've been looking for and striving toward honesty and insight. That's more complicated and terrifying than it sounds. Striving for honesty and insight—a pretty glib thing to say. You say enough things like that, you can get yourself subsidized. A little government money to enrich the culture. You start genuinely *doing* it and they shut you out. You become a non-person. The cookie jar is placed on the top shelf, out of your reach. You wind up living naked in the forest, gnawing roots and mumbling to yourself. No one wants to wind up like you.

And I don't want to wind up like no one. I've run out of heroes and even in my worst moments I don't wish to be anyone other than myself. I write what I damn well please. I've made under $500 doing it. I'm mid-40 years old. I'm a window washer. I make $10 an hour doing *that*. As editor of *Vagabond*, I also publish what I please. In limited editions, it goes without saying. *Vagabond* carried me thru a lot of tough places. When the writing isn't going right, putting out a book of someone's writing that *is* going right helps. I'm sympathetic towards rebels and visionaries. They're easy to spot because they don't travel in packs. I write to survive. There's not much more to say about it. Read the books.

John Crawford

West End Magazine

John Crawford

John Crawford was born in Los Angeles in 1940. After overcoming a childhood bone disease, he received a BA from Pomona College, an MA and PhD in English from Columbia Univ. After teaching college seven years, he founded *West End* magazine in 1971. Since 1976 he has been editor and publisher of West End Press. He is currently teaching at the Univ. of New Mexico.

The Company We Kept

Seated on my desk, like a Victorian stuffed monkey, is what I have left of it, a baker's dozen issues of *West End* magazine. The bibliographer in me makes a neat summary: Volume 1 is missing; Volumes 2 and 3, under my editorship (Summer 1973-Fall 1975—we tried to do four issues a year); Volume 4, under joint editorship with Gail Darrow Kaliss, from Spring 1976-Fall 1977; and Vol. 5, no. 1, a Midwest People's Culture Anthology Issue, with Gail as editor, me as Contributing Editor and Jim Dochniak of Minneapolis as Guest Editor, Summer of 1978. The magazine is not officially dead: Gail has been trying to get out Vol. 5, no. 2 since late 1978. But for me, at least, the turmoil is ended. West End Press, which I started in 1976, took away my attention.

I can reconstruct the beginnings. In 1971, I was 31; my life went through changes. I got a Ph.D., my marriage broke up, I got fired from my teaching job, was beaten up on a picket line. It was a time of psychiatrists and roses, wrecked cars and love affairs, the sort of year you are lucky to have once and live through. The magazine was named one day in the West End Bar and Grill, Broadway and 114th Street, New York City, when I was brooding about Spengler's *Decline of the West.* It was to be a journal of "personal and social change"—personal because I thought *I* needed it, social because I thought the world did. Soon, I was to declare myself in step with "the necessity of history." (That line wound up in a friend's poem, parodying me.) My friends at the West End—Michael O'Brien, Bill Zavatsky (he had a babyface then), Mark Weiss, Bill Wertheim and others—viewed me with anxiety as I went ahead. I had discovered the paper plate process (75¢ a double-page sheet) and enlisted the services of Christopher Washington, a printer in a youth program in East Harlem and one of the most patient men I ever met.

Help in putting out the first issue came from Alison Colbert, then a writer with a few poems out and a fresh interview with Allen Ginsberg for *Partisan Review.* She got Allen to donate the leavings from the *Partisan* interview to my journal. Mary Oppen, who with George had befriended me in the mid-'60s and remained supremely loyal in the years following, gave me a number of poems. They were her first published writing, I believe. Both Mary's work and Allen's interview (fugitive reflections which the intellectuals around William Phillips probably couldn't make hide or hair of) spoke well for the "personal change" part of my formulation. I hadn't gotten to the politics yet, though a picture of Karl Marx playing the guitar *did* adorn the cover.

The whole history of *West End* was to be one of overcorrections; that began with the second issue. Alison broke with me over it, saying, "You could have made this a fine magazine. Instead, you blew it," over a steamy table one night at the West End. I think she would have preferred editorial content which might have challenged *Partisan* (this was the time of Richard Kostelanetz' drafts of what was to be *The End of Intelligent Writing*, a highminded attack on the *Partisan* crowd when it didn't come out like monkeys on typewriters). I had something different in mind—I wanted to democratize writing at any cost. Perhaps both Allison and I would have amended our positions later on. But this was Spring 1972, and nobody was giving much intellectual ground if they could help it.

So the second issue was a "street issue," featuring lots of poets (a double issue) but guided in spirit by three from California. Julia Vinograd, once a Flower Child, had become a street vendor of her own poems. She is still out there on Telegraph Ave., so far as I know. Gary Spenser was a self-styled Marxist balladeer, not much for frills, who never even got his copy of the magazine—it bounced among California hotels before coming back to me. The featured long-poem of the issue was "Ode to Robert Duncan While Bending the Bow," by gay activist Paul Mariah. Long out of print, the issue (produced in New York) is a curious collection of avant-garde Californians, with a voice a little guttier than the average.

Closing out the first volume was my own "slim volume of verse," *Sun Man Shadow Man*, long since o.p. and, if the truth were known, self-suppressed. I was dealing with the pangs of self-awakening which had led me to start the magazine itself: among other things, a newly discovered libido. The title poem is perhaps indicative. "Shadow Man" ends "I come when you least expect me./ I leave when I can./ With what I can."

216

With Volume 2, beginning in Summer 1973, new things started to happen. The first issue had a stylized map of the Maine coast on the cover, and a long diary piece by Jean Stewart inside. How Jean and I sweated over that one! We composed it on a linotyper because she liked the delicate typeface. It appears now to have been 9 pt. with 2 pt. leading—this was still going onto paper plates. The piece insists on the supremacy of the feelings in an almost Proustian way, and perhaps for that reason seemed good for the magazine. The same issue, rather ironically considering the difference in form, had a poem by Denise Levertov, "Goodbye to Tolerance." It attacked her friends in poetry who had started to twit her for her radicalism. "Your poems/shut their little mouths," she commands, in fractured syntax, and accuses the "genial poets, pink faced/ earnest wits" of murdering the oppressed: "It is my brothers, my sisters,/whose blood spurts out and stops/forever/because you choose to believe it is not your business."

We put Denise's declaration of war to our own uses—something which she had approved. Friends had counseled me from the beginning of my magazine that "poetry and politics don't mix"—gently, the Oppens, who had been both Communist Party members and poets, but not at the same time; less gently, people like Horace Gregory, whose hands, it turned out, were not very clean; and my old friend, Michael O'Brien, who quoted Keats: "We hate poetry that has a palpable design upon us." Denise's poem drew the predictable fire. Ted Enslin wrote us, for publication, "She is one of the most thoroughly naive people I ever met" and added, "Who the hell are you to call some of the most important impulses in men 'petty-bourgeois'?" (These arguments, of course, are not over. But at that point in the history of *West End* many of us were uncommonly ready to say rather bizarre things in defense of our views. My favorite was Enslin's nomination for the perfect collectivist state: *Iceland*!)

Also in the Summer 1973 issue, I had printed a number of poems by Ray Lindquist, "who writes close to the feelings of the people he lives with." Lindquist, a Presbyterian minister who lived close to Attica prison, and wrote poems about the guards there, broke with me over the next issue, Fall 1973, which had a sketch of Allende on the cover, a poem from Neruda which ended "I want to see them punished," and the first lit-mag treatment of the fascist coup in Chile. Communist propaganda, sniffed Ray, and our friendship was over. I began to realize that even if I was starting to say things right, I was going to lose friends over it. That was an unforeseen consequence of a concern with "personal and social change."

The Fall 1973 issue is significant for introducing some Bronx voices, from where I was teaching, at Lehman College: Lorraine Sutton, whose poem "Oye Gloria" captured the sounds of South Bronx street life very well; and Virginia Scott, whose essay "Radio Religion" is still screamingly funny, relevant, and full of Virginia's strong working-class feeling. There was to be more of Virginia in the Winter issue: her autobiographical poem "Affirmations," "beginning with the/affirmation of *my own/pain*," was to become the basis of her own book, *Poems to a Friend in Late Winter*. This was near the beginning of her Sunbury Press, which now includes ten issues of a poetry magazine and a number of

217

chapbooks. (If I have one accomplishment of pride as editor of *West End*, it is that I supported Virginia Scott early on. She has done wonderful work as an editor, teacher, and independent thinker.)

The Winter 1973 issue was probably the best edited of the early run. It features student writing from the Bronx, poems about growing up in the Midwest, experiencing American justice, and being a soldier in Viet Nam. The most striking material comes from Carolyn Dow, a welfare organizer in Bangor, Maine. It is touchingly direct: "My whole life long/i've been a whore/sold my soul for/a pat on the head/a smile/a kind word." Her friend, Gail Kaliss, supplied the main direction of the issue in a letter: "If fighting must come, it will, and we will have to fight for our lives. But in the meantime we need not just to show how bad things are . . . but how they could be . . . with a system that responds to people and their needs."

In the next issue, two poets who had been steered to us by Denise Levertov took over the whole magazine. Mark Pawlak wrote the poems that made up *The Buffalo Sequence*—later a book in its own right, from Copper Canyon Press. And Richard Edelman published a longpoem, *The Printer's Testament*, which included a memorable, strikingly romantic image of Che Guevara's face emerging like an icon from his press.

Gail Kaliss of the Winter 1973 issue was to become *West End*'s co-editor and finally its editor; Mark Pawlak and Rich Edelman, two of the magazine's best friends over the years. These young writers graced the latter days of the anti-war movement with their clarity, idealism and human concern.

The first two issues of Volume 3, produced in Summer 1974 and Spring 1975 respectively, continued my attempt to thread between the "personal" and "political"-now under the banner of the end of the Vietnam War and the meaninglessness of a peace without national restoration here at home. The magazine seemed to enter the same period of drift as did the nation. We were dealing, it seemed, with options both lost and found. Gail Kaliss wrote a good poem on her miseducation ("I am blind, I am deaf/with a mind like a tap/turn it on, turn it off/stop the body from running"); George Oppen wrote a striking short note "On Resistance," in which he defended his decision to go to war against the Nazis. The Spring 1975 issue had a funny piece called "I Don't Want the Word 'Capitalism' in My Poem" by Hilton Obenzinger; a fable of the Tupamaras by Margaret Randall, who corresponded with us tirelessly in this period; a good poem by Joan Colby, who seems to me one of the best writers of that "silent" decade; and some remarkable work by Jean Tepperman, including one poem ending: "I got in the bathtub/and looked at my foot./This foot needs blood/ with food in it, air,/a shoe for city broken glass,/rest and a clean sock./No reason why/this foot/doesn't deserve/all that." When I first read this, with Gail Kaliss, we both thought that Gail's prayers had been answered; the poets had begun to show "how (things) could be."

My period of sole editorship ended with a chapbook by Kip Zegers and a "Boston Issue" around the busing struggle in 1975. The Boston Issue was timed

218

for the beginning of the Fall term of public school; there was concern that the racists in the City Council might provoke a bloodbath. We tried to solicit poems directly related to the struggle. We didn't get many—most were, instead, "contributions" to the issue by progressive-minded poets. I wrote a report on the racist attacks, Margaret White did conversations in a South Boston bar where she was a waitress (to show there were honest working people in that part of town, too) and Anne Sadowski did a successful poem about working in a Boston book factory, where "workers don't read/through thousands upon/thousands of words pass/through their fingers/each day like sand/inside an hour glass." But my favorites were two: a left-wing poem of real fervor by Meatcutters Union rep John Mitchell, ending "Struggle is a constant/and the dialectic is forever!" and a poem on grief by first-time author Maureen Molta, ending "Cut the evil root—prune, then flourish," which really *could* have served as the poetic statement for Boston then. We gave a party when the magazine came out; Molta, new to such things, got as far as our front steps and her courage ran out. She was a generous, hardworking woman who subsequently started organizing writers, I believe in Brighton. I hope she is still at it.

The period of co-editing with Gail Kaliss, comprising Volume 4, was the most successful for the magazine. I redesigned the cover—ironically, it looks like *Partisan Review*—and we gave up on paper plates and went to a regular printer. We had a seemingly infinite variety of new authors: interesting pairings like Marxist poet Antar Mberi and Ntozake Shange, later of Broadway fame; Patricia Eakins and Margaret Randall ("Motherhood" and "Prime Stroke to Completion"); Bernadine Oliver, on Harlem, and feminist theorist Batya Weinbaum, on Coney Island; a gentle Ed Ochester and a ferocious Meridel Le Sueur. Most of all we opened the pages, under Gail's influence, and let some fresh air in: a host of working-class writers finding a home, perhaps for the first time in an "established" small press publication. (How strange the word would have seemed.)

In 1976-77, Gail and I saw some dramatic moments. We interviewed Walter Lowenfels when Walter was dying and too thoughtful of the feelings of his young guests to explain why his tongue was slowed and his spirits sagging. We broke with Denise Levertov, who had wanted to edit an issue for us and couldn't tolerate our insistence that we participate with her in the process. Finally, we even argued with each other, when Gail wanted to pull out material already typeset because it contained sexist and racist statements, and I wanted to get the issue out, because it was late already, and deal with consequences later. Probably other things were pressing on us: my rootlessness was becoming an impediment to my judgment, while Gail's biggest problem was earning a living. The magazine as I had known it ended with a Midwest issue which spoke of great revivals in that region: But that is another story, one I have been living in Kansas City and Minneapolis since 1977, and will tell in some other place.

In looking back over this magazine, my greatest enthusiasm for it lies in the company we kept. We made friends and enemies (often the same person, as things evolved). We made some alliances which we should not have, and lost some friendships which ought to have been cherished and nurtured. Arrogance lies behind many such mistakes; these things cost, over the years. But we also had fine successes. We established a good climate and a place for many authors. Our sense of our work, especially at the end, became more one of collective sharing. Writers like Mark Pawlak, Kip Zegers, Susan Epstein, Patricia Eakins and many more actually helped us in the process of publishing the magazine. We went to readings together, and directly confronted social issues rather than speak only from the page. And so it came about that indeed the "poetry" and "politics," the "personal" and "social," had come together.

When I participated in a panel called "From Writer to Reader" at the American Writers Congress (New York, 1981), I was gratified to see, in a small room, eight writers once published by *West End*—from eight cities! And they are still out there, organizing and writing. That was what we came for—to pass the word, and to keep it moving on.

Facts and some sentences to end this. An issue of the magazine cost me less than $100 in 1971; it came to somewhere around $700 at the end. We started with 150 copies or so, never distributed much above 500. Many went out free to friends; we sold a few at newsstands, mostly in New York, and a few through the mails. More poets were submitting to us later on—whether because there were more out there, or due to improved communications, I'm not sure. We were never grant-dependent to any degree until the end, and even then the crucial production factor was not money but available time and energy. Publishing a little mag became a life-style: it meant going to COSMEP meetings, book fairs, and bookstores, and visiting writers. We did these things willingly, and acquired many friends in the small press world, but we lived a double existence too, because our primary interest was in the socially engaged writers. We joined others in the fight for grants and for the grant process, for true democracy in giving; but we are not too dismayed at the outcome in these Reagan years. Those who fought hardest alongside us seem to be surviving, because they believe in something beyond their egos, and they work hard. We are concerned about the survival of alternative literature not so much for its own sake, in any case. We are concerned more about the survival of a world we want to live in, and its improvement. The vision has not changed, though the means of arriving at the end of the road may seem quite different.

WEST END

MIDWEST

PEOPLE'S CULTURE

ANTHOLOGY ISSUE

VOLUME 5   NUMBER 1

ONE DOLLAR

Marvin Malone

Wormwood Review

Marvin Malone

The *Wormwood Review* goes on and on and on . . . and continues to exert an influence beyond that expected of a little magazine printing only 700 hand-numbered copies. In addition to being the editor of *Wormwood*, Marvin Maline is a professor of pharmacology and toxicology, a serious collector of little magazines, and a part-time artist/poet. Born in Nebraska in 1930 and married there in 1952, he lived in New Jersey, New Mexico, and Connecticut before settling in Stockton, California. There he teaches at the University of the Pacific School of Pharmacy. The curious can pick up other life details from: *California Librarian* (34/4: 230-235, 1970), *TriQuarterly* (43: 388-397, 1978) and the current edition of *American Men and Women of Science: Medical Sciences*. The bearded, balding professor's opinions on God, politics, sex and loss of innocence can be inferred from his commentary below.

The Why and Wherefore of *Wormwood*

The first issue of *Wormwood* was set up in the winter of 1959 in a cold Connecticut barn where it was printed on an antique letterpress powered by gin-fueled graduate students. Now, fulfillment of subscriptions is guaranteed personally through and including issue 96. Since issue 5, *Wormwood* has been essentially a one-man operation, with the editor functioning in all capacities—reading submissions, editing, typing camera-ready copy, designing/preparing cover art, maintaining correspondence and subscription lists, addressing mailing envelopes, plus functioning as clerk, accountant and fall guy. This feat of nearly 100 issues requires persistence most of all (especially when one is committed for life's essentials to doing another full-time job well). This also implies a continuing infatuation with the printed word.

A love of books and magazines and a facility for reading and writing date

223

back to the editor's earliest childhood memories and cannot be explained either by heredity or congenial environment—probably a counterbalance to the realities of the Great Depression. About 1949 and by chance, the *New Directions* annuals were discovered. They revealed the existence of the classic literary mags such as *STORY, transition, Contact, View, Poetry London* and Connolly's *Horizon*. Once identified, these exemplary mags were each searched out and devoured. This search led to the discovery of mags such as *Golden Goose, Black Mountain Review, Origin, Merlin* and *Zero*. These sequentially pointed toward the true, low-budget little mags being printed at that time such as *The Deer and the Dachsund, Naked Ear, Inferno, existeria* and *Hearse*.

Correspondence was started with Harold Briggs' little shop Books 'n' Things (New York City), Judson Crews' The Motive Bookshop (Ranches of Taos, New Mexico), Larry Wallrich's Phoenix Bookshop (New York City), Frances Steloff's Gotham Book Mart (New York City) and eventually Jim Lowell's Asphodel Book Shop (Cleveland, Ohio) and Henry Wenning's elegant shop (New Haven, Connecticut). Each of these bookmen was fond of little mags, knowledgeable and a good teacher. Each had a different perspective and taste. An orgy of reading and collecting little mags was launched with Hoffman, Allen and Ulrich's *The Little Magazine: A History and a Bibliography* providing backward perspective and James Boyer May's magazine, *Trace*, providing current addresses and information. After a decade of spending spare time on such activities, becoming an editor was inevitable.

All of the above-mentioned magazines are quite different, yet all have influenced the editorial attitude manifested in *The Wormwood Review*. The influences are probably not all that apparent to the casual reader—but that is as it should be. This decade of preparation had also established some guidelines in the editor's brain about what was necessary for a little magazine to function successfully. These guidelines became the philosophy behind *Wormwood*: (1) avoid publishing oneself and personal friends, (2) avoid being a "local" magazine and strive for a national and international audience, (3) seek unknown talents rather than establishment or fashionable authors, (4) encourage originality by working with and promoting authors capable of extending the existing patterns of Amerenglish literature, (5) avoid all cults and allegiances and the you-scratch-my-back-and-I-will-scratch-yours approach to publishing, (6) accept the fact that magazine content is more important than format in the long run, (7) presume a literate audience and try to make the mag readable from the first page to the last, (8) restrict the number of pages to no more than 40 per issue since only the insensitive and the masochistic can handle more pages at one sitting, (9) pay bills on time and don't expect special favors in honor of the muse, and lastly and most importantly (10) don't become too serious and righteous. Ignoring the above ten commandments appears to lay the ground for a mag's self-destruction. Very few little mags are terminated by outside forces—they self-destruct! It is unrealistic and romantic to believe otherwise. Undoubtedly, *Wormie* will self-destruct some day, but it's not possible for the editor to predict when that will be. Every three years the editor rereads the magazine as he prepares a three-year index and debates whether *Wormwood* continues to have a function. There is no wish for continuation as an end in itself. The responses of readers and contributors, the number of reprint requests, the number of new poets found, etc. are considered. If this analysis is positive, subscription fulfillment is guaranteed for another three years and one proceeds on.

The average little mag is organized as a spontaneous publishing vehicle for the editor and his/her friends. Very few items written by this editor have appeared in *Wormwood* and all of those have been short and written on the spot to fill a blank space when photo-ready copy was being prepared—all appear under one of several assumed names. While this stance does seem to assure some degree of editorial honesty, it (of course) does not assure editorial taste. Taste seems to be acquired no other way than by reading acknowledged classics and then a *lot* of contemporary work and then following one's best instincts. Honestly edited one-man mags may or may not have "taste" but practically all such are interesting for what they reflect about the editor. It is probably true that collectors like "interesting" mags while the professors like mags with "good taste." Taste on a national/international scale does change with time, and the present editor refuses to worry about whether history will find *The Wormwood Review* to be "interesting" or "tasteful." *Wormie* simply exists to publish what the editor chooses to think is important.

Originally published in Storrs, Connecticut and for the last 13 years from Stockton, California, *Wormwood* has been produced in towns virtually lacking a writing/publishing community—but since *Wormwood* has never attempted to be a community or a specialized magazine, it has never had to depend upon local or specialized talent. It has never had significant local support (presently one paid subscriber from Storrs and two paid subscribers in Stockton) and it would be unrealistic to expect such, considering the present TV-oriented culture in the United States. This insularity has proved to be a blessing since it has cut down on the time-consuming and nonproductive small talk, gossip and posturing which seem to be the preoccupation of most "literary" groups—and it has not cut down on productive communications with like-minded individuals elsewhere. The United States Mail still functions reasonably well although becoming progressively more expensive and erratic!

Communication with others has been through personal correspondence and the exchange of magazines. The exchange of mags is considered to be especially important for maintaining editorial perspective and editorial health. *Wormwood*'s exchange list usually ranges from 100 to 120 English-language and foreign-language magazines. *Wormie* balks at exchanges when the other mag is committed to vanity publishing or to selling some cause other than literature. This continuing dialog with authors and other publishers means much to this editor and therefore constitutes a major reason why he continues to publish a little magazine—nothing more than a variation of the pen-pal syndrome.

Wormwood is self-funding and nonprofit. Library subscriptions constitute the backbone of the income—their renewals are reasonably predictable and this allows the stability needed for long-range planning. Since the libraries want four issues a year, *Wormie* takes care to provide four issues a year. Although issue dates are irregular and although two issues are mailed out at a time (obviously this cuts the postal bill and mailing work in half), four issues are produced religiously per year. What is earned *per year* is exactly correlated with the number of pages and the quality of printing used *per year*. *Wormwood* has been printed by letterpress (first and fourth issues), commercial letterpress (second issue), paper-plate offset (the lean years) and presently by traditional offset means. In the first decade, mimeographed sheets (devoted to news, reviews and commentary) were stapled in with the other sheets, but this has not been done since the press was moved to Stockton (a mimeograph is not easily accessible here). The editor's time is donated wholly to balance the press's budget. Since his professional salary cannot support a magazine and a family of four, the mag must earn its way in the so-called good old American tradition of free enterprise. Any dependency on funding agencies, such as CCLM or NEA, is resisted. To encourage individual subscriptions, the yearly price is kept as low as possible. Because of the recent postal rate increases, the cost has just been raised from $4.50 to $5.00 for four consecutive issues. This virtually guarantees that any person (who really wants to) can subscribe.

There are very few individually crafted products these days that sell four for $5.00. The economically sad truth is that the reading audience of little magazines is very limited if one ignores the audience associated with library subscriptions. This audience is almost exclusively limited to active writers (of all ages) with egos strong enough to read and enjoy others' work plus, of course, the rare individuals who are little mag readers and collectors by preference. The audience is select but the market limited. The $5.00 subscription price and the limited audience dictate that one must use offset processes for printing a 40-page magazine, use saddle-stitching, and restrict oneself to one-color printing. Then (and only then) will income balance expense. If one mimeographs the entire mag, then a profit is certainly possible. A fancy, slick-paper, multicolor format will definitely sell copies in bookstores and newsstands where impulse buying is common, but magazines such as *TriQuarterly* and *The Paris Review* are frequently bought only for coffee-table display and not for reading. One copy can last for years if the colors fit in with the decor! However, *TriQuarterly* and *The Paris Review* (generally considered to be successful magazines) also do not make a profit. This editor believes in the principle that a little mag is nothing if it is not read. *Wormwood* is after a live audience even if limited in size. The editor frequently dreams of publishing a magazine with the present editorial policy (plus prose) packaged in a format with the physical heft and feel of *Botteghe Oscure* and illustrated with very well-reproduced photographs of contributors—but this is clearly a dream.

Wormwood does not distribute to bookstores or newsstands simply because it cannot afford to. During the first ten years, serious attempts to do this were made, but these businesses almost universally regarded it as good business not to settle accounts with such a small operator. Their philosophy seemed to be that little magazines always fold—so why turn good money back to a doomed operation? Such a philosophy is fool-proof good Yankee business sense, but it does insure that the small mags do fail. One key to a magazine's survival is to just not attempt such distribution and concentrate on getting subscribers. It is this editor's impression that the real audience for little mags does not do much impulse buying—they seem to browse in libraries first and then subscribe to the 4-6 mags that most satisfy their literary appetite. These individuals also tend not to discard their little mags—which makes them amateur collectors. A word-of-mouth recommendation from these "fans" does sell subscriptions, and in our subscription list it is possible to trace the "genealogy" of a new subscriber back several "generations."

Cid Corman once indicated in a letter that he thought it useful to have each issue of *Origin* associated in the public's mind with one poet, so that readers spoke of the new "Charles Olson" issue or the "Creeley." This concept appealed and so *Wormie* instituted its yellow-paper center sections of 8-24 pages devoted to one poet or one idea. Subscribers like the idea and it does provide an unusually good showcase for a young poet. Twenty to forty copies are signed by the featured author and half are retained by *Wormwood* to distribute to patrons and friends of the press, while the remaining half become the signer's property. Poets featured to date have been: David Barker (issues 75 and 84), John Bennett (55), Harold E. Briggs (40), Charles Bukowski (16, 24, 53, 71, 81/82), William S. Burroughs (36), Judson Crews (19, 58, 83), John Currier (44), Sanford Dorbin (42), Ian Hamilton Finlay (14), Hugh Fox (32), Don Gray (26), Oliver Haddo (27, 28, 39), Alred Starr Hamilton (61), Dick Higgins (25), Gloria Kenison (23, 26), Jim Klein (scheduled for 86), Ronald Koertge (29, 35, 51, 63), Carl Larsen (11), Lyn Lifshin (47, 59, 65, 78, 85), Gerald Locklin (31, 50, 64, 67, 76), Leo Mailman (77), Wilma Elizabeth McDaniels (scheduled for 87), Al Masarik (57), Ann Menebroker (54), Jack Micheline (37), Joyce Odam (49), Christopher Perret (21, 30), Ben Pleasants (38, 52, 72), Bern Porter (41), Ray Puechner (27, 28, 39), Steve Richmond (43, 70), Kirk Robertson (60, 69), Paul St. Vincent (74), Walter Snow (46), Richard Snyder (56), Charles Stetler (48), Brian Swann (68), Richard Vargas (73), William Wantling (15, 36), Charles Webb (62), Jon Edgar Webb/*The Outsider* (45), and Phil Weidman (33, 79). The writing styles of this group are disparate in the extreme as are their ages, personalities and backgrounds—all deserve a greater reading audience. Issue 17 was devoted to the Le Metro poets; issue 34 to female poets; and issue 80 to *Wormwood*'s "birthday" celebration.

The most bittersweet award an author can receive today is the annual Wormwood Award "for the most overlooked book of worth for a calendar year." Certain of the awardees are now well known, but were not at the time of the award. A single review in some other magazine can disqualify one. Here is the list: 1961: Alexander Trocchi, *The Outsiders* (Signet); 1962: Kurt Vonnegut Jr., *Mother Night* (Gold Medal); 1963: James Drought, *The Secret* (Skylight); 1964: Russell Edson, *The Very Thing That Happens* (New Directions); 1965: Christopher Perret, *Memoirs of a Parasite* (Hors Commerce Press/Jim Callahan); 1966: Stanley Crawford, *Gascoyne* (Putnam); 1967: Peter Wild, *The Good Fox* (The Goodly Co.); 1968: Ian Hamilton Finlay, *3 Blue Lemons* (Wild Hawthorne Press); 1969: Charles Bukowski, *Notes of a Dirty Old Man* (Essex); 1970: Lorine Neidecker, *My Life by Water* (Fulcrum); 1971: Jonathan Williams, *Blue & Roots/Rue & Bluets* (Grossman); 1972: Gerald Locklin, *Poop, and Other Poems*

WASP WOULD STING YOU - 62

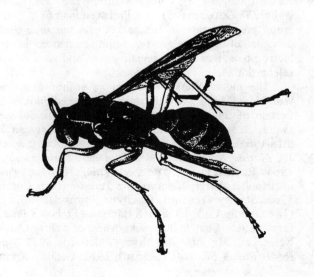

(MAG Press); 1973: Ronald Koertge, *The Father Poems* (Sumac); 1974: Steve Richmond, *Earth Rose* (Earth Press); 1975: Lyn Lifshin, *Shaker House Poems* (Tideline); 1976: Phil Weidman, *After the Dance* (Orchard Press); 1977: Joseph Nicholson, *The Dam Builder* (The Fault); 1978: Charles Webb, *Zinjanthropus Disease* (Querencia Press); 1979: Michael Kasper, *Chinese English Sentence Cards: A Novelette* (Imaginary Press); 1980: Wilma Elizabeth McDaniel, *Tollbridge: Poems* (Contact II Publications). Certainly these books should not have been ignored, and the editor does enjoy the reading that is necessary to make a selection. Nominations are gratefully accepted by mail.

The present little mag scene appears reasonably healthy, but it does not have the pure excitement and dedication of the 1960-70 decade when anyone with a mimeograph was in business and fiercely independent. In the 1970-80 decade, many magazines shifted their focus from the art of the printed word to the art of grantsmanship—these arts are not equivalent. *Wormwood* has never wasted its limited space on scholarly, semi-scholarly, or non-scholarly criticism, preferring to print the stuff that criticism feeds on. Instead, *Wormie* has always run extensive free listings of new mags and little press publications. The general philosophy was to push the art of the word, the idea of subscription and purchase—and to push the concept that the little mag scene was large and varied enough to provide each reader with something desirable, no matter what his/her taste might be. Infighting for prestige, grant monies, positions on review boards, etc., did not seem to be what *Wormwood* was all about. Consequently, *Wormie* has never battled for literary turf . . . preferring to let history decide.

Consequently, we missed much of the fun of the '70s. Literary infighting now is quite common and the object appears not to be literature but the control of federal/state monies for writing and publishing. Government functionaries are not kindly disposed toward creators of the printed word—literature's allocation of monies is only a very small fraction of that dumped on the performing arts. A larger audience is needed in the United States for contemporary literature, and a significant advance in this regard has been made since 1960—due exclusively to the little publishers and not due to the big publishers of New York City and environs. If the infighting within the little magazine/small press scene continues and becomes more public, both the developing audience and the scraps of federal/state monies will surely be lost. When the infighting involves writers it is very easy for the contenders to use choice adjectives as weapons and then have the words picked up by the press. The scraps of money doled out for literature are hardly worth fighting about in the final analysis.

Although probably a controversial opinion, this editor believes that the very steady increase in the number of little mags which began in the 1950-60 decade and which flowered in the 1960-70 decade was due more to better communication between editors and between editors and authors than to grant monies and the increased availability of low-cost printing services—after all, the mimeograph had been around a long time before the so-called "mimeograph revolution." Whether one is an author or editor, there is no greater stimulation than the discovery of a like-minded editor in the next town, the next state, or in England, or in Brazil. This facilitation of communications can be correlated with the founding of the little magazine called *Trace*, which served originally as a little magazine/small press directory. Prior to this time, accurate, up-to-date addresses were difficult to find, especially for foreign publishers. Later on the magazine decided to print literature in addition to functioning as a directory and was not too successful in this regard. After its failure, the directory function was taken over by Len Fulton who launched the *Directory of Little Magazines* in 1965. Issued annually, this essential book is now titled the *International Directory of Little Magazines and Small Presses*. In 1973 another book was produced which has facilitated communications within the national literary community: *A Directory of American Poets*, published by Poets and Writers Inc. of New York City. Prior to this time, such listings were restricted to established and fashionable individuals and the addresses were usually in care of some agent. In 1976, the same group published *A Directory of American Fiction Writers*. These books tend to hold the little mag/small press scene together and allow outsiders to sense the dimensions and vitality of the contemporary literary community. A condensed (but quite comprehensive) appraisal of the little mag scene of the 1960-70 decade from the viewpoint of this editor/collector has been published in *Vagabond* (No. 19, pp. 43-51, 1974). The trends begun in that volatile decade are just now beginning to surface in the products of the establishment presses.

As television has tended to wipe out distinct dialects within the United States, so also has TV tended to spread corruption of language to all levels of society. Merchandizers write words to sell products (corn flakes, politicians, electrical appliances, attitudes, automobiles, life styles) via the national media and, if the products sell, these writers are valued and generously awarded with cash. Such writers usually make no claims that their output constitutes truth or high literature even though it is successful in moving/manipulating people. The public (using the same logic) measures the worth of creative writers (those aspiring to high literature) by media reports of the magnitude of their cash advances and whether or not there are secondary contracts for soft-bound editions and movie/TV versions. It is ironic that true poets and wordsmiths can now owe their reputations more to merchandizing (the words of others) than to their own verbal and creative skills—Orwell's key year of 1984 is here. The little magazine/small press scene seems to be a healthy antidote to all of this. On the last page of issue after issue, *Wormwood* has reprinted this quote from poet/artist Jean Arp's "Dadaland"—it seems to sum up the role of the little publisher in modern society:

> We were seeking an art based on fundamentals to cure the madness of the age and a new order of things that would restore the balance between heaven and hall. We had a dim premonition that power-mad gangsters would one day use art itself as a way of deadening men's minds . . . .

Montana Morrison 1985

Diane Kruchkow

Zahir & Stony Hills

Diane Kruchkow

Diane Kruchkow was born in Stamford, Conn., in 1947; grew up in the '60s in New Hampshire, New York, and New England; still growing up in Maine, in an old farmhouse. Writing, editing, teaching—gardening, & mothering. She has been a member of the Board of Directors (and Chair) of COSMEP; was founder and coordinator of NESPA; founder and editor of *Zahir, Stony Hills*, and *Small Press News*. She has served on the Literature Panel, Maine State Commission of Arts and Humanities, and the CCLM Grants Committee (1977). Her publications include numerous essays and poems, and the chapbook *Odd Jobs*.

A Short Literary Biography of an Idealist

Back in 1969, I sat up one night, after having seen "The Shoes of the Fisherman," and had some sort of religious experience (periods of crying, clarity, my mind and emotions cartwheeling) and knew by the next morning that I would publish a magazine. I didn't quite know what type of magazine, but I knew there was a lot wrong with the world and somehow I wanted to pounce in there and try to fix it up.

I was in college at the time, in New Hampshire, looking for commitment under those tall elms and maples in one of the prettiest campuses in New England. It was in the midst of the student ferment and I was becoming "involved" and would soon become very involved in the student strike and other politics. I was also an English Lit. major taking an Honors course in Expatriate writing and gossip of the '20s (I'd read *Being Geniuses Together* or *Shakespeare & Co.*, transport myself into the scene, get to know the folks, then go tell stories about the period to my Honors professor who usually chuckled a bit and gave me an "A").

But I was more involved in the Philosophy Dept., since it seemed to understand the ferment of the time, while the English Dept. pretty much ignored it. Even the Philosophy professors whom I admired, however, went their own middle-class way after preaching how one should live the truest life possible. It was disappointing. I knew my deepest commitment was to literature. Good literature told how it really was. Good literature, to paraphrase Hemingway, cut through the baloney. It revealed what was going on behind uncommunicative eyes.

Things were coming together for me pretty quickly back in 1969. It was, as they say, a formative year. One day in my roamings through books about the Expatriate scene, I discovered *The Little Magazine* by Hoffman, Allen & Ulrich. It traveled right to the core, became a bible. I wanted to edit a little magazine, find my "green isle in the sea" and change the world.

The summer of 1969 I went to England, to Oxford on a summer study scholarship, and while I was there I received word that an experimental college at the University had gotten funded and was going to begin when I returned there for graduate school in the fall of '69 (under a Ford Foundation Fellowship for future professors). I had proposed to teach a workshop on the small press if, in fact, the university became a reality. Now, here I was knowing very little, but burning to find out.

My first touch with the modern-day small press was through a letter from a nearby publisher, Bob Fay, who then lived in Ogunquit, Maine. He had published a couple of issues of his magazine, *eikon*, and, small world that it is, had also started up some papers in Maine with his good friend Len Fulton. He even worked on Fulton's magazine, *dust*, for a while in California before moving back to Maine.

Bob's first letter was typed (on an old black Royal, I subsequently discovered) with no capitals and was full of self-examination. I had never read anything like it. There I was gearing up to be a university professor, being expected to write exceptionally dull papers on Milton and trying to read *American Scholar* and into the scene came a human being with hassles and problems trying to discover and accept his situation. It seemed real. If this was what the little mag scene was like, I wanted to join in.

While I was a graduate student and meeting with my experimental college crew of freshmen and sophomores over wine and popcorn in my basement apartment just off campus, reading poetry and discovering current magazines, I also saw a lot of Bob and his world. It was not only diametrically different than the stiffness of university life, but was also at the other end of the scale from my upbringing in Fairfield County, Connecticut, an area which never took hold on me.

In mid-semester, the workshop decided to put out its own little magazine. Its title, *Zahir*, came from a short story by Borges, in which a character got so involved with a coin—the Zahir—that he became oblivious to all else around him and went mad. (Subsequently I learned that "zahir" was a Semitic word which meant "something very intense.") We sent flyers around to various places and were soon inundated with manuscripts.

The students read and decided upon the manuscripts while I tried to figure out how to put out a magazine, spending semester break talking with the printer. I spent days trying to get the pages in order and, for the cover, sketched out a long "Z" with the rest of the name riding on its tail—something probably set loose from the old "Zorro" days. The University paid for the first two issues, which are now out of print.

Bob told me that out in California Len Fulton had started an organization for little mag editors. That, of course, was COSMEP. In its early days COSMEP was exciting: It was The Scene. It was how the wild and wooly got to know and meet each other—how friendships and long- (and short-) term relationships began. COSMEP to me helped create the modern-day equivalent to the '20s Expatriate scene, uniting those in the '60s who had somehow become expatriates in their own country.

I wrote to Len. I wrote to Richard Morris. I traveled all night and into the morning on a Greyhound bus to get to the Buffalo conference in 1970. It was just what I was looking for: real writers and people involved with the underground and commitment. Allen Katzman of the *East Village Other* was there, as well as Claude Pelieu and Mary Beach, Ray Bremser and Allen Ginsberg whom everybody seemed to know. Lawrence Ferlinghetti sent a resolution that we refuse government (i.e., NEA) money. At my lunch table one afternoon sat George Plimpton and Peter Ardrey who were being castigated for censoring the *American Literary Anthology*. My roommate, Sue Sherman, took me to see "Battleship Potemkin" which I had never heard of. On the walls of SUNY at Buffalo where we met were revolutionary slogans in red paint. I felt I was at the heart of movement and change in this country and it cleared out my synapses and prepared the way for a whole new perspective.

Naturally, I decided to drop out of graduate school after that, and find out what I could find out about literature and publishing and change. I moved around the northeast a lot in the early '70s: from New Hampshire to Cambridge, Mass. (having been accepted to, then dropping out of Radcliffe's Publishing Procedures Course, because the small press emphasis was nil) to New York City (where I did my first layout—Zahir No. 3—telling the printer in California to fix it if I did it wrong but it turned out I did it right) to Maine, then New Hampshire again and down to Massachusetts, all the while taking *Zahir*, in 13 cardboard cartons, with me. It was a traveling publishing company, although I never considered myself a publisher.

In 1972, I hitchhiked out to the conference in Madison, Wisconsin. It was put on by Morris Edelson at the Univ. of Wisconsin and he had provided a keg in the corner and had us all sit around in a circle and things got happening. What happened that year was that many women who had traveled great distances to get there did not get enough notice and rebelled and said nothing was happening and they felt uneasy talking to the men. I remember there was a 9:30 a.m. meeting in which Carol Bergé stood up and made this point and that was the start of the women's movement in COSMEP, which lasted many years.

I never really got involved in the women's movement in COSMEP because I never felt uneasy talking to the men. Harry Smith was Chair in 1972, and granted, Harry is a little hard to talk to, but if you know human beings you can

235

talk to Harry. He's a kind and generous man and I never once had problems asking him anything. I found that true of most of the male hierarchy of COSMEP, even of those not so kind or so generous. Somehow, and to this day I don't truly understand it, I was usually treated with great respect. In fact, one of the secrets of my longevity in the small press is that there's always been a certain magic there for me which has worked coming in and going out.

In 1973 I was elected to the Board of Directors of COSMEP and voted "Chair No. 2"—a position which lasted only a few years. Len Fulton was Chair that year, and the conference was in New Orleans. Ted Gay, whom I was then (and still am) living with, and I hitchhiked to New York state and drove down with Joe Ribar. Memories from this conference include staying at Tulane (celebrating my birthday with a mint julep), attending a party at John ("Planet of the Apes") Corrington's, meeting Darlene Fife and Robert Head of *NOLA Express*, and listening to Anne Pride prophesy that soon COSMEP would change its nature and direction, a natural progression for all organizations.

I didn't think much about that at the time. COSMEP was still exciting and here I was with Fulton and Hugh Fox and Carol Bergé and others on the Board, eagerly awaiting the controversies. (In '71 or so Carol Bergé had photocopied a year's worth of Board correspondence which anyone could obtain for $1.00, and it proved fascinating.)

By 1974 I was elected Chair of COSMEP. I remember watching TV in our fourth or fifth residence in Newburyport, MA, where Ted and I had lived since 1972, when Richard Morris called up and said I had been elected to the Board. The meeting was in New York City (Columbia) that year, and it was on a boulder in Central Park that the Board elected me Chair. I was glad, although it meant a year of photocopying and sorting Board Correspondence for me, with not a whole lot of progress or change. At least, I think, I held things at an even keel. I was working part-time at a local bookstore at the time and we were getting long letters from A.D. Winans and others to deal with. George Mattingly, Paul Foreman, Darlene Fife, Jackie Eubanks, Mary MacArthur, and Hugh Fox were also on the Board back then.

One thing I instituted was a voting chart, so Directors could know at a glance what was happening and what had happened. There wasn't any revolution that year, but I think right after my term COSMEP did change a lot, going in the direction of "non-literary" publishing. Maybe I just held that change off for a year.

Zahir by this time had developed into a somewhat respectable poetry magazine, with one or two issues appearing annually. I was not too concerned with subscribers, but did manage many personal trips to stores and libraries wherever I went and spent some memorable time hawking issues at Harvard Square back when Harvard Square was interesting. *Zahir* and I also became involved in many regional and national distribution ventures, such as the Book Bus, the COSMEP Distribution project, the NESPA catalog, and the NEA-sponsored national meeting of small press distributors held one weekend in Fargo, South Dakota, which culminated in a network of distributors called "Bookmovers" which never really got off the ground.

236

I was getting over 100 manuscripts per month, which wasn't a tremendous amount, but did take quite a bit of time to answer, all in longhand (I've never used printed rejection or acceptance slips). *Zahir* was my education in poetry; I felt I had to know why I accepted or rejected each poem—often telling the writer such details in the rejection/acceptance slip—causing my rejection slips to receive many good reviews.

Most issues were general poetry issues, but from time to time I included such oddities as a theory of physics by Will Fontaine, the mailing and visiting regulations at Florida State Prison, or a letter from Madeline Murray O'Hare, as well as the Spanish Diaries of Hugh Fox and a debate on Immanentism. *Zahir* No. 6 (a web-offset tabloid) focused on short fiction and the last two issues were chapbooks of longer poems by Connie Fox (her first) and Guy Beining, with collages by Tom Sutton, a professional cartoonist who wanted to experiment with other forms. Many poems from *Zahir* have been reprinted and many of its poets and writers have gone on to further fame if not fortune.

I always felt that *Zahir* & I attained a healthy symbiosis. While I put much time and effort into editing, producing, designing and (yes) marketing, *Zahir* helped me learn about the publishing and writing scene, large and small, and helped me work toward a niche for myself that might be fun, unique and even, perhaps, important. (*Stony Hills* and *Small Press News* have furthered that search, but more on them below.) While we did not change the world, I did, I feel, take a few steps towards the relation with it I'd like to have.

Along with my involvement with *Zahir* and COSMEP, grew my involvement with the New England Small Press Association (NESPA), an organization Ritchie Darling (Green Knight Press in Amherst, MA) and I set up in 1969. Ritchie had written to Bob about forming a New England organization and Bob had turned the letter over to me and we took it from there. The organization was quite active during the early-mid-'70s, holding meetings, readings, putting out a catalog and books, and fomenting statewide efforts (for example, the Maine Writers & Publishers Alliance grew out of this). Towards the end of the decade it petered out, and is presently defunct.

One day, though, in a lunch line in some cafeteria, Ritchie said, "Hey, wouldn't it be nice to have a review of New England small press publications." I took it from there and began *Stony Hills*, a tabloid small press review which originally concentrated on New England. It was inevitable, though, that *Stony Hills* would cover the national scene, since so much of my involvement was on a national basis. We (royal "we") did have pretty thorough coverage of New England presses in early issues, with interviews with Dick Higgins (then in Vermont), Val Morehouse, and the Waldrops of Burning Deck. In our first issue, we had reviews by Hugh Fox, Charles Plymell, Anne Pride (reviewing *Sports and the Macho Male*), Robert Abel, Karla Hammond, Joe Bruchac, Tom Montag, Roberta Kalechofsky and others, plus "Notes from Prison" by James Lewisohn (still incarcerated in Maine) and a listing of small presses in Mass. Our second issue had photos of the '77 COSMEP Conference in Lenox, MA (I traded in my brownie camera for a Konica 35 mm) and reviews and essays. Issue No. 3 began a serial interview with Larry Eigner, a series on small press "Groundbreakers" by

Merritt Clifton and my "Story of Seattle"—a write-up of the controversial CCLM meeting in Seattle in '77 in which, without any prior consultation at all, John Bennett, Harry Smith and I, the three elected members of the grants committee, decided to divvy up the money equally to all the applicants. (A lot has been made of this decision, but it was based simply on our individual dissatisfaction with the way grants had been handed out.)

In our fifth issue, we had the usual reviews, interviews, plus photos of the '79 Book Affair in Boston, notes on the CCLM meeting that year and an article from Brazil from Hugh Fox. The magazine developed issue by issue, through layout (all done by me except for No. 7, done by Doug Mumm), typesetting and contents. By issue No. 8 we ran a complete index and extensive short review section. By issue No. 9 our subtitle changed to "News and Reviews of the Small Press," leaving out the New England emphasis and becoming a national publication. In this issue (1981) we ran one of the first-ever major reviews of Meridel LeSueur (by Curt Johnson) and my own statement on how-to publishing books within the small press ("I *am* bothered by the how-to surge within the small press . . . for basically *how-to books tell how to fit into a system . . . ."*). During the '80s the magazine has developed along these national lines, acquiring Contributing Editors Lynne Savitt, Curt Johnson, John Bennett, Hugh Fox, and Mark Melnicove, and recently changing its subtitle to "Reviews of the Literary Small Press" to emphasize its concentration on fiction and poetry. And to cover all the immediate news and commentary on small press happenings, I began *Small Press News* in 1981, a newsletter appearing ten times per year.

It is quite clear to me that by this time, having gone through a few magazines, a few organizations, and a few years of living (now including motherhood), that the small press is, was, and will be a tool through which I feel I can deal with life in the truest way for me. It has never been an end in and of itself. There is something beyond the small press and it's not Random House: It's Plato's perfect circle. It's the human potential; it's a coming together. It's for reasons such as this I can't hanker to competition within the small press, or even take seriously much of the marketing and how-to talk. That's all OK in its place, but its place has gotten out of hand. It's not the Real Thing, but few publishers bother to look behind (beyond) it. The Real Thing is what I found back in "Shoes of the Fisherman"—something much more spiritual: a hunger of the soul.

I frankly miss the relating (corrosive or congenial) of the early days of COSMEP. I miss the controversy, the energy people had then to speak out, to hold the stultifying forces of bureaucracy and growth off for a few more years. I grew up with the small press, hand in hand, but while I still feel (somewhat) young, I'm afraid the small press has turned middle-aged. While many of the books are still exciting, there's something about the whole scene that's turning stale. I'm continually hoping for a certain freshness, looking for a new generation coming down the pike searching for the human spirit behind the computer chip, those who

go after all those vague dissatisfactions, to get at the core of them . . .
keep [their] eye on it and keep moving toward it until [they] hit it,
[they] strike that chord that lies deep inside all of us and [they] say
something that is true and always has been true and always will be true
and cannot be compromised and rationalized and frittered away . . . ."
(John Bennett, preface to *Vagabond Anthology*).

I'm sure they are there and can help us keep the vision clear.

Curt Johnson

Afterword

Curt Johnson

Curt Johnson (b. 1928 in Minneapolis, Minnesota) has been editor of *December* magazine since 1962. He has had four novels, a novella, and a collection of essays published, and has edited or co-edited four anthologies of little-magazine fiction, among them *Writers in Revolt: The "Anvil" Anthology*, with Jack Conroy. A freelance editor and writer who began with *Popular Mechanics* in 1953, he is currently publisher of *Who's Who in U.S. Writers, Editors & Poets: A Biographical Directory*.

I. December Magazine/December Press

I. The first condition of the freedom of the press is that it is not a business activity.–Karl Marx

Mostly it comes out of my pocket: $96,000 outgo in 24 years (up to this number), $51,000 income. Everybody's time is donated.

But it was never a hobby, though from the start I felt there would be patrons of the arts, lovers of literature, who would lend their support. As it turned out, there weren't.

I don't know—I tried to finagle money, but I have no talent for it. Early on I sent begging letters to the wealthy culture elite on Chicago's Gold Coast and North Shore but nobody wrote back. And just five or so years ago I had two very wealthy Chicago heiresses on the verge of kicking in some significant cash but then I got disgusted with what I was doing and intimated that they were possibly dilettantes (which they were), and that's all she wrote.

No private foundation has ever put up a nickel, and I've badgered a dozen of them, including the Rockefeller, the Playboy ("Mr. Hefner is not interested in associating in ventures wherein he does not exert complete editorial and financial control"), the Ford, the Old Dominion, and the Carnegie Corporation.

I first asked the Illinois Arts Council (IAC) for support back in 1968. They wanted ten free copies for their Advisory Panel members to review. I sent the books right away and the next thing right away I heard was *No*. ("The reason for this action is that the Council's funds are completely committed at this time.")

Same thing, same reason, in 1969, so—my ox not ungored, so to say—I wrote an article on the Council's activities for *ChicagoLand* magazine. It wasn't a complimentary article and the reply to my 1970 request for support was: "The question of funding small literary publications has been tabled." This from the $30,000-a-year Executive Director who—before the article appeared—had suggested (while I was interviewing him for the article) that I'd be a splendid person to serve on a panel to study that very question.

In 1971 the Illinois Arts Council gave $500 to a Michigan distributor of little magazines who was also getting support from the National Endowment for the Arts (NEA). This distributor used his support money to paint his house and chicken coop and never did get around to distributing. Honest. *December* got: "We are sorry to inform you . . . ."

In 1972, the same, and I vented some spleen in Chicago's *Literary Times*. The excellent writer Jim Harrison sent me a letter:

> Liked your fine, specific rage in the new *Literary Times*. In Michigan nearly all of the Arts Council money went to a hokum project called "ARTRAIN"—a bit of surrealism in everyday life wherein for about $70,000 a few carloads of "art" are trucked along the state's railroads. As with all Arts Councils not a single "real" artist is a member of the council . . . .

In 1973 December Press got a $150 IAC award for publishing *The Bonnyclabber* by George Chambers, who also got $150. *TriQuarterly*, the big, school-sponsored (Northwestern Univ.) little got $500 just for being.

In 1974, nothing; in 1975, another cash award ($200, I believe), this one for publishing Jay Robert Nash's *On All Fronts*; and in 1976 an award of $200 for Bob Wilson's *Young in Illinois*.

In 1977 I submitted a grant application to the National Endowment for the Arts via the IAC. (The state arts council people like you to go this route: it helps to justify their existence.) Jennifer Moyer was in charge of lit projects in the IAC pyramid by then and she called to advise me to revise my application—"flesh it out." I said I'd be pleased if she'd submit it as wrote. She warned me I would regret my laziness; all the other Illinois presses were submitting lengthy, detailed applications, and mine was bare bones. Didn't I realize I was importuning the federal government?

The application required only a single IAC signature—the head man—and it could be sent to the NEA. The deadline was March 1. Now Ms. Moyer, or her minions, had a bad habit. If a state awards program submission was due, say, by

242

June 15th, the announcement of the awards would be mailed the 9th, arrive the 12th, leaving you a scant three days to comply and the USPS to deliver your response. Repeatedly the IAC office barely got its mail out under this low tight wire. So I called the IAC a week after I sent the NEA application to it, early in February, not wanting them to miss the NEA deadline. (We were dealing, after all, with the federal government!) I called twice more, the last time on February 15, and on this occasion, my application still unsigned and unmailed by them, I fear I used an Anglo-Saxon verb for tilling the soil as I queried various, including Ms. Moyer, who responded to my invective with "I don't have to submit it at all."

March 3 I got a note from Jennifer Moyer: "This is to notify you that your small press application was sent to the NEA on February 22, 1977, ahead of the March 1 deadline . . . . I feel your rudeness to the receptionist, my secretary and to me was unnecessary and I hope that our relations can be more cordial in the future."

Imagine my embarrassment when December Press's turned out to be the only Chicago-area application to score. (Moyer couldn't believe it either.) That grant helped to publish five books.

II. Everything seems to be one gigantic mistake . . . . But it is we who are mistaken, not history. We must learn to look reality in the face; if necessary, we must invent new words and new ideas for these new realities that are challenging us.—Octavio Paz

As the '80s began, International Harvester Company had a loss of $1.6 billion for the year 1980 and its chairman and CEO, Archie R. McCardell, resigned his half-million-a-year post. (Some reports say $2-million-a-year post.)

On quitting, Archie received $600,000 from the company, plus IH products worth $28,000. He was also forgiven a $1.8 million loan that IH had made him to purchase 60,000 shares of its stock. He also had his life, accidental death, medical, and dental insurance benefits continued for one year, and Harvester returned to him his contributions to its savings and investment program and pension plan.

Have you ever quit a job or been laid off or fired? Were you handsomely rewarded at the time?

On resigning, Archie—who in 1977 had received a signing bonus of $1.5 million for his deigning to favor IH with his management expertise—said of his stewardship: "I know, in my heart, I did a lot of good things for the company, and the company is a lot better off."

Horse hockey, as J. Pierpont Morgan, who put IH together a century before, might have said; when Archie left, IH had debts of 4.2 billion, and mounting. Today, the company doesn't exist (which must have founding father Cyrus Hall McCormick wreaping in his grave), and, naturally, a whole slew of its former workers are unemployed.

Not entirely thanks to Archie, of course, but he contributed, he and many other top-top IH execs with him, experts in management all, men with eyes only for the bottom line, as they would express it . . . . You and I might call

243

Archie (and those with him and like him) a jerk—not to put too fine a point on it—were he not a captain of industry.

It is the captains of industry of this country—men like Archie— who have twice run and won with Ronald Reagan for their President. (And ours.) Their master plan for the economy of the country has virtually eliminated the corporate income and the estate tax, bestowed substantial benefits (such as windfall profit tax deductions) upon industry, and allowed profitable companies to "lease" the losses of unprofitable companies (like IH) so that neither corporate winners nor losers pay taxes, thus creating a tax system in which revenue is raised almost exclusively from individuals who *work* for a living. (As for the unemployed, Reaganites would as lief *their* entitlement was starvation. This is astounding, but true.)

Equally satisfying to the men who rally 'round Reagan is the ease with which corporations are now able to persuade unions to renegotiate worker contracts downward—"or else we'll close the place." In the instance of U.S. family farmers, they have foreclosed.

And yet the workers and the farmers, and damn near everyone else, have twice voted for the policies Ronnie says he espouses. Apparently, it would seem, quite possibly, maybe perhaps, Americans never will get a bellyful of pie in the sky. Or of Norman Rockwell rhetoric like this: "How can families and family values flourish when big government, with its power to tax, inflate and regulate, has absorbed their wealth, usurped their rights and too often crushed their spirit?"

That's the present President of the United States asking that, the President who in 1982-83 gave the Department of Defense (originally, you will recall, our Department of War) $10 billion more than its $206 billion wish list, and keeps giving more of the same for weapons year after year ($293 billion for this year— 1985—28% of *all* federal spending)—and running up the national debt astronomically while piously praising the goal of a balanced budget, and . . . .

But what's the use? We've known all along that Ronald Reagan is a smiling, mindless hypocrite, and an affable demagogue, haven't we? And that the cant he speaks is spoken to further enrich his already mega-wealthy friends and supporters.

Are Ronnie and his pals good for us or our children and grandchildren? Was the captain of the *Titanic* a good sailor?

III. Truth and reason are opposed to common sense and public opinion.—Erich Fromm

Ronald Reagan's domestic and foreign policy programs and his hypocrisy about both have everything to do with little magazines and small presses.

On the other hand, a cynic might say that the editor of a litmag or an independent small press is much like the fellow wheeling an empty wheelbarrow in and out of a barn. The fellow believes he is doing something useful; inside the barn is a load of wet hay; he is wheeling shade from inside the barn outside into the sunshine, sun from outside into the dark barn.

Given the present state of our society and civilization, and the set of mind of our leaders, the cynics may not be far wrong, but they are exceedingly foolish as to their own best interests, I think, to let matters stand as-is and as-tending without attempting to change them.

Yet given long-term trends in the United States, it cannot but seem to many —including many litmag editors and small press publishers—that there is little that can be done to remedy matters. This attitude C. Wright Mills pegged 30 years ago when he characterized the "alienation" of the free intellectual as "a lament and a form of collapse into self-indulgence."

The "rationalization of the free intellect," according to Mills, made it harder for intellectuals "to locate their external enemies than to grapple with their internal conditions. Their seemingly impersonal defeat has spun a personally tragic plot and they are betrayed by what is false within them."

So that we have had many little magazine editors and their writers retreating into art for its own sake, and then cursing the world because the world pays no heed to their contrivances and irrelevancies.

It has always been the thought here that what is false, invidious, destructive, unjust in American civilization ought to be resisted—however inadequately that thought has been expressed in December Press publications. Which is also to say that well-wrought fiction is fine and necessary, and poetry is pretty, too, but exploration of the interior self will be an exercise in futility if the exterior ultimately finds itself starving and in chains.

The independent small press in these States these days is the only press that will mention, or might even have the faintest inclination to show our present predicament for what it is. And suggest remedies. That's to say, the excesses of our present system now manifesting themselves won't kill the system. They will kill us, and our children.

IV. . . . you could bring the mag out twice in a month and then once in two years and everything would be fine if the stuff between the covers was good; you could bring it out on gloss paper using a letterpress or on a mimeo using recycled paper and it didn't make any difference; my God, you could print the magazine with rubber stamps and that wouldn't matter, that would not make it bad and it would not make it good, the method by which you got the word out was incidental, the important thing was to . . . keep your eye on it and keep moving toward it until you hit it, you strike that chord that lies deep inside all of us and you say something that is true and always has been true and always will be true and is not and cannot be compromised and rationalized and frittered away, can only be lost from sight—you say it and do it and it is a poem, no matter what the form.—John Bennett

Jack Conroy had the right idea. The motto of his bi-monthly *Anvil* (1932-35), the pioneer of proletarian magazines devoted solely to creative work, was: "We prefer crude vigor to polished banality."

In 1935 Conroy ("The Sage of Moberly") appended the following note to his masthead:

245

With this issue *The ANVIL* reaches a circulation greater than that attained by any other so-called "little magazine" ever published in America . . . .

The average "little magazine" prints some 500 copies an issue. The late *Pagany*, financed by a millionaire, never achieved a circulation greater than 1,000, we understand. *Blast* stopped at a similar total. *The Windsor Quarterly*, which is suspending, and *Manuscript* are reported to be in the 1,500 class. *Partisan Review* has been printing 2,000 copies. *The Hound and Horn*, with influential backing, stopped at the 3,500 mark . . . .

The ANVIL began with a 1,000-print order . . . . The current number attains the 4,000 mark.

But some 3,500 of those copies represent newsstand and bookstore distribution, 2,300 in New York City . . . . Lacking an endowment, a magazine must appear monthly to win the steady stream of subscriptions to finance its continued publication.

To make *The ANVIL* a monthly is our goal. Will you aid us . . .?

It was not to be. William Phillips and Philip Rahv—the Bobbsey Twins of pre-WWII leftist literature—wrested the *Anvil* from Conroy and, with its sub list and sales as a base for their *Partisan Review*, went on to 50 years of polished banality and propaganda. *PR* became de rigueur for the coffee tables of alienated U.S. intellectuals, and as recently as the late 1960s was boasting to potential advertisers of a circulation of 19,000, a boast quickly deflated to 9,000 when the *American Literary Anthology* editors announced a limit of 15,000 circulation on magazines expecting to qualify for one or more of their National Endowment for the Arts awards.

But Conroy's 1935 representative circulation figures apply with accuracy to today's leading littles. (Though the "average" little magazine today probably prints only 1,000, give or take 500.) Meanwhile, in 50 years the population of this country has doubled.

Ten years ago Harvey Swados lamented the fact that though his creative writing students did not read little magazines, they planned to publish their work—where?

. . . in the quarterlies and little magazines which few read regularly and to which none subscribes. One gets the impression that for them these periodicals exist, not because of any intellectual or spiritual commitment on the part of their editors or readers, but rather as a kind of neutral depository for creative efforts . . . .

For three years in the '60s I traveled the country meeting with college English profs on textbook matters—and none of the many teachers of lit with whom I talked, negotiated, and got drunk had ever heard of more than Harriet Monroe's *Poetry* or Margaret Anderson's *The Little Review* or *Partisan* or *Paris reviews* . . . and not all that many had heard of *them*. Over a span of 20 years I hand-addressed and mailed some 30,000 *December* promo fliers to English profs and in all that time only 30 or so subscribed.

Worse, those few (creative writer) English profs who *do* know of the littles generally send out their own stories and poetry and SASEs via their department's postal meters and can't even get around to asking their schools' libraries to subscribe.

Do I mean to imply that English profs have an obligation to support little mags? You goddam right I do—they make their well-paid livings off literature, and little mags are right where it all begins.

As for creative writers, English profs and otherwise, submissions to *December* over 20 years would—I guess—total about 40,000 from—I guess again—some 15,000 individuals. Of these 15,000 creators who wished to be published in *December*, a round dozen have subscribed. (Medical doctors, lawyers, and psychiatrists have outnumbered writers two-to-one as subscribers.)

December is neither well-known nor prestigious. But if its address has been found and used by 15,000 writers, I'd guess there must be at least 75,000 "serious" writers in this country of 225,000,000. That may be a conservative estimate—to which you can also add knows only God how many more dabblers. Do they *all* have an obligation to support little mags? You goddam right they do—if they want to get published, or want their betters to.

The solution is simple: All little magazines should require all contributors to enclose, with each submission, letters (xeroxed) from at least two of this country's thousands of littles, on those magazine's letterheads, addressed to the individual contributor, stating that they are current-year subscribers. No such tickies, no readings.

This put-your-money-where-your-mouth-is plan is as nearly fool-proof a solution to low litmag sub totals as I can devise, and it is a serious proposal.

V. New York was not a stable center, and high culture for its own pure sake was not what it was about. It was becoming a national and international culture market, engaged in organizing, processing, marketing and exploitation . . . .

Here in Chicago we should make the most of our backwardness. Not to be with it is an advantage when it is mad.—Saul Bellow

As a simple country boy, I am all for regionalism—on a national scale—culturally. Where I come from is the heartland of the heartland and I heartily endorse my region's egalitarian spirit, and its individualism, not to mention its pride in taking care of itself and its own.

I speak of the Midwest, of course, certainly the city of Chicago, where the littles started, with *Poetry* and *The Little Review*, but also of the whole region which gave us Twain, Dreiser, Hemingway, Fitzgerald, Hamlin Garland, Sherwood Anderson, and Richard Wright (via Memphis)—wot-the-hell, for a long time there two-thirds of our best and most of the next-best, including Sandburg, Masters, Lindsay, Hecht, Farrell, Conroy, Algren, Lardner, and LeSueur.

About 15 years ago I indulged myself by trying, on assignment from Theodore Solotaroff's commercial *New American Review*, a culture-survey of U.S. little magazines. There was the East Coast and the West Coast, I knew that much, but for the Midwest I was stuck for a catch-all designation. I used "Third Coast," which I either stole from a Milwaukee little mag, or anticipated. The style of the survey was the best I could manage in imitation of a slick, hip, with-it prose that, at the time, I thought well of because I thought it would sell. (It didn't to Solotaroff; Morris Edelson later printed the piece in *Quixote*.) A piece of the piece went like this:

The West Coast confronts the Establishment, makes guerrilla war on it. The East Coast *is* the Establishment. It samples all experience, flirts with power, wearily judges the West Coast outrageous and naive, the Third Coast manipulatable.

The East Coast prints beautifully done stories on trivial subjects, trivially done poems on childish subjects, and weighty criticism about its culture heroes (who are Henry James). The West Coast prints only poetry, millions of lines of it, though only one of every 30 of its writers of poetry is a poet. The Third Coast? Honest work in all genres, God save the thesis.

The East's flirtation with power becomes a commonlaw marriage and it pockets federal money covertly and overtly, spends most of that money directly on itself or its consuls, and with the balance publishes volumes (edited by its proconsuls) of the "best" (the *American Literary Anthology*) from the nation's little magazines, at least half of the favored being its own. The West is scandalized, protests mildly, at last agrees to cooperate with the East to prevent future scandal. The Third Coast sighs "co-option."

The East Coast delivers a considered, condescending judgment: "It is the character of the bumbling, well-intentioned Good American, too good to be wasted in the aluminum-siding business, but not of course good enough to compete with sensibilities of real literary delicacy and accuracy." (This sort of thing is memorized for cocktail party chit-chat —then forgotten by all but a few.) In its next breath the East cancels the reputations of three fairly respected names by denouncing "that same nervous, apologetic relation to what he has made that has embarrassed and perverted countless American writers, including Whitman, Twain, and Hemingway." The West Coast, never having heard of these three scribblers, continues its mimeo pamphleteering. The Third Coast devoutly continues to read Brautigan and remains silent.

Finally, it may be said in further gross oversimplification, since there is overlapping, intermingling, and moving between the coasts, since there are good guys and bad guys on all (some one issue, some the next), and since some little magazines and their editors are in their place but not of it, that the East Coast looks inward, has resources and contacts, can be dryasdust while striving for cool, practices incest, is vain, and indulges in old polemic. The West Coast looks outward, is young and underground, has no resources, practices hysteria, is alive, indulges in even more incest than the East (but innocently), and makes new polemic. The Third Coast? It watches its flanks, waiting . . . . The East Coast has faith, based on its power. The Third Coast has hope—and the West Coast has charity, and Charles Bukowski.

That's the way I saw it 15 or so years ago—but I think it is still as true as most general impressions. True then, and now. What it leaves out is the South and its litmags—which are about what you'd expect: aristocratic, genteel, and sometimes very damn good, but seeming to function within a tradition (form, logic, reason, restraint) long before scuttled off all the coasts. It also leaves out the poets of the Pacific Northwest, who do not belong to the West Coast (that's California, all by itself), and who for a quarter century have been the best in the country but who are much too far from the seat of literary power (NYC) ever to be recognized.

All this meant to convey some of what *December* has been about lo! these many years and some of what this book is meant to be about—and with an apology to my co-editor, whose idea this book was in the first instance and who hails from New England, which—like the Pacific Northwest—can be exempted from its coast when sweeping generalizations are swept.

VI. Magazine starting is an act of passion, not one of consideration—careless, heedless, and irreverent. Work out the probabilities and you will never start one.—Vance Bourjaily

What this book is about, as you surely realize by now, is the little mags and small presses of the '60s and '70s—the independent, alternative, *literary* press in our country—and what they did and who—representatively—they were, as Diane Kruchkow has set forth in her Foreword. The straitjacket questionnaire sent those who wrote articles for this book is given question by question with the responses of Alta of Shameless Hussy Press, in its alphabetical place.

I don't know how many little magazines and small presses there are, but Len Fulton at Dustbooks (Box 100, Paradise, CA 95969), who chronicles and tracks the small press and independent publishing movement, does know. The latest Dustbooks *International Directory* I have seen is the 19th, for 1983-84. It has 3,535 entries. Lot of people out there working to get the word out. (In 1965, when the *Directory* was first published, there were 250 listings in the 40-page, $1.00 a copy guide.)

Of the thousands over the years, a minority (Fulton could tell you how many) is sponsored by a college or university. The worst of these school-sponsored littles, unfortunately, are about as lively as a C-minus paper in English 101, though perhaps this is inevitable, since the school-subsidized littles (or "literary journals" as their schools' fund-raising officers prefer to call them) depend for money on the goodwill of conservative boards of regents, trustees, and alumni, and unless their editors possess uncommon skills, tact, and persuasive powers—

249

together with luck—they can continue as editors only by publishing literary criticism and "safe" poetry and fiction.

The best school-sponsored—*Western Humanities Review, Confrontation*, for example, and those in this volume—are very good. But overall, as David Dempsey put it in 1967, "Creeping respectability has overtaken most of the academically-sanctioned literary magazines; they no longer die to set verse free . . . . The note of protest is muted."

The independents, on the other hand, can also be deadly dull, especially when they consist exclusively of the work of the editor and his or her friends.

For its part, *December* magazine has concentrated on fiction. As to that, I quote at length from Vance Bourjaily's article, "Notes on the Starting of Magazines," which appeared in 1958 in Vol. 1, No. 1 of *December*. It states beliefs we hold firmly.

When I started my own magazine, *Discovery*, I had everything to learn about the editorial process, and much of that learning was surprising.

For example, I had to learn that selection of manuscripts is not, as I had thought, a critical function but its opposite. Where the critic is reluctant, the editor must be eager. Where the critic is careful, the editor must be rash . . . . I seldom bought a story which I didn't know I was going to buy the moment I finished reading it; there was a sensation I seldom know as a reader, which . . . was a specifically physical sensation; there was tingling in it, excitement, and relief—relief that here, out of the pages and pages of material submitted, was something I'd enjoy publishing . . . .

I have often thought that the decline of fiction in larger magazines was largely due to the fact that their selections are made by boards of editors, each with a vote, and with words to say or write; it's safe that way. The larger the board, the more different minds contributing words, the less risk there is of ever making a mistake, publishing something really bad, outrageous, offensive . . . .

At least a year is spent selecting material for a regular issue of *December*, sometimes more. And when I have an issue almost ready to go, but feel that it's not *quite* all there, I wait. Invariably, at the very last moment, a story comes in that is a *must*—and that sets the tone for that entire issue.

Of course this means that all the other contributors must wait and wait and wait . . . . But they are amply rewarded for their patience: two author's copies of the issue, plus as many more, within reason, as they want and have the presence of mind to ask for.

VII. The three astronauts did not reach the moon but they reached the hearts of millions of people in America and in the world. They reminded us in these days when we have this magnificent technocracy that men do count, the individual does count.—Richard M. Nixon

250

Apropos of BS, you remember that they reconstructed the astronaut's words when he finally did put his foot upon the moon, don't you? Understandably nervous, the poor fellow garbled his prepared line ("One small step for mankind . . ."), but they fixed the tape. And you recall that the bronze plaque with Dwight D. Eisenhower's farewell address affixed to a door of the Pentagon has the entire speech, word for word—except for the passage in which Ike denounces the perils of a U.S. military-industrial complex, right?

Anyway, would it not be beneficial for the health of our culture *and* that of little magazines if little magazines were to be used in college courses in contemporary lit? Yes, but they are not generally so used, if at all. The reasons for this hinge on the kind of people who determine what texts can be used, and, also, the general ignorance, referred to earlier, of the existence of little magazines by teachers of English. And the fact that no teacher's guides accompany litmags, as they do conventional lit texts; to teach from litmags would require effort.

In 1965 I wrote a letter to the Director of the Cooperative Research Program of the U.S. Office of Education, asking how I could undertake, under provisions of Public Law 531, 82nd Congress, a study that might bring solvency to little magazines and sanity to contemporary lit college courses by using little mags in those courses. In reply, I received 14 pages of grant-application instructions, from which I drew up an 11-page small contract proposal (15 copies required), enlisting as sponsor, Gene Garber, a fine writer then teaching at the University of Iowa, and as transmittor, John C. Gerber, the Twain scholar and then head of the English Department at Iowa.

Proposed was the sending of a self-mailer questionnaire to 27,000 teachers of college English, alerting them to the existence of litmags and asking them if they thought they might not profitably use such magazines in their teaching. Responses were to be summarized, results disseminated to the little magazine community, and Garber was to write an article on the survey for a professional journal, probably *College English*. A grant of $4,329 was requested to do this, mostly for printing and mailing. Seven months passed, then the verdict.

I later talked to one of the members of the committee—college English teachers all—that reviewed the proposal. He said that only one of the committee's ten members—Jim Miller of the University of Chicago (whom I'd personally lobbied)—had okayed it. The rest, he said, including himself, viewed the proposal as a "promotion scheme."

Onward and upward with the arts.

VIII. The morally overwrought quality of much liberal thinking derives, I believe, not merely from indignation but from the strain of trying not to perceive that capitalism's logical tendency is to preserve inequality, deplete resources, pollute the elements, keep an underclass out of work, and tyrannize over the economies of other nations.—Frederick Crews

The U.S.A. has 8,337 public libraries with 387 million books. The U.S.S.R. has 130,653 public libraries with 1.5 billion books.

People in the United States, old and young, have quit reading stories, novels,

251

poetry—books. Television is responsible. When we spend our lives in equal thirds per day—sleep, work, TV—there is no 25th hour in which to read.

Those who *can* read have quit, that is; there are 23 million U.S. adults (1 in 5) who *can't* read. (They read at less than 3rd- to 4th-grade level.) The United States has dropped from 18th to 49th in literacy since the '50s (out of 158 U.N. nations). And a recent study of 100,000 high school seniors showed that only 1,000—1 percent—could write two consecutive sentences without a mistake.

I'm not going to let all this upset me. Not when our country can still—despite what carping critics like to point to as "shortcomings"—can still produce such citizens as Cornelia Guest, 1982's "Deb of the Year." Cornelia is the god-daughter of the Duke of Windsor. At 3:30 in the afternoon she wears black leather pants and a coyote fur coat to an interview—and orders champagne to sip —at Manhattan's Cafe Reginette. She is a blonde cutie and at first she thinks she went to 500 parties last year. She wants to be an actress.

Her father was the polo player Winston Guest, an heir to the Phipps steel fortune. Her mother is a friend of First Lady Nancy Reagan and has thousands of orchids in several greenhouses and a very nice apartment on Park Avenue.

Cornelia is (in 1982) 19 years old and her ambition is to win an Oscar for acting. At 15, Cornelia dropped out of Foxcroft, a Virginia boarding school, to ride horses. She loves horses. She has a 42-year-old Peruvian real estate developer for a boy friend. She amends the 500-parties figure downward to 365.

Cornelia has been told about her country's recession (it began about 1982), but she doesn't feel guilty about it. "Well, no, how hard is it? I don't think it's very hard to go out and buy a new dress every day. You take a credit card to Bergdorf's and you go and say, 'I want that.' And you put it on, and if it looks okay, you take it."

A friend corrects the 365-parties figure to "maybe 300, of which 250 you could never recall, or 275." Cornelia often dances at Studio 54 until 4:00 a.m. and among her many friends is Mick Jagger.

What parties does Cornelia remember?

"The Christmas party where I sang—at Xenon last year. Then Lester's 'Save the Trees,' where we showed up without a tree. This was in Studio 54. Um, where else?"

"That was 'Save the Children,' " her friend reminds her. "Not 'Save the Trees.' " ('S okay: she showed up without a child, too.)

I don't think Russia could produce a little princess like Cornelia. At least not since 1917.

IX. Sow all the words you can
    For in a better age
    Men shall judge the harvest
    By its intrinsic worth.
            —Lady Nijō

I've made the workaday living that supports *December* by editing and rewriting for commercial publishers. I learned the basic skills my first six months (editing how-tos at Popular Mechanics Press). Once a month every month since, sometimes more frequently, I've discovered anew that when you hear a man say, "It's not *who* you know but *what* you know," he's a liar. But that, of course, is the world of commerce for you.

Reed Whittemore, founding editor of the *Carleton Miscellany*, wrote a pamphlet on little magazines back in 1963 in which he said, "Sometimes a celebrated poet can't be sure whether he owes the celebration to himself or to his powerful friends." And that's the world of belles lettres for you.

One time the head of a famous Midwest writers' workshop, a young poet, told me, "We must disabuse the students in the workshop that it's who they know that gets them published." I could only nod. What else is a simple country boy to do?

A year later I saw the young poet standing in line around a lectern at the MLA meetings in Chicago waiting to shake hands with Robert Lowell after Lowell had given a talk. When he saw me he asked for George Hitchcock's address so he could write him to say how much he enjoyed *Kayak*. I told him the address would probably be in his latest copy of that poetry magazine.

I remember another teacher from another writers' workshop telling me with satisfaction about the famous woman poet, who was also an advisor to a New York publisher, who had through his initiative given a reading on his campus: "So I drove her to the station after her reading and mentioned that I had a book of poems ready. We had a drink, and you know . . . . Now they're publishing it." . . . We have an expression out here for all of the foregoing, and it isn't "Sucking eggs." Another expression we have, freely translated, goes: "There are fewer writers made between the covers of a book than between the sheets."

I know, I know; this verges on a descent into mere gossip (or a dissent into mire godspel), so onward and upward once more, and at flank speed.

The study of the question of Illinois Arts Council (IAC) funding of small literary publications I mentioned earlier finally concluded that only non-profit magazines or presses were eligible, leaving the independent *December* (run as a small biz) out, but Northwestern's Univ.-supported *TriQuarterly* in—for $6,000.

Before Jennifer Moyer left the IAC she coordinated a little mag exhibit for the public. The exhibit was stuck so far away in a corner of the basement of the Chicago Art Institute that I don't believe even the building's architect could have found it. The next year she coordinated a book fair—open to presses from wherever in the Midwest—held in Chicago's downtown "Cultural Center." For the event, an *extremely* loud electric blues band was hired for $1,000 (a figure given me by a member of the band down in the parking lot after closing while we were getting our cars). Jim Hanson, editor of *In the Light*, wrote of this book fair:

> During the band's break, I said, to the band, "As long as you keep playing, there is no possibility that any of us will do what we came here to do: to contact people and to sell books." An encounter with Jennifer Moyer of the Illinois Arts Council near the bandstand followed. I asked her, "Are you going to allow all this to continue?" She said yes. I said, "Then you are shortcircuiting any possibility of a viable small press conference." She replied, "Then you can go."

253

Shortly after, Jennifer Moyer herself went, moving up and East in the culture bureaucracy to CCLM (Coordinating Council of Literary Magazines) as its Executive Director. (CCLM is the 1966 successor to ALMA, the Association of Literary Magazines of America, founded in 1961.)

When I took on *December* (1962), there were no government grants. But since they began to be given ('66?), I have had great good fortune in getting them. I have tried to figure out the reason for this; the only explanation I can give is merit.

Were it not for grants from the CCLM and the NEA—and a couple of low, low interest loans from my parents—there would have been quite a few years in the past 24 of no publication. And not once have any of *December*'s benefactors interfered in any way with what I sought to publish—though several times my parents have given me hard looks for what I did publish.

Some individuals in the small press community, including some of my closest friends in that community (and in this volume), have refused to take CCLM or NEA money. For myself, I take the money and run my press. If I'm corrupted, it's not government money doing it.

The good fortune began early. In 1965, when I was still brand-new to the litmag "game," I was invited to a three-day symposium on little magazines at the Library of Congress, and there first met the fabled little literati. The next year or the year after (I've lost the records), *December* was one of the first 13 literary magazines in the country to receive a support grant from CCLM (which got the money from the NEA); the other 12 recipients were biggies. These kindnesses to *December* I believe were due to the good offices of Reed Whittemore, Poetry Consultant to the Library of Congress in '65 and a leader in ALMA-CCLM's affairs and with whose *Carleton Miscellany* I had been exchanging my fledgling *December*. (*CM* was published out of Northfield, Minnesota—the Midwest.)

In the early '70s I wrote so much on what I saw to be the evils of CCLM and the NEA that it is surprising I continued to receive grants. The burden of my complaint was that the lion's share of the money went to cronies of those giving it (or to the givers themselves) and also that far too much was spent administratively. And that this was unfair because it was all taxpayers' money—*our* money—which *they* were controlling for their own benefit.

Besides the recommendations for remedy that I made back then, I think the only thing I have to add today is that maybe the government should pay a lot of our practicing writers and poets (see XI, below) not to practice, however much they may need it.

XI. The cheap values and the irresponsible actions of the literary world are very much the creations of a society in which originality, spirit, and radical vision are almost outlawed. We would be fools to forget that this very same society thought the atom bomb spelled the dawn of a new civilization and not the death of man.—Chandler Brossard

Yes, the NEA literature program has had grant panel judges giving awards to their buddies. Here's a recent, decade-ending example: In 1979-80, no fewer than 15 poets who taught at the "Jack Kerouac School of Disembodied Poetics" each got $10,000 NEA grants (total: $150,000). Said Steve Katz, a member of the NEA selection panel (and NEA winner of $12,500 in 1981): "The luck for them was that Ron was on the panel."

"Ron" is New York poet Ron Padgett, a former NEA grant recipient and a former instructor at the Disembodied Poetics school. (He also knew most of the other NYC poets who got grants.)

A $10,000 NEA grant for fiction went to one Tom Veitch. On the general panel awarding this grant sat—you guessed it—Ron. Ron has two pen names according to a 1977 Who's Who in Poetry he listed himself in: Harland Dangerfield and Tom Veitch. Did Ron really make *himself* a grant? Wouldn't that be going a bit *too* far?

According to Ron, his Who's Who listing was all a hoax; Tom Veitch is only a good buddy with whom he co-authored a book of poems and for whom his Full Court Press published a book of poetry.

Do you think it is an easy thing   Whoops, here's God
To make a tuna salad sandwich   (I felt the orgasm
Shall I smash this pie in your face   under my finger.)
the face of God?

One of the specimens of poetry above is by Ron, the other is by Tom . . . . They write a lot alike, don't they. Maybe they *are* the same fella! . . . The pity of all this is not that Ron and Tom are grant-sharing buddies, but that neither Ron nor Tom can write poetry for sour apples.

I have never been appointed to any NEA advisory selection panel—and damn glad of it—but ten or so years ago I was elected to a CCLM grants committee. We met in Phoenix, Arizona, and in between all the social events we spent a day sweating out grants to the applicant magazines, with CCLM then-Director Gail Kong keeping frantic track of the accumulating total on her pocket calculator.

After we'd dispensed the available money to what we felt were deserving magazines, we dispersed. Shortly after returning home came a letter from Ms. Kong saying that $20,000 in additional funds had turned up immediately *after* our meeting and that the CCLM Board (non-elected) had decreed that the extra $20,000 would go to magazines which had been awarded matching grants—proportionately to the biggies: *Antioch Review, Carolina Quarterly, Chicago Review, Massachusetts Review, Ohio Review, Partisan Review, TriQuarterly*, und so weiter. (Magazines which received smaller grants and asked to be made a part of the matching post facto were refused.)

It's as the horsedealer said when a horse he'd just sold dropped dead before his very eyes: "Can't understand it. He never did that before."

XII. If the radical movement had been permitted to follow its natural course it would never have become entangled with the freewheeling, grassroots tra-

255

dition. It would have been urban, intellectual, and critical.—William Phillips

Now, a question for future investigation by Ph.D. candidates and other scholars and historians: How directly were the nation's politics and literature linked the past 30-40 years? Or why were we in Vietnam?

James Angleton was a dedicated anti-Communist, a granite-hard hardliner, convinced that the Soviet KGB had penetrated deeply into U.S. society. As the CIA's Director of Counterintelligence, he fought the Cold War on all fronts, illegally amassing surveillance files on at least 10,000 U.S. citizens, opening their mail to do it when he thought that was necessary. But in addition to his CIA work, he was also a prize-winning orchid grower and a poet. He had contacts on all fronts.

Testifying before a Senate committee investigating CIA activities, Angleton said, "It is inconceivable that a secret intelligence arm of the government has to comply with all the overt orders of the government."

James Angleton was born in 1917 in Boise, Idaho. His father owned the National Cash Register franchise for Italy, and James spent his summers in Italy, attended college in England. In 1937 he entered Yale, serving there on the editorial board of the *Yale Literary Magazine* ("An organ of the intelligent intelligentsia"—Eugene V. Rostow) with McGeorge Bundy, the future national-security adviser to Presidents Kennedy and Johnson and a future head of the Ford Foundation.

In the summer of 1939, Angleton co-founded a magazine of verse, *Furioso*. "Jim was the go-getter," said Norman Holmes Pearson, professor of English and American studies at Yale, "he had the contacts." These contacts included Archibald MacLeish, E.E. Cummings, Richard Eberhart, William Carlos Williams, and Ezra Pound, shining stars among the roster of *Furioso* contributors recruited by Angleton.

In 1943 he joined the OSS, training in London, then going to Italy. In 1947 he joined the CIA and in 1954 he was authorized to set up the agency's counterintelligence staff, whose personnel and activities here and abroad increased exponentially through the '60s under his dedicated direction. But in 1973, after Watergate, his staff's illegal domestic activities came under scrutiny and in December of 1974 he was fired.

"Jim was smart and imaginative," said Pearson, the Yale English prof, "but Reed was the one who wrote." "Reed" was Angleton's co-founder of *Furioso*, and roommate, E. Reed Whittemore, Jr. . . . Curioso.

"My own aesthetic inclinations at the time . . .," wrote Whittemore for *The Little Magazine in America* (1978), "was to write about the futility of action." (Cf. C. Wright Mills on the alienation of the free intellectual.) "And despite its campaigns, *Furioso* was, after the war, a magazine oddly dedicated to incapacity."

Not so his roommate, James Angleton, as we know.

William Phillips was once a fire-breathing socialist. He has been editor of *Partisan Review* since 1934, an advisor to NYC publishers, and an English prof.

Over the years both he and his magazine have changed—radically, to use a term that long ago used to please him.

Reacting to Lillian Hellman's charge in her book *Scoundrel Time* that he, among others, had not admitted that his Cold War anti-Communism in the late '40s and '50s had been "perverted" by the Right, he said, ". . . My anti-Communist reaction probably carried me a little too far . . . ." How far was too far has yet to be fully gauged.

Partisan Review was founded as a John Reed Club journal in the mid-'30s. It retreated from Communist Party propagandizing very soon after it appropriated the subscription list of the more successful *Anvil*, then quickly moved from Trotskyite class-struggle polemics to alienation via Freud to Jacobite nitpicking via neurosis, and emerged—supported by an Eastern institution of higher learning—as the pre-eminent Cold War coffee table ornament of liberal intellectuals and English Department comers the nation over. It did this, one suspects (to use *PR* phraseology), by taking a political stance that suited the U.S. government's shadowy appendages in charge of what might be termed "thought control."

In 1946 Phillips and his co-editor of *PR* announced that "We have in our midst a powerfully vocal lobby . . . embarked upon nothing less than a policy of appeasement with Russia."

By 1955 Phillips was saying, "I, for one, see no reason to countenance the activities of the American Communist Party." In this, he had influential fellow travelers: J. Edgar Hoover, for one; James Angleton for another.

In 1967 an ex-CIA official revealed that money for the English magazine *Encounter* had for years come under the table ($15,000/year) from the CIA and that the CIA had installed its own agent as editor of *Encounter*, as well as an agent in the European-based organization called the Congress for Cultural Freedom, founded in Berlin in 1950. The Congress had quasi-official, publicly-known status through the German magazine *Monat* (which was founded after WWII by the U.S. State Department), and its editor had been a member of the OSS. *Monat* was almost certainly supported by CIA funds also.

The year before the *Encounter* revelation, in 1966, William Phillips became Chairman of CCLM, the successor to Reed Whittemore's ALMA. Phillips was already a member of the Board of Directors of the American Committee on Cultural Freedom, an affiliate of the European Congress, and *Partisan* had been receiving financial support from the Committee since 1959.

The Cold War party line—its philosophical core and aesthetic ideology, as developed at the 1950 Congress—was, according to the cultural historian Maxwell Geismar, that "liberalism in itself leads only to communism, hence a new kind of Cold War liberalism, or shall we say liberal-fascism, must be developed cogently and held to dogmatically. Any critical premise or judgment (just as any work of art) outside or deviating from this Cold War 'philosophy'—the philosophy designed to save the 'Free World' from the Communist menace—must be attacked, repressed, liquidated, ignored."

Which accounts for statements about the bumbling American judged good enough to do better than sell aluminum siding but not good enough to compete with sensibilities of real literary delicacy, and for the denigration of such as Whitman, Twain, Hemingway—as well as Parrington, Dreiser, and Sherwood Anderson. These pronouncements are the East Coast's, set forth in *Partisan*.

The 1967 disclosure of CIA meddling in cultural affairs on a global scale upset our leading intellectuals by compromising them. So much so, that they had no comment. But they did not close up shop.

In an essay titled "The Cloud of Certainties," the novelist R.V. Cassill observes:

Let us recall (the) revelations about the CIA . . . . Anyone keen enough to infer, from that glimpse through the clouds, the magnitude of engineered misrepresentation that has alienated us from the political realities of the last decades would be, I think, keen enough to note also how quickly the clouds were closed again. And worry about this at home. And bother with analogies between political and literary ideologies. (Did the CIA really subsidize Jack Kerouac in a cunning attack on the novel?) And wonder if anyone else had noticed.

About the time of the CIA disclosures, *PR* held a symposium on Vietnam. The symp's participants observed that "Most of the criticism of Administration policy . . . has simply taken for granted that everything would be fine if only the Yanks would go home. It is not clear whether these critics . . . really care what happens to the people of Southeast Asia so long as America gets out."

Of course we know what happened so long as we stayed.

PR's talkers (highest-ranked writers and intellectuals all) concluded their Vietnam session with: "Obviously, the time has come for some new thinking," though they failed to provide any. Or, as Phillips, a signatory to the symposium's statement, unwittingly remarked in bewildered tones only yesterday: "We've confined ourselves so long to abstract and moral questions concerning the past or the future—and to those which lend themselves to cocktail party agitation—that we have cut ourselves off from the means of affecting the present."

Not quite. In 1972 the Ford Foundation (McGeorge Bundy its head) awarded a $50,000 grant to the by-now infamous English *Encounter*. Phillips attacked this grant as discriminating against U.S. magazines, and in early 1975 the Ford Foundation announced a $500,000 grant to CCLM. This grant Phillips did not attack.

Here, from a review of Noam Chomsky's *Toward a New Cold War* (1982—the review is by George Scialabba in the *Village Voice*) is a way of looking at U.S.-U.S.S.R. relations since 1917 that is seldom attempted:

The United States tried to strangle the new Soviet regime by financing a civil war and a foreign invasion; imposed an economic boycott and withheld diplomatic recognition for 16 years; . . . colluded with Britain to insure that Russia would bear the main burden of fighting Nazi Germany, at horrific cost; refused postwar reconstruction aid on reasonable terms; whipped up anti-Soviet hysteria at home to justify creation of a peacetime military establishment; trained and airlifted operatives into the Soviet Union from 1949 to 1952 to organize insurrections; and, in an unprecedented violation of international law, regularly overflew Soviet territory with high-altitude spy planes. In October 1962 the United States accepted . . . a near-50 percent probability of nuclear war in order to establish the principle that the United States has the right to maintain missiles on the perimeter of the Soviet Union, while the Soviet Union has no corresponding right.

Who was responsible for this U.S. foreign policy? Noam Chomsky says that "few if any interest groups, outside of business, have generalized influence on the broad range of (U.S.) foreign policy."

And thus we have Ronald Reagan saying: "In your discussions of the nuclear freeze proposals, I urge you to beware the temptation of pride, the temptation to . . . label both sides equally at fault, to ignore the facts of history and the aggressive impulses of an evil empire, to simply call the arms race a giant misunderstanding and thereby remove yourself from the struggle between right and wrong, good and evil." . . . Is he saying that U.S. business interests . . .?

XIV. Talent, imagination, brilliance, originality are so many meaningless nonfactors in this literary myth-making enterprise. . . . What's relevant is the total business machinery of American publishing overpowering all aesthetic values.—Leslie Woolf Hedley

Facts-of-life items in no particular order of precedence with reference to commercial (trade, as opposed to small press) publishing:

1. Book best sellers are the result of market research and promotion dollars (engineered hype). Quality is not part of the equation—just as Leslie Woolf Hedley says.

2. The chain bookstores—B. Dalton, Waldenbooks, Crown—which do 50 percent of the U.S. book business done today, will tomorrow do 90 percent. They will, thus, exert an even greater deleterious effect on what is published than at present—that is, only books that sell in huge quantities will be stocked (also known as the self-fulfilling prophecy).

3. The never lucrative market for quality short stories in the United States was nevertheless still fairly widespread and open 25 years ago. Today it is virtually closed and nearly non-existent in magazines of the newsstand.

4. For all practical purposes, the even less lucrative market for poetry in the United States closed out 25 years ago.

5. Trade publishers today are directed by salesmen—most of whom couldn't edit their way out of a comic book—and owned by conglomerates. And those publishing houses that still accept unsolicited or unagented manuscripts—and there are only a few—continue the odd publishing tradition of having such mss. read first—and passed upward or rejected outright on that decision—by the newest and least experienced persons on their staffs.

6. The salesmen directing trade publishing houses today report to conglomerate accountants who in almost every instance know even less about the many

aspects of publishing than the salesmen. Care less, too.

7. In 1967, a staff member of the U.S. Information Agency (USIA) described to the Senate Foreign Relations Committee its "book development" program. Under this program, from 1956 to 1967 at least 104 titles were published by U.S. trade publishers—from Praeger through Farrar Straus through Doubleday—with direct subsidies to authors from USIA or purchase guarantees to the publisher. Distributed to U.S. bookstores and through U.S. book clubs by their publishers, as well as abroad by the USIA, many of these titles were originated, and funded, by the CIA. Nowhere in these books is an indication of government sponsorship or subsidy.

8. Conglomerate money, methods, and management have changed U.S. publishing so greatly that it is today nearly useless as a civilizing force in society. Is, in fact, a counter-civilizing force.

9. That conglomerates own all of the largest trade publishing in the United States is just as injurious to the purpose of publishing as would be exclusive ownership by the Moral Majority or the Communist Party.

10. Conglomerate publishing executives regularly use such non-standard words in their writing and speaking as "measurable end products," "prioritize," "effectuate," "interface," "input," and "over-arching." This renders communication difficult—which is the intention.

11. Twain, Dreiser, Hemingway, Fitzgerald, Algren, Farrell, Lardner: Perhaps one of these authors could make a living at writing in today's fiction markets.

12. The quantifiable information that conglomerate managers base their decisions on—in publishing as in other fields—is distinctly inferior to qualitative information so far as producing beneficial results.

13. Conroy, Sandburg, Masters, Lindsay, LeSueur: Not one of these writers could support themselves with their writing specialties—then, and never now.

Facts-of-life items in no particular order of precedence:

1. In 1978 a jailed radical on the "Barney Miller" ABC network TV show was scripted to say: "The Vietnam war wasn't fought to preserve freedom. It was fought to preserve the oil companies and Dow Chemical and DuPont." ABC's corporate lawyers deleted this speech from the script. Money makes the mare go.

2. On the "Three's Company" ABC network TV show allusions to oral sex and getting and losing an erection were common, as you may recall. This drop-your-pants cheap humor is OK with ABC's corporate lawyers. Who are well paid.

3. Yes, if you can afford the tuna, it is an easy thing to make a tuna salad sandwich, good God!

4. In the U.S.S.R., a writer's first book typically is printed in an edition of 10,000 copies and sells out. Second printings range from 25,000 to 75,000 copies. A book of poetry written by a recognized and talented poet will sell out nationally in 20 minutes at the bookstores.

5. In 1982, General Electric closed its Ontario, California, plant and moved those operations out of the country. Its accountants had decided that paying a

260

worker in Singapore $43 a week or a worker in Brazil $68 a week was cheaper. The dispossessed GE worker in California—to take an example—who had planned his/her life around a pension of $1,000 a month when they retired will have to settle for $175—and try to find another job. It was not only the much lower wages abroad that prompted GE's move; it was also the avoidance of pensions that the move afforded. Which is also the reason prime pension candidates (people over 40) are seldom hired by corporations, and why companies maneuver to unload younger employees before their pension rights become vested.

6. In 1934, William Phillips spoke at a John Reed Clubs convention in Chicago. Meridel LeSueur was there: "(He was) practically saying that the people, the farmers, the workers . . . had no power or culture . . . . And I got up and said . . . we were the basis of culture . . . the intellectuals were the betrayers of culture."

XV. The hard-bought American belief that literature can be made only by a willingness to take one's own chances was sold piecemeal by individual surrender.—Nelson Algren

Regular issues of *December* and December Press books are usually published in editions of 1,000 copies. Jerry Bumpus' *Anaconda*, today an underground classic, had a print-run of 1,000 hardbound, 2,000 soft. It took ten years to sell or give them all away. *The Otis Ferguson Reader* which we published to universal approval by its audience (connoisseurs of prose, plain speaking and the arts, lively and literary) was rejected by 35 trade and university press publishers over 10 years. With regret in each instance, but rejected. They would have given their eyeteeth for the notices that book got. No guts.

December Press books are put out as special issues of the magazine to capitalize on *December*'s library subscribers, which in 1978 reached a high of 174, today number 112. Half of these library subs are from the Ebsco and Faxon subscription agencies, however, and thus are discounted 20 percent. Individual subscriptions reached a high of 204 in 1965, today number 19, two more than when Jeff Marks gave me the magazine in 1962. Bookstores get maybe 100 in all, seldom pay. Small press distributors get maybe 100, seldom sell. The rest go to authors and exchange magazines and as review and other comps and to writers in prison.

Anaconda was, I believe (and I'm probably wrong about this), the first novel in the last quarter century to be published by a little magazine, thus establishing (in my mind, at least) the modern era's small literary press. There was a need for that to be done; by 1967—*Anaconda*'s year of publication—it was quite clear that commercial publishers were abdicating their responsibility to quality fiction.

George Chambers' *The Bonnyclabber* is the only December Press book that looks well-designed. It is also the only really experimental book the Press has published. I had to read it five times to figure out what Chambers was doing and to realize how extremely well he had done it. (N.B.: The first page of *BC* is blank except for a footnote; librarians returned copies claiming they were defective.)

261

The U.S. Postal Service has raised its rates 1000 percent over the last 25 years and lowered its service at least as much . . . . *December*'s cover price has increased 300 percent in 25 years . . . .

John Bennett's *Vagabond Anthology* ($10.95, Vagabond Press, 1 Morris Way, Ellensburg, WA 98926) and Morty Sklar's *Editor's Choice* ($14.50, The Spirit That Moves Us Press, P.O. Box 1585, Iowa City, IA 52244) are both excellent intros to litmag content, prose and poetry, in the '60s and '70s. Excellent. . . . Good also, some say, is any volume of Bill Henderson's *Pushcart Prize* annuals, and these are available commercially.

XVI. It ain't no use to sit and wonder why, babe.—Peter, Paul, & Mary

Louis Vaczek was born in 1913 in Budapest, the son of a diplomat. He graduated from McGill University, Montreal, in 1935 with a degree in chemistry and then worked in Egypt and Saudi Arabia as a chemist/manager. In World War II he served as a pilot in the Royal Canadian Air Force. After the war, as a volunteer for the American Friends Service Committee, he helped rebuild Warsaw.

In this country, he taught at the New School of Social Research and at Chicago's Roosevelt University, concentrating on the relationship between science and art. He wrote a chemistry textbook (*The Enjoyment of . . .*) and four good novels, and made a living as a teacher and as a science editor for encyclopedias.

Louis was one of the handsomest men I've ever known, and one of the most personable and friendliest. In 1983, the year of his death, at age 69 (looking 49), he was still single-handedly sailing the Atlantic Ocean, literally and figuratively. He was one of the founders of *December*.

James Drought, rebel and maverick, was one of the first fiction self-publishers in this country to almost break even. Illinois-born, he died June 2, 1983, in Norwalk, Connecticut, at the age of 52 of a heart attack—his second, I believe.

He thought he was the grandson of B. Traven (*Treasure of Sierra Madre*). He may have been. He thought that U.S. book distribution was controlled by a restrictive monopoly. It probably is. (In 1968 he asked the Department of Justice to take anti-trust action on this; it wouldn't.) He thought his fiction had been suppressed (which was why he self-published) and that when, as in the case of his *The Gypsy Moths*, he did at last gain some access to commercial exposure (a mass-market paperback edition, a movie), the men of commerce cheated him. I think they did.

He was a good friend to *December* over many years. More important, and most regrettable, he was a major American writer who because he told the truth in his fiction (and with art) was never heard by all of the audience that should have read him.

Bob Wilson died July 11, 1983. He was 55. He had grown up in Lincoln, Illinois, and spent most of his adult life in Chicago. He was a writer and editor best known for his collection of short stories and essays, *Young in Illinois*, and for *The Film Criticism of Otis Ferguson* (Temple University Press), which he co-edited. For the last 19 years of his life, Bob Wilson was also the movies editor of *December*.

Bob's last 10 years were tortuous for him mentally and physically, I think, but he bore them with fortitude. Those who have read his *Young in Illinois* would know he would not complain.

Young in Illinois is a beautiful book, steeped in bittersweet nostalgia, beautifully written. I once had to give a talk to high school student writers in Crete-Monee and asked them to read an essay from the book, "Life and Art in the Thirties," as preparation. These writers were born at least 25 years after the time Bob spoke of in his essay, but so evocative and skillful was his prose that when we discussed it *they* told *me*—at length—about all the many good things the essay had and did.

Without Bob Wilson *December* magazine would have been quite different than it was and would never have lasted through to this year.

He cared about good writing, scotch whiskey, injustice, movies, basketball, jazz, his parents, and his daughter, Sue Young Wilson. Not at all in that order. And any man who hated two women and one man as he hated had to be a good man. And good men are harder and harder to find.

The last time we were together in Chicago we spent an afternoon and evening talking, eating, drinking, and carousing and parted late at night to go our respective ways with our respective ladies of that evening. We rejoined at my apartment the next morning, a Saturday, about 10:00 o'clock. For breakfast I finished what little bourbon I had in the place while he started to work on a nearly full quart of scotch, which tastes, as is well known, like medicine. When I ran out of bourbon he shared his jug with me. He paced and I paced and we talked about our plans for *December* and about people and writers we'd known and things we'd done together, and let the sunlight stream into the room and got closer that Saturday to saying to each other what we really believed than we'd ever gotten in 25 years of knowing each other.

He had for 10 years been trying to sell *The Otis Ferguson Reader*, a book ms. he'd co-edited, to commercial and university press publishers. Finally he asked me if I wanted it for December Press. *The Reader* is a collection of Ferguson's jazz pieces, among much else. I know nothing about jazz and Ferguson is best known as a film critic. But *The Reader* was good writing, even I could tell that, and if Bob said it was worth publishing I knew it was well worth publishing. (He had incorruptible standards; once I asked him to select my 10 best short stories out of 50 I'd had published so I could submit a collection to a contest. "I would," he told me, "but you haven't got ten that good.")

But that Saturday, at one point in our long, peaceful, continuously refilled discussion, I said that if I had to pay his co-editor (Dorothy Chamberlain, Ferguson's widow) more than I'd paid other December Press authors in the past for their work (almost nothing), to hell with it.

He frowned and half-smiled and paced, lit a cigarette, stopped his pacing, cleared his throat, frowned and half-smiled and said, "You have to, Curt. It's my book."

I saw him off to Lincoln about 3:30 that afternoon, both of us with a happy, mild buzz on. That Saturday was the only day in my life I ever enjoyed scotch.

The Ferguson book was published late in 1982. It is the only December Press book to get reviewed all over—*The New Yorker, The New York Times, Harper's, The Village Voice, Downbeat*—and favorably, and the only book in 25 years to make a nickel for the Press. Bob waited seven months after its publication, until all the enthusiastic reviews were in, and then he spread the *Chicago Sunday Tribune* out on the kitchen table in Lincoln, Illinois, late Sunday evening after supper on the 10th of July and started through it and that Monday morning at 3:30 his mother found him slumped over the papers, his head on his arms on the table, and bigod I miss him.

The world of arts and letters—such as it is or they are today—will miss him, too.

XVII. The World is a raft sailing through space with, potentially, plenty of provisions for everybody; the idea that we must all cooperate and see to it that everyone does his fair share of the work and gets his fair share of the provisions seems so blatantly obvious that one would say that no one could possibly fail to accept it unless he had some corrupt motive for clinging to the present system.—George Orwell

Finally, two things: (1) I don't mean to single out Archie R. McCardell or William Phillips as the arch-enemy, but they may be. And (2) the reason George Plimpton (see headnote to *Paris Review* article, in its alphabetical place, this volume) is as churlish as I find him to be in his permission for his piece herein is that ten or so years ago I put the knock on the early volumes of the *American Literary Anthology*, which he co-edited. Inordinately large sums of NEA (taxpayers') money were spent on those volumes and their selections were inordinately East Coast-weighted—the dreaded Literary Establishment was at work. . . . I know—Never knock anyone else's racket, sure, but the thing is, you don't have to play politics if your side has already won, do you?

I remember talking to George's co-editor after the first volume came out. The *ALA*'s stated purpose was "to provide recognition for writers whose work appears in literary magazines with small circulation . . . ." I suggested that the *New York Review of Books* (circulation 84,000) and *Evergreen Review* (circulation 150,000) did not appear to qualify as small-circulation literary magazines and that the judges who made selections from them for *ALA:1* were perhaps not playing with a full deck—or dealing from the bottom, whichever. The co-editor first set me straight on *that* (it was a mistake of some kind, and probably would not be repeated), then intimated that even *I* had been suggested as a future judge, then said that—in his judgment—the most recent issue of my own magazine, *December*, had some perfectly splendid pieces in it and that he—personally—was going to go through it yet again, prospecting for *ALA:2*, and that possibly—well, you never knew.

Unlike a great many small press people, I do not secretly envy George Plimpton and (as some do) knock him in public. I openly envy Plimpton his writing skill, his adventures, and the Grevy's zebra skin rug in his Manhattan study—and knock him in public. For example, it seems to me that to carry on as he does for pay in TV commercials is biting clear through the shank of the silver spoon that has been clenched between his teeth from birth.

Actually, George owes me. Back in 1965 I did him a very large favor. During the rather frenetic cocktail party held at the close of the Library of Congress get-together of little magazines, I was standing behind him at a pay phone in the hotel lobby, waiting to make a call. When he finished his call he turned away, leaving behind his little black book of names and addresses. I hesitated, and then, against my instincts, I called to him and returned his little black book to him . . . . I still regret that.

You see, Plimpton and I are approximately the same age. (We were then, back in '65, too.) I was tall and slim then. So was he. And he had not long before been designated by *Esquire* as America's Most Eligible Bachelor.

For all I know—and counterfactuals are hard to disprove—I could have lived high off the hog for several seasons with that little black book in my possession.

It's like John Dos Passos said a long, long time ago: "all right we are two nations." (Which is what F. Scott Fitzgerald meant when he said the very rich are different; Hemingway, unfortunately, missed that point.)

What I've meant to say in this essay is that I never met a rich man I really liked—nor one who'd ever heard of the alternative press. And I don't expect to.

Publishing a lit mag or small press publications is not a business, no. But it can never be a hobby, either, if the effort is to achieve anything worthwhile.

The drive and energy of the '60s alternative press, and its dedication and grasp of possibilities, began to dissipate across the '70s. I hope to see it revive, but that the small press directory has expanded from 250 to 3,535 listings in 20 years does not impress me; the most of the newcomers seem to be non-literary (many, how-to) publishers who, I think, if they had their druthers, would not remain small. More power to them, but wot the hell—*How to Make a Bigger Buck?*

It seems to me that what's needed once again is a commitment to oppose the cant of that other nation, those who have sold out or would like to or those who needn't sell out because they already own or can buy all they survey.

What's needed, I know, is a commitment to oppose the rich at every chance, because the rich bully the poor and kill the weak. In real life and in lit matters, too. A commitment to oppose in order to change. Without that, why bother?

Montana Morrison 1985

mR

MISSISSIPPI REVIEW
SOUTHERN STATION
BOX 5144
HATTIESBURG, MS 39406
$10/$18/$26   1/2/3 YRS

33:
LITERARY CRITICISM

34/35:
BISHOP, CAMOIN, CAPONEGRO,
CHAMBERS, COVINO, CROWELL,
DOVLATOV, DUNLOP, FRYDMAN,
GORDETT, GROFF, KOLANKIEWICZ,
MOORE, MORRIS, NOLAN, OSAMU,
PACHECO, PEACOCK, SOLHEIM,
ZARANKA, ZEIDNER

36:
BENSKO, BRUCE, BURGIN,
DIXON, DOTY, DUNNE, DUVALL,
JANOWITZ, KAPLAN, KNOLL,
KUNSTLER, LOPATE, MAGOVERN,
MARELLO, MAYES, MILLER, SHIRLEY,
SPIELBERG, TATE, THOMAS

37/38:
TRANSLATIONS

december

SWEET GOGARTY, a novel by Matthew Hochberg (illustrated), $4.00. "A splendid display of deadpan grotesqueries. Hochberg's novel remains dramatically outrageous (or outrageously dramatic) through its final bittersweet page."—*New Haven Register*

DESTINY NEWS, stories by Robert Fox (illustrated), $4.00. "The most enlightening and enlightened surrealism I've read since Franz K."—Lee Wallek

YOUNG IN ILLINOIS, stories by Robert Wilson (illustrated), $4.00. "It consists of five stories that read like a novel, slowly written, beautifully executed over the last 20 years. They are stories of youth and manhood, with all the pain, agony, loss, and acceptance."—*Chicago Tribune*

THE SECOND NOVEL, by Norbert Blei, $6.00. An exploration of what it's like to be a writer in this country in these times, by one of the Midwest's most widely published writers.

THE FORBIDDEN WRITINGS OF LEE WALLEK (illustrated), $6.00. "This volume should be in the possession of all those who have an interest in literature and criticism and can read."—Dr. Merton Smile

WHY GIRLS RIDE SIDESADDLE, stories by Dennis Lynds (illustrated by Kay Cassill), $5.00. Ten stories of restrained sorrow and acceptance by the author—under pen-names—of 25 suspense novels and science-fiction novels.

HONEYMOON/MOM, two novellas by Hugh Fox (illustrated), $5.00. An exhilarating nightmare of a honeymoon in which the protagonist approaches the inner sanctum of the horror of horrors—inability to consummate—and of what follows after.

ABSTRACT RELATIONS, stories by Thomas E. Connors (photo-illustrated by Diane Schmidt), $5.00. Ten stories of conflict—marital, familial, man against himself, woman against herself—and of memory.

IN EMPTY ROOMS: Tales of love—stories and a play by Henry H. Roth (illustrated), $5.00. Six stories and a probing play by one of the most widely published and perceptive writers of the last quarter century.

THE OTIS FERGUSON READER, $10.00. " . . . One of the outstanding collections of jazz essays currently in print. . . . He used language with an elegance."—*Down Beat*

Send name, address, remittance, and books wanted (postage paid) to:

December Press
3093 Dato
Highland Park, IL 60035

Order all ten books, deduct $15.00 from total list price.

the
wormwood * review

$6/year * from
box 8840 * stockton
ca * 95208

SAMISDAT writing distinguishes itself through passion, purpose, and commitment. We live to encourage life, and to oppose whatever destroys life, on whatever pretext. We respect the laws of nature, not of government; the morals of practical consideration, "do unto others as ye would have others do unto you," not those of superstitious dictate. We salute no flag, obey no draft, neither take nor contribute to public funds, kneel only to tend our garden, and thumb our noses at all propriety.

Regular issues contain from 3 to 7 short stories, 15 to 40 poems, an essay or two, and considerable original artwork. Between regular issues we publish single-author books and chapbooks addressing similar themes. Since 1973, we have averaged over one publication per month. No. 100 appeared in mid-1980.

We mail to subscribers in bundles, semi-quarterly.

Box 129
Richford, Vermont
05476, U.S.A.

Please send me:

_____ Sample copy ($2.00)
_____ Sample copy plus our
          philosophy of writing ($2.50)
_____ Next 500 pages ($15.00)
_____ Next 1,000 pages ($25.00)
_____ All future items ($150.00)
(An average year's production is about 750 pages.)

My check or money order accompanies. My address is:

STONY HILLS

THE NEW ENGLAND ALTERNATIVE PRESS REVIEW

$1

— Single copy — $1.00 + 50¢ post-
age and handling
— Back copies — 75¢

ISSN 0146-2067

Subscriptions:
$3/3 issues — Individuals
$4.50/3 issue — Institutions

Box 715
Newburyport, MA 01950

"One of the best of the now several reviews of small press items."

-Bill Katz, Library Journal

". . . the hope for the future seems to lie out in the sticks."
—Stanley Kunitz, Library of Congress Conference, 1975

Morrison 1985